Teaching Historical Empathy

Katherine Perrotta and Jennifer Curl

Teaching Historical Empathy

Bridging the Past and Present

PETER LANG

New York · Berlin · Bruxelles · Chennai · Lausanne · Oxford

Bibliographic information published by the Deutsche Nationalbibliothek. The German National Library lists this publication in the German National Bibliography; detailed bibliographic data is available on the Internet at http://dnb.d-nb.de.

Library of Congress Cataloging-in-Publication Data
Names: Perrotta, Katherine, 1984- author | Curl, Jennifer, 1962- author
Title: Teaching historical empathy : bridging the past and present /
    Katherine Perrotta, Jennifer Curl.
Description: New York, NY : Peter Lang, 2025. | Includes bibliographical
    references.
Identifiers: LCCN 2025008207 (print) | LCCN 2025008208 (ebook) |
    ISBN 9781636677873 paperback | ISBN 9781636677927 pdf |
    ISBN 9781636677934 epub
Subjects: LCSH: Education, Secondary--Curricula | Empathy--Study and
    teaching (Secondary) | Social sciences--Study and teaching (Secondary) |
    Language arts--Correlation with content subjects
Classification: LCC LB1628 .P44 2025 (print) | LCC LB1628 (ebook) |
    DDC 152.4/1--dc23/eng/20250429
LC record available at https://lccn.loc.gov/2025008207
LC ebook record available at https://lccn.loc.gov/2025008208

Cover image: Jones Bridge by Katherine Perrotta
Cover design by Peter Lang Group AG

ISBN 978-1-63667-787-3 (print)
ISBN 978-1-63667-792-7 (ePDF)
ISBN 978-1-63667-793-4 (ePub)
DOI 10.3726/b22881

© 2025 Peter Lang Group AG, Lausanne (Switzerland)
Published by Peter Lang Publishing Inc., New York (USA)

info@peterlang.com

All rights reserved.

All parts of this publication are protected by copyright.
Any utilization outside the strict limits of the copyright law, without the permission of the publisher, is forbidden and liable to prosecution.
This applies in particular to reproductions, translations, microfilming, and storage and processing in electronic retrieval systems.
This publication has been peer reviewed.

www.peterlang.com

Contents

Acknowledgements vii
Praise for *Teaching Historical Empathy: Bridging the Past and Present* ix
Introduction 1
Chapter 1   Literary Analysis 21
Chapter 2   Digital Media 57
Chapter 3   Music and Recording Arts 89
Chapter 4   Films and Documentaries 117
Chapter 5   Photographs and Visual Arts 149
Chapter 6   Place-Based Education 175
Conclusion 209

Acknowledgements

This book is truly the result of the collaboration of teachers, students, critical friends, and mentors who are committed to historical empathy and excellence in teaching and learning for all students. We extend our deepest thanks and gratitude to Ali Jefferson of Peter Lang who believed in our book and supported us every step of the way. Thank you to Robert Assante, Jason Endacott, Annie Evans, Kristen Jenkins, Sara Karn, Elizabeth Keohane-Burbridge, Rebecca Llungren, Karalee Wong Nakatsuka, William North, and Leah Panther for taking the time out of their busy lives to provide their feedback, insights, and expertise to make this book accessible to ELA and social studies teachers, preservice teachers, graduate students, coaches, instructional specialists, and teacher education faculty.

Katie would like to extend her love and gratitude to Steve, Julianna, her parents, Jennifer Curl, Taha, Bethanie, so many dear friends and colleagues, and all the teachers in her life that made writing this book possible.

Jennifer would like to convey her thanks and love to Dave, Duncan, Kate, Steve, Mark, and Katie Perrotta, and also, to the many colleagues who over the years illustrated what great pedagogy truly is.

This book is dedicated to all of our students, who are very much co-authors of this book.

Praise for
Teaching Historical Empathy: Bridging the Past and Present

"Dr. Perrotta's and Dr. Curl's book *Teaching Historical Empathy: Bridging the Past and Present* fills a void in history pedagogy books. This book offers easy to implement lessons that will fit all levels of history and ELA classes. The authors collected great lists of sources, teacher friendly websites and digitized archives that will help teachers find primary and secondary sources to fit any topic. Building historical empathy practices into one's curriculum will be seamless with these ideas."

Jennifer Baniewicz,
Social Studies Teacher,
Charger Learning Center at Amos Alonzo Stagg High School

"Practical, thoughtful, and deeply engaging, *Teaching Historical Empathy: Bridging the Past and Present* offers a valuable guide for educators looking to connect historical empathy with effective teaching in ELA and social studies. Dr. Perrotta and Dr. Curl provide clear strategies, interdisciplinary connections, and a range of useful resources to help teachers inspire critical thinking and empathy in their students. By combining historical context with literary analysis, this book serves as a practical tool for creating meaningful and engaging lessons that encourage students to explore diverse perspectives and develop a deeper understanding of the past and its relevance today."

Dr. Franklin Allaire,
Associate Professor,
University of Houston Downtown

"Katherine Perrotta and Jennifer Curl's *Teaching Historical Empathy: Bridging the Past and Present* is a much-needed tool for teachers in the classroom. In today's ever-changing world, it is a welcome salve that can help teachers lead students to become more empathetic critical thinkers that can truly put themselves in others' shoes. If you are struggling to bridge history with ELA instructional practices, this is the read you need."

Colby Williams,
English Language Arts teacher

"In *Teaching Historical Empathy: Bridging the Past and Present*, Perrotta and Curl provide a powerful and timely exploration of historical empathy as an essential framework for teaching social studies and English Language Arts. By bridging disciplinary divides, they offer educators practical strategies to engage students in critical inquiry, historical analysis, and civic reflection. This book is an invaluable resource for those committed to fostering deeper understanding, empathy, and active participation in our democracy. A must-read for educators seeking to make history and literature more relevant, meaningful, and transformative."

Dr. Shirley Marie McCarther,
Editor of *American Educational History Journal*,
Chair and Associate Professor, Educational Leadership,
Policy and Foundations, University of Missouri- Kansas City

Introduction

Brainstorming Activity

- What do you think historical empathy is?
- How can historical empathy relate to teaching ELA and social studies?
- Do you think you have implemented strategies to promote historical empathy? If so, were they effective? If not, are you interested in learning more about these approaches to teaching ELA and social studies?

Introduction: Why Historical Empathy?

The term empathy has made the rounds on the internet as memes, videos, blogs, and news stories concerning popular culture, politics, current events, and perspectives on an array of issues for several years. "Why can't we get along?" "I feel your pain." "We are in this together." "Your truth." The circulation of these memes is not a huge surprise, given the turmoil people around the world are facing in the wake of the COVID-19 pandemic. Cries for greater empathy from educators, parents, civic organizations, politicians, and other public and private entities have been a response to deep political division concerning matters of social justice movements, racial violence, mass shootings, gender inequities, immigration, global pandemic, economic volatility, terrorism, war, and threats to democracy. These are complicated issues for adults to grasp, let alone children. Although living through these fraught times could lead people to be willing to learn about others' perspectives and experiences when coping with these issues, teachers, curriculum developers, school leaders, parents, and educational leaders are struggling with how to promote empathy in an age of "cancel culture," "fake news," and "divisive concepts laws."

Empathy is defined by Merriam-Webster as "the action of understanding, being aware of, being sensitive to, and vicariously experiencing the feelings, thoughts, and experience of another of either the past or present without having the feelings, thoughts, and experience fully communicated in an objectively explicit manner." Engaging in empathy takes time and practice; it is a life skill that develops over many years from experiential knowledge, listening, feeling, and making reasoned connections to those with whom we empathize. However, with greater calls for promoting civics and socio-emotional learning in schools, teachers are facing a major conundrum: how do you teach content and curricular skills that also promotes empathy for students living in this confusing world?

Historical empathy is not a new concept. In fact, historical empathy as an instructional strategy can be traced back to late-19th century and early 20th century Progressive Era social, economic, and political reforms were reshaping the purpose and need for history and social studies education (Perrotta & Bohan, 2018c, 2020). Building upon the works of important scholars, philosophers, and educators such as, but not limited to, John Dewey (1910, 1916), R.G. Collingwood (1946), Rachel Davis DuBois (1942), Edwin Fenton (1967), Allan O. Kownslar (1967), Jerome Bruner (1960), O.L. Davis (2001), Elizabeth Yeager and Stuart Foster (2001), Peter Lee and Rosalyn (2001), Kaya Yilmaz (2007), Keith Barton and Linda Levstik (2004), and Jason Endacott and Sarah Brooks (2018), we, Katie and Jennifer, define *historical empathy* as the three-pronged approach to teaching social studies and ELA that promotes the cognitive and affective engagement in historical thinking through:

1) Examination of socio-economic, political and cultural aspects of historical contexts of texts
2) Analysis of how historical contexts shape the perspectives, beliefs, and actions of those in the past
3) Making reasoned affective connections to texts based on experiential knowledge and historical content, while acknowledging how the past and present differ, in order to take feasible informed action in the present.

Teaching social studies and ELA from a *historical empathy* approach takes history, geography, civics, economics, writing, literature, and grammar instruction beyond pedagogy. Historical empathy is the active process of humanizing the curriculum through engaging students in the *cognitive skills* (or also referred to as intellectual or academic skills) of analyzing multiple types of primary sources and texts through connecting to their *affective* or *emotive* responses to what they learned, which can include connections to prior knowledge, feelings, and life experiences when examining how the past and present often interact. We are sure that you are already teaching to promote historical empathy with your students and do not even realize it. We share our experiences about teaching from a historical empathy approach to show you that these approaches to teaching social studies and ELA are feasible, powerful, and meaningful.

Often, historical empathy skills are housed in social studies standards for history and civics, which makes sense given the aim for promoting youth for active participation in democratic society. The National Council for History Education (NCHE) History's Habits of the Mind (HHM) framework specifically highlights *historical empathy* as the process in which the examination of perspectives, historical contexts, problems, and decisions through source analysis can promote historical empathy and civic engagement. Additionally, the National Council for the Social Studies' (NCSS) Executive Summary defines social studies as "promotion of civic competence—the knowledge, intellectual processes, and democratic dispositions required of students to be active and engaged participants in public life." (https://www.socialstudies.org/standards/national-curriculum-standards-social-studies-executive-summary) The dispositions NCSS outlines as being central to social studies education are using knowledge of students' communities, nation, and world to engage inquiry through data collection and analysis to solve problems and make informed decisions. Although these skills involve deep research and investigation of source evidence, heavily implied in the NCSS definition of social studies is historical empathy— the intellectual and emotive ability of students to consider differing perspectives from the past, even those they may disagree with, to actively participate in contemporary democratic society and civil discourse.

Throughout the years, we would talk about teaching and share approaches we used with different types of primary sources and literature to engage students in inquiry-based learning. Ultimately, we realized that our content areas, though unique, are very closely related. Social studies is not simply the nonfiction branch of ELA. ELA is more than the technical aspects of spelling, grammar, and syntax of language. Great works of literature, poetry, creative writing, and informational texts, which include historical documents, share a literary tradition that cannot be truly appreciated or understood if ELA and social studies were treated as separate entities. For instance, the Declaration of Independence is an inspiring work of writing with eloquent prose, assertive arguments, and infamous quotes regarding equality that shaped legal precedents in this nation and others since 1776. From a social studies standpoint, examining the Declaration with historical empathy strategies can involve analyzing the historical context of 1776 and why the document was written, scrutinizing the various perspectives concerning what Thomas Jefferson should include and omit from the final document, and reflecting upon how one feels when they read the document and makes affective connections to what they live and learn about history, especially when not all men and women have been treated equally despite the immortal lines in the document. Including the ELA perspective into analyzing the Declaration from a historical empathy approach makes analyzing this document so much richer and engaging. Without exploring the historical contexts of the Enlightenment and the writers of that time, students may miss how the works of Locke, Rousseau, Voltaire, and Montesquieu influenced political thought and theory regarding the relationship between a government and the people.

Moreover, without the literary analysis of colonial literature of the 18th century, such as the poetry of Phillis Wheatley, students may not grasp the breadth and depth of the American Revolution as not just a political dispute, but a socio-economic and cultural divide that set the course of this and other nations on a trajectory of grappling with what freedom and equality means. The fact that Wheatley, along with generations of African Americans, women, indigenous Americans, and marginalized groups fought for, and still fight for, equal rights despite the words that Jefferson wrote in the Declaration in 1776. Engaging students in the analysis of the historical contexts and perspectives of people in the past with non-fiction and fiction works can be a powerful way to promote historical empathy in an interdisciplinary way. This book is meant to be a one-stop shop of teaching strategies and resources that social studies and ELA can use, hopefully together, to build bridges that connect historical empathy to active engagement in learning English and social studies that supports student development into active, informed, and caring citizens.

Historical Empathy: A Timeline

Before we talk about why this book can be an impactful tool for ELA and social studies teachers to promote historical empathy, we need to outline some of the curricular and pedagogical context of historical empathy. Grounded in works of historians, teachers, theorists and philosophers from the 20th and 21st centuries that we mention above, historical empathy challenged "traditional" historical research by emphasizing the role of the researcher's subjectivities when analyzing how historical contexts of the past shape perspectives of the past, and the extent to which a researcher's feelings, emotive responses, and experiences impact how they discern historical significance. As a result, history and social studies instruction shifted from being a passive to an active learning experience for students to examine historical contexts and perspectives through analysis of multiple sources and making relevant connections to their own lives, feelings, and prior knowledge.

In the United States, progressive social studies instruction through implementing historical empathy methods was quite prevalent from the 1950s throughout the 1970s during a time when hundreds of "new social studies" curricula focused on highlighting marginalized narratives and analyzing social problems through examination of experiential knowledge of youth. However, the pedagogical pendulum swung in the 1980s when the government report *A Nation at Risk* (1983) caused deep political debate over the failure of schools and how progressive teaching was a major reason why the U.S. was falling behind competitor nations during the end of the Cold War. Although the 1989 Bradley Commission, which was comprised of historians, educators, professors, and then- Education Secretary Diane Ravitch, convened to make recommendations for history instruction, persistent debates about what the history and social studies curriculum should focus on— a multicultural approach of America's diversity or assimilation perspective of American exceptionalism— stymied efforts in the 1990s to establish a national history curriculum.

When the U.S. Congress reauthorized the 1965 Elementary and Secondary Education Act (ESEA) in 2001 with No Child Left Behind, (NCLB) curricular and instructional emphasis shifted to math and ELA, particularly in elementary and middle school grades, for all American students to obtain 100% proficiency in these areas by 2014. Despite this goal, the numerous critiques of the aims and implementation of NCLB to achieve this proficiency rate include the lack of regard for historic issues such as (but not limited to) racial segregation, gender inequalities, lack of high-quality special education, and disparate numbers of school counselors and community supports such as meals, books, and internet for children in high-need areas. Without basic acknowledgement of these issues, let alone policies that empathetically explored these issues in order to create meaningful solutions, the complete demonstration of math and ELA proficiency on high-stakes exams was woefully unrealistic, even though policy makers and elected officials on both sides of the political aisle championed for NCLB, and later Race to the Top (RTTT) federal grants for science, technology, engineering, and mathematics (STEM) initiatives in the states. Absent from these reforms were sustaining curricular initiatives to promote social studies.

In 2002, $1 billion in federal Teaching American History (TAH) grants were included in appropriations funding for NCLB, which funded local educational agencies (LEAs) to provide professional development for history and social studies teachers. Katie was fortunate to have attended a couple of TAH-funded professional development workshops at the Museum of the City of New York when she was a middle grades social studies teacher working in the New York City Department of Education. Many of these professional development offerings highlighted how teachers can find and use primary sources and other historical entities such as museums to support teachers' content knowledge of history, students' aptitude on state exams, and preparation of K-12 social studies teachers. TAH grants were funded until 2012 when H.R 1891 was passed, which repealed "ineffective or unnecessary education programs in order to restore the focus of Federal programs on quality elementary and secondary education programs for disadvantaged students" (https://www.congress.gov/bill/112th-congress/house-bill/1891/text). Despite the fact the U.S. economy was recovering from the

2009 Great Recession and budget concerns were very real, the repeal of TAH grants and other programs such as character education, economics education, indigenous education, foreign language instruction, mental health, and women's educational equity led to a widening gap between the support, funding, and emphasis of social studies, and empathy, in K-12 schools.

Around the same time, the National Governor's Association created the Common Core Standards Initiative (CCSI) in 2010. The CCSI provided a standardized framework of curricular skills that students in all participating states should be able to demonstrate literacy proficiency in math and ELA. Skills such as analyzing source evidence, understanding different perspectives, citing evidence to support arguments and claims, and evaluating the reliability and credibility of sources that are often taught in social studies and history courses are embedded in the CCSI ELA standards for grades 6-12. Conspicuously, there are no history standards included in the CCSI ELA standards for grades K-5. However, the CCSI (2010) notes that among the important literacy skills for history is to understand diverse experiences and perspectives across cultures through reading, analyzing, and critiquing diverse texts.

All these debates and changes to the social studies curriculum had direct and indirect impacts on ELA teachers. To support these social studies standards, the National Council of the Teachers of English (NCTE), along with the International Reading Association, updated their ELA standards in 2009 to create a strong foundation of language learning and literacy "to ensure that all students are offered the opportunities, the encouragement, and the vision to develop the language skills they need to pursue life's goals, including personal enrichment and participation as informed members of our society" (NCTE, 2009, p. 1). The standards emphasize the need for ELA to include literacy instruction for verbal, written, and visual forms of language because of the importance of preparing students for life, careers, and citizenship in a rapidly changing technological society. Since the standards highlight those forms of language such as "film and television, commercial and political advertising, photography, and more" are vital to rigorous and relevant ELA instruction, we find that these forms of language are relevant to promoting historical empathy. Primary sources come in various textual and literary forms, and we contend that social studies and ELA teachers have much in common when supporting the curricular and content goals of their instruction. Although the skills of historical empathy are largely implied throughout the NCTE standards, the aims of engaging students in analyzing the complexity of language very much parallel the goals of social studies standards.

In response to the implementation of the CCSI, the NCSS issued the College, Career, and Civic Life (C3) Framework in 2013 to complement states' adoption of K-12 social studies standards that were in alignment with the ELA standards. The C3 Framework is fashioned to promote historical thinking through implementation of its Inquiry Arc's Four Dimensions of 1) Driving Inquiries through Compelling Questions, 2) Making Content Connections to Civics, History, Economics, and Geography for elementary, middle, and high school grades, 3) Analyzing Primary Source Evidence, and 4) Using Evidence to Communicate Conclusions and Taking Informed Action. The C3 Framework has been the hallmark of NCSS professional development and teacher materials that are published in their journals *Social Studies and the Young Learner*, *Middle Level Learning*, and *Social Education* for almost a decade. A major curricular aim of the C3 Framework (2013) is to promote student engagement in analysis of multiple perspectives to gain "historical understanding requires developing a sense of empathy with people in the past whose perspectives might be very different from those of today" (p. 47).

Former Secretary of Education Arne Duncan called for "empathetic leadership" in response to school closures due to COVID-19 (Rotherham & Zhao, 2020). In the wake of the January 6, 2021 Capitol insurrection, Duncan and former Education Secretaries urged for the adoption of the Roadmap to Educating for American Democracy (READ) initiative, which would "renew the study of history and to rebuild civic education from the ground up, by providing guiding principles for states, local school districts and educators across the U.S. They, in turn, can establish their own standards and tailor curricular materials to their local communities." Created in 2021 by organizations such as Harvard University, Tufts University, iCivics, Arizona State University and funded by a grant from the National Endowment of the Humanities and U.S. Department of Education, this initiative is meant to "complement, not compete with, the C3 Framework" by providing seven themes and five design challenges that are specific to history and civics instruction (p. 2). The READ initiative essentially provides specific compelling questions related to the C3 Framework Dimension 2 history and civics standards that can guide teachers and students through the process of historical empathy by examining the role of government in the lives of individuals and societies, the challenges people and groups face, the "multifaceted" historical and civic narratives of American democracy, and discuss potential avenues for solving problems (EAD, 2021, p. 16). You can download a copy of the READ report and standards from their site (https://www.educatingforamericandemocracy.org).

Why This Book

The HHM, READ initiative, C3 Framework, and CCSI offer several pedagogical approaches to fostering historical empathy in social studies. Additionally, the historical empathy skills of identifying historical contexts, examining past perspectives, and making reasoned affective connections to the present are extremely relevant to ELA instruction as outlined in the NCTE standards. However, with so many approaches to choose from, many teachers may find these choices to be overwhelming. Making things even more confusing is searching on the internet for guidance on how these frameworks can be used to support students' empathy as an academic and personal skill. A simple Google search of the term historical empathy yields over 38 million results. Teachers cannot simply read millions of websites and articles about historical empathy so that they can adapt these strategies to their classroom instruction. As a result, we wrote this book for teachers, pre-service educators, curriculum specialists, professional development facilitators, museum educators, and other educators as a "one-stop-shop" for historical empathy resources and strategies to deepen your ELA and social studies instruction.

Historical Empathy: Katie's Story

When I was a kid growing up in New York City, I was mesmerized when I learned about the discovery of the African Burial Ground in Lower Manhattan. Excavation for construction of a building was halted when human remains were found. This was in 1991, and as an elementary-aged child, I had no idea about the legacy of enslavement in New York, let alone in the north. Fast forward to my undergraduate experience in college, I was taking history courses and learning more about the deeply entrenched history of slavery and segregation in the history of New York City. Again, I was shocked because I did not know anything about the slave rebellions during British rule, the role of African Americans who fought in the American Revolution, or the 1863 Draft Riots where Irish immigrants rioted against conscription into the Union army, lynching Blacks and burning a colored orphanage in Manhattan. I was majoring in education and striving to be a middle school social studies teacher. My goal was to return to the New York City public schools and teach; a way of giving back as a result of the good education I received as a student. I realized that I needed to teach history differently from the way I learned it. How could I live in a place my whole life and be unaware of the experiences, challenges, perspectives, and accomplishments of so many people in history that I never heard of?

After graduating from State University of New York College at Oneonta, where I studied New York City history, I began my first full-time teaching job in a middle school in a predominantly Latinx immigrant neighborhood in Brooklyn. I started my teaching career five years after 9/11 and two years before the Great Recession. I was coming of age during a confusing time after the terror attacks on the World Trade Center, wars in Afghanistan and Iraq, and suspicions of anyone who looked "different" from the status quo. While trying to make sense of these events in my young career, I was also trying to figure out how to make the social studies curriculum I was teaching engaging, interesting, and relevant to my students. My first year of teaching was incredibly challenging. I had pretty much zero classroom management and very low confidence that I could be a good teacher. I literally cried every day for three months, lost a lot of sleep and weight, and doubted whether I chose the right profession.

Around Thanksgiving, I had a realization that I had to find a way to teach the curriculum and standards in a way that engaged students to want to learn social studies. I also realized I needed to be human, a scary proposition given my total lack of classroom management. I started talking with students about my hobbies and interests, and asked them questions about what they liked and disliked about social studies. They asked me about my background and my interests. Once rapports and relationships were developed, I began experimenting with using primary sources that had some connection to students' lives, interests, and community where they lived. I started with the obituary of Charles O. Dewey, whom the school was named after, and students began to ask about the significance of names of streets, buildings, and landmarks around Brooklyn. I found documents such as speeches, diary entries, photographs, music, maps, and art from time periods like the Great Depression, World War II, and Civil Rights Movement to show that diverse people always existed in the United States who held different perspectives and had experiences. I survived my first year of teaching having learned a lot not only about my skills as a middle school teacher, but the community where I was working.

During my second year of teaching, I worked with the Brooklyn Public Library to assist me with finding documents about the neighborhood where students lived in order to make their studies of U.S history relevant to their lives. I also began taking students on field trips to historical sites in Manhattan such as Federal Hall, Castle Clinton, the Museum of Natural History, Prospect Park, and Greenwood Cemetery. I assigned projects like creating postcards, brochures, board games, and historical narrative writing where students used examples from primary source documents to write from the perspective of someone from the past, and to reflect on how this research can connect to their lives. I created long-term projects where students researched issues such as gentrification, immigration, economic recession, and a presidential election using primary sources and proposing at the end of the project how their research can be used to create a solution to the problems. Gradually, I noticed that students were more eager to come to social studies class, asking "what are we doing next,

Miss?" and being excited to display what they learned. At that time, I did not realize that what I was trying to do was to promote historical empathy through my social studies instruction.

I discovered historical empathy during my doctoral studies in social studies education after I moved to Atlanta. I relocated with my fiancé (now husband) at the height of the Great Recession when he took a new job down South. A major aspect of being in a Ph.D. program is identifying an area of research that needs greater exploration that makes a significant contribution to student learning. I was stuck on a topic that I could not let go of. While I worked in Brooklyn, I was pursuing my master's degree in history in order to obtain my professional teacher certification, a requirement in New York State. I was on my way home from a Teaching American History (TAH) grant professional development workshop at the Museum of the City of New York in 2007 where I stumbled upon the story of Elizabeth Jennings in a book about Lower East Side tenements. The caption stated that the Lower East Side, where present-day City Hall is located, was the location of a "little known site for racial progress." I never heard of Jennings or this milestone before.

I felt transported back to when I was a child learning about the discovery of the African Burial Ground. I started going down the rabbit hole of the mid-aughts internet to find out who Elizabeth Jennings was. Based on some brief articles and blogs, I read that she was a Black school teacher who was forcibly ejected from a streetcar in 1854 on her way to church. Her abolitionist father Thomas L. Jennings hired the law firm of Culver, Parker, and Arthur to represent her in a lawsuit against the Third Avenue Streetcar Car Company. Future president Chester A. Arthur argued Elizabeth's case in New York Supreme Court, asserting that as a paying customer, her ejection from the streetcar violated her common carrier rights. During the antebellum period in New York and other northern cities, privately-owned transit company instituted racial segregation policies. Jennings won her case, which set a legal precedent for Blacks in the north to challenge racial segregation before the Civil War. Even as I retell this story 15 years later, I still get chills because I had no idea segregation, de jure and de facto, existed in the north. I knew I had to bring this story to my students, and possibly write about Jennings for my Master's thesis. Alas, at the time, I could not find enough documents to write a full thesis. I was running out of time to finish my degree before my impending move to Atlanta. So I wrote about something else, and put Jennings aside...until it was time to write my dissertation study. I kept going back to Jennings and her story and my ignorance to her story and had a revelation sitting on my couch one evening---- why should we care about this story?

INTRODUCTION

Then I had the ah-ha moment. I grabbed my copy of Sam Wineburg's (2001) *Historical Thinking and Other Unnatural Acts* and lo and behold, found this quote:

> In the words of the Bradley Commission, the report that launched the current reform movement in history education, students should enter 'into a world of drama— suspending [their] knowledge of the ending in order to gain a sense of another era— a sense of empathy that allows the student to see through the eyes of who were there (p. 8).'"

I read on, finding that Wineburg (2001) cited researchers Roslyn Ashby and Peter J. Lee's works on historical empathy and how this is a process in which learners, children and adults alike, engage in not only analyzing the past, but trying to understand the past on its own terms, not solely from our presentist lens. For example, we can look at how Elizabeth Jennings' ejection from a moving horse-drawn streetcar from a 21st-century perspective as being an example of how people may be quick to act to a situation like this. Today, we could take cellphone video and post online by livestreaming the incident on social media, which could compel others to march, protest, sign petitions, and take up donations to support Jennings' legal defense and other medical expenses. However, no one intervened in 1854 except a German immigrant who helped her up off the sidewalk after she was forcibly thrown from the streetcar. From a presentist lens, which means that we judge the past on today's terms, we may be compelled to say, "the people on that streetcar were racist! They didn't care!" And that could very well have been the case. However, 1854 New York was different from today. A city with a high number of immigrants who were in competition for jobs and housing with poor whites and freedmen, it is plausible that the bystanders did not intervene due to fears of getting involved in a situation that could lead to job termination if they took the wrong side of the conflict. Passengers might have been too scared to get involved for fears of getting hurt themselves, as the lower East Side Bowery section of Manhattan was notorious for gang activity (yes, those "Gangs of New York"). The acknowledgement of historical contexts, perspectives, and how the past and present differ, while condemning acts such as racism by making reasoned affective connections to this history is the process of historical empathy. We can't know how to address a present-day issue if we don't look to see how people and groups faced challenges and overcame them.

As a result, I created a curriculum using primary and secondary sources about Elizabeth Jennings' incident and conducted my dissertation study on whether middle and secondary students' engagement in this unit about Jennings as an underrepresented historical figure could promote historical empathy. I found that students could demonstrate cognitive aspects historical empathy when studying ordinary people and lesser-known historical events in local and national history through analyzing primary sources and deliberating a response to the driving question, "is it ever OK to break a rule or a law?" with narrative writing, mind mapping, and debate activities (Perrotta, 2022; Perrotta, 2018a). I also found evidence of a historical empathy gap, where students who identified themselves as white, Asian, and male displayed lower rates of the affective responses to historical research as compared to students who identified as female, Black, Latinx, or of Middle Eastern descent (Perrotta, 2018b). So, I was left with the question, how do students' identities impact the extent to which they demonstrate historical empathy? I am still working on an answer to that question, along with other historical empathy scholars and social studies teachers. Identity is personal and collective, unique and controversial, what we strive to be and what we understand. I hope teachers who read this book also think about these questions, and how we can work together to promote historical empathy to support the next generation of this nation's leaders, thinkers, and doers.

Historical Empathy: Jennifer's Story

In my fifteen years of teaching high school English Language Arts (ELA), for over half of those years I have taught American Literature. While I love teaching most literature, I particularly enjoy teaching American Literature. I tell my students that they should be able to find their story in American Literature, whether they sit in the class as American-born citizens, immigrants, or refugees. American Literature should offer the story of each of us. That's the idea, and yet, as good as I think I am at offering opportunities to my students to find their stories, and by that, I mean presenting a broad sampling of literature and invitations to explore, do I teach the language of that exploration? Do I give them a map to follow, and do I suggest that they may find multiple stories that may cross in unexpected ways? In other words, it is not enough to present a survey of literature if our end goal is to ask our students to own it. We need to consider what tools they will need to question the purpose of the writers, examine the motivations for those purposes, and yes, be prepared to challenge the arguments.

Since 2021, many state legislatures across the country passed laws that prohibit teaching about "divisive concepts." As a teacher and resident in a state where this type of law was passed, the implications of these legal actions concern me greatly. Over the years, I have enjoyed open academic discourse with my students over texts; discourse that could not have occurred without the assurance that I was protected as long as I did not in any way direct my students toward a specific political or philosophical agenda. Teaching diverse populations, I attempt to remain sensitive to all my students' cultural backgrounds, offering them a safe place to participate in discussion around texts from *The Adventures of Huckleberry Finn* by Mark Twain to *Native Son* by Richard Wright; from *Passing* by Nella

Larson to *Dear Martin* by Nic Stone. The language of these laws are ambiguous and thus, easily interpreted in ways that could criminalize the very discussions I have entertained about the diversity of American literature and history in my ELA classes for years.

During the 2019-2020 school year, I attended the National Council for Teachers of English (NCTE) annual conference in Baltimore. Each year at its conference, NCTE recognizes teachers across the country for outstanding work in and outside of the classroom. One such educator was Georgia media specialist Cicely Lewis who was awarded the NCTE and Penguin Random House National Teacher Award for Lifelong Readers for her Woke Reading initiative in which she challenged students to read books that challenged social norms and offered young protagonists that represented populations often neglected in literature. She encouraged students to read narratives that included characters like themselves but also very different from themselves. I realized I possessed an opportunity to do something similar, perhaps on a smaller scale, but equally important to my students.

At the time I was teaching in a school represented predominantly by students of color and a significant population of students who were immigrants and refugees. I wanted to give my students the opportunity to read books in which they felt represented but also challenge them to read about others and other experiences different from themselves and their experiences. When I returned home to Georgia from the conference I reached out to my principal and shared the idea. He loved it and told me to go forward with it. I started a GoFundMe, raising enough money to purchase over 60 titles. Our media specialist was very helpful, offering suggestions for new titles that students were requesting. It was serendipitous that our media specialist organized a book fair that fall semester. This allowed me to include my students in the book selection giving them further voice in their reading. The project was a huge success. Students loved being included in the process and felt invested. I challenged my students to read three books: one that offered a protagonist they could relate to, one that offered a protagonist very different from themselves, and one that challenged their ideas.

After students completed at least one book, we held book talks. Students could not wait to share their books and their reactions. Many times I heard a student comment after hearing a classmate's discussion, "I really want to read that now!" I invited my principal and other administrators and teachers to observe some of our discussions. No one expressed concern. In fact, reactions were quite the opposite. My principal loved the student engagement and the level on which they were able to discuss social issues and make connections to other works. One student exclaimed, "I have never read a book in school that had characters who spoke my language." Other students made connections to classic works we read in class such as Arthur Miller's *The Crucible*. Those older works now possessed more relevance for them.

When Katie approached me about co-authoring this book, I quickly said "yes" to the opportunity. English Language Arts (ELA) courses possess a natural connection to social studies. For me, it has always felt natural to teach through a new historian lens; offering historical context to the works I present to my students so that they hopefully glean a better understanding of the social, political, and cultural movements at the time the work was penned. Teaching Shakespeare's final play, *The Tempest*, becomes more than the last play of a 17th century playwright when students can engage in the history of the time. It was the Age of Discovery and early days of what would become the building of the British Empire. Conversations about colonization become the elephant in the room if ignored, but if engaged, become opportunities for students to make connections and explore their own understandings and experiences. It helps them to begin to understand that literary texts offer writers' devices like figurative language to explore the complexities of power, justice, leadership, government, society and culture. Fictional writers offer readers the opportunity to frame historical events through multiple lenses and interpretations. In the same way, non-fictional works can present a variety of perspectives on a single subject.

I love stories. I chose narrative inquiry for my dissertation study because it offered a methodology that allowed me to tell a story. History is full of stories that fiction and non-fiction writers have framed in various ways, through multiple perspectives, to help readers engage in empathy. When students ask, "Why do we have to read this?" I answer simply, "So that you can stand in someone else's shoes." For these and many other reasons, it has always made sense to me that social studies and ELA teachers work in tandem to present historical events. One of the reasons I have always loved teaching American Literature is that it is the one high school ELA course that is taught (in most schools) the same year as its history counterpart, American History. Students have told me multiple times that they appreciate the "double dipping" these two courses offer, especially when both are taught chronologically. Many times throughout the year, my students have reported learning about a period in American history while reading a fictional or non-fictional text from the same period.

A friend who was born in Somalia and educated in Kenya, told me that much of her education was through stories. These stories imparted history and cultural relevance. Given this educational tool, her parents, especially her mother, used stories to explain a situation or help her with something with which she was struggling. She explained to me that these stories frequently helped her navigate difficult situations. I immediately thought of my hopes for my ELA students. Social studies and ELA courses possess the language and context through which students can develop historical empathy and hopefully gain a greater and broader appreciation of the world around them.

What is Available and What is Needed

Our stories highlight how ELA and social studies teachers are already implementing historical empathy strategies in their curriculum and instruction. Grounded in historical empathy research over the past 20 years, this book is geared towards teacher practitioners who can conveniently identify strategies that can be used to promote historical empathy in social studies and ELA. We provide NCTE and NCSS C3 Framework-aligned lesson plan examples in each chapter with examples of learning activities and resources that teachers can readily adapt and use with their students. We recommend that you read this book as the foundation for why historical empathy is important for ELA and social studies education.

This book offers a one-stop-shop to support teachers, instructional coaches, curriculum developers, and educational leaders on how to effectively promote not just empathy, but historical empathy, in ELA and social studies education. We focus on historical empathy, not just empathy, in this book because historical empathy encompasses both the cognitive and affective responses to the experiences of people's experiences in the past and present through source analysis. We can't go back in time to ask Elizabeth Jennings about her ordeal. We can support students, and encourage ourselves, to dig deep into our prior knowledge of social studies, language, literature, current events, personal experiences, and vicarious knowledge of others' experiences to analyze how historical contexts shaped the perspectives of those in the past, and how that historical significance interacts with our present world.

Historical empathy is not just simply imagining what life was like in the past. Historical empathy is not just rattling off dates, names, and events in class. Historical empathy is not feeling sorry for victims of injustice in the past, nor is it condoning bad acts no matter the time period in which atrocities occurred. Historical empathy is the intertwined process in which students' emotions, feelings, reflections, identities, and experiences--- among the things that make them human--- simultaneously impact historical thinking through primary source research.

Historical empathy is a process that may take years for students to develop. Moreover, historical empathy is not a linear experience, as students may have strong affective and cognitive responses to content to certain topics versus others. However, isn't the goal of teaching to support students' cultivation of skills and content knowledge throughout their lives, not just during their time in compulsory school? The aim of historical empathy is to promote students' competence in ELA social studies literacy so that they can grow up to be prosocial participation in democratic society. Given the diversity of experiences and assets that students bring to your classrooms, as well as the expanse of issues, technology, texts, and primary sources that can be incorporated into ELA social studies instruction, we outline the process of unpacking what historical empathy is and how teachers can promote these skills in the following chapters that connect to the NCTE standards and NCSS C3 Framework. Each chapter includes brainstorming activities and reflection questions for you to consider as you think about how you can implement historical empathy strategies in your classrooms.

Chapter Outline

Chapter 1: Literary Analysis highlights some approaches on how to use literature analysis when teaching historical empathy in social studies. Many approaches to interdisciplinary connections to English language arts will be made in this chapter, since numerous curricular standards and skills that support historical empathy in social studies are complemented by the CCSSI standards, as well as the NCTE Standards. Specifically, this chapter will start you on your journey when teaching to promote historical empathy by exploring how the reading, research, and writing skills in social studies and ELA can support students' development of their cognitive and affective skills of identifying historical contexts and perspectives from works of fiction and non-fiction literature.

Chapter 2: Digital Media focuses on how to choose and use web-based primary and secondary sources when fostering historical empathy in social studies. Piggybacking on literary analysis, we share examples of effective and impactful primary and secondary sources from credible and vetted websites and digital media outlets that teachers can use when planning historical empathy inquiries with their students. Discussion of news articles, social media, and contemporary issues and current events that are posted on digital platforms will be included with regard to discerning credibility, validity, and accuracy of information. We highlight in **Chapter 3: Music and Recording Arts** how songs, lyrics, and audio recordings can be played with students to foster historical empathy. Music is said to be a universal language, and Katie and Jennifer zone in on the recording arts as primary sources that can support students' development of intellectual and emotive skills of historical empathy. In **Chapter 4: Films and Documentaries**, we provide suggestions and tips for using motion film, television shows, and documentaries as secondary sources that can be analyzed by students for historical contexts in which visual arts are created, the perspectives of those creating these films, and how the information presented in these films can support their understandings of how the past is interpreted in the present.

Chapter 5: Photographs and Visual Arts details how to engage students in historical empathy through examination of illustrations, portraits, paintings, photographs, and cartoons. In particular, pictures and portraits can serve as primary and secondary sources. We discuss analysis techniques that teachers can implement with students to determine how the contexts and perspectives by the artists, and the images they portray, can support students' academic and emotional connections to historical content. Chapter 6: Place-Based Education outlines several ways in which virtual and physical museum exhibits, cultural institutions such as botanical gardens and libraries, and local history sites can provide community resources that students can analyze historical contexts, perspectives, and purpose for preserving historical and cultural locations. We end with our Conclusion where we provide some answers to the "so what?" question about why historical empathy is an important aspect of ELA and social studies instruction. Why should anyone care about the past? Why should we bother reading old documents and stories? Why should we spend time analyzing old photographs or listening to music or watching film? We hope that this book provides space where teachers and students can discuss the age-old question about schooling: "why do we need to know this?" by thinking about the ways you can implement historical empathy in your instruction and be part of pushing this pedagogical field forward as we face challenges that are yet unknown in the 21st-century.

An Invitation: How to Use this Book

We ask the question again, *how do you teach content and curricular skills that also promotes empathy for students living in this confusing world?* as a jumping off point for teachers, curriculum designers, coaches, educational leaders, and pretty much anyone who cares about children and the health of our democracy to think about how their own understanding and demonstration of historical empathy that prepares students for life in the 21st-century. You will notice that some of our chapters are long because we wanted to provide teachers with as many resources and ideas as we could to support their creativity when implementing historical empathy with their students. We encourage readers to skip around chapters, check out the materials in the call-out boxes, and consider trying out the examples of materials, standards, and lesson plans that most resonate with you and your students. Each chapter has a list of cited references and suggested resources. This book is meant to be a tool that can help teachers and students engage in historical empathy not only during classroom instruction, but when they venture out into the world.

INTRODUCTION

Haim Ginott's (1972) quote, "I've come to a frightening conclusion. I am the decisive element in the classroom" resonates with us because if we want to promote historical empathy in our teaching, we as teachers need to model those skills and self-reflection. If we expect the future generations to solve our world's complicated problems, then let's take a deep dive into our own experiences, perspectives, assumptions, and understandings of what historical empathy is, so that we can model what historical empathy can be in our classrooms.

References

Barton, K., & Levstik, L. (2004). Teaching history for the common good. Lawrence Earlbaum Associates.

Bruner, J. (1960). *The process of education: A landmark in educational theory.* Harvard University Press.

Common Core State Standards Initiative. (2010). English language arts & literary in history/social studies, and technical subjects. https://www.thecorestandards.org/wp-content/uploads/ELA_Standards1.pdf

Collingwood, R. G. (1946). *The idea of history: Revised edition with lectures, 1926–1928.* Oxford University Press.

Davis, O. L. Jr. (2001). *In pursuit of historical empathy.* In O. L. Davis, Yeager, E.A., & Foster, S.J., Eds. *Historical empathy and perspective taking in the social studies, pp. 1–12.* Roman & Littlefield.

Dewey, J. (2024, 1916). *Democracy and Education.* Columbia University Press.

Dewey, J. (2019, 1910). *How we think.* Anados Books.

DuBois, R.D. (1942). *Get together Americans: Friendly approaches to racial and cultural conflicts through the neighborhood-home festival.* Harper& Brothers.

Educating for American Democracy. (2021). *Roadmap to Education Americans for Democracy Report.* https://www.educatingforamericandemocracy.org/wp-content/uploads/2021/02/Educating-for-American-Democracy-Report-Excellence-in-History-and-Civics-for-All-Learners.pdf

Endacott, J. L., & Brooks, S. (2018). Historical empathy: Perspectives and responding to the past, in Manfra, M.M. & Bolick, C.M., (Eds). *The Wiley international handbook of history teaching and learning,* 203-225.

Fenton, E. (1967). *The new social studies: Implications for school administration.* Curriculum Report: National Association of Secondary School Principals 51(317), 62–76. doi:10.1177/019263656705131709019263656705131709

Ginott, H. (1972). *Teacher and child.* Avon Books.

Kownslar, A. O., & Frizzle, D. (1967). *Discovering American history.* Hold, Reinhart, and Winston.

Lee, P., & Ashby, R. (2004). Empathy, perspective taking, and rational understanding, in Davis, O.L., Yeager, E.A., & Foster, S.J., Eds. *Historical empathy and perspective taking in the social studies*. Roman & Littlefield, pp. 21-50.

Miller, A. (1953). *The Crucible, a Play in Four Acts*. Heinemann Plays series. Notes and questions by Maureen Blakesley. Oxford: Heinemann.

National Council for History Education. *History's Habits of Mind*. Retrieved from https://ncheteach.org/Historys-Habits-of-Mind

National Council for the Social Studies. (2013). *College, career, and civic life framework for social studies state standards*. https://www.socialstudies.org/system/files/2022/c3- framework-for-social-studies-rev0617.2.pdf

National Council of Teachers of English. (2009). *Standards for the English language arts*. https://cdn.ncte.org/nctefiles/resources/books/sample/standardsdoc.pdf

Perrotta, K.A. (2022). A wholesome verdict: Using historical empathy strategies to analyze *Elizabeth Jennings v. The Third Avenue Railway Company* of 1855. *Social Education- the National Council for the Social Studies 86*(1), 47-56. https://www.ingentaconnect.com/content/ncss/se/2022/00000086/00000001/art00008#trendmd-suggestions

Perrotta, K.A., & Bohan, C.H. (2020). Can't stop this feeling: Tracing the origins of historical empathy during the New Social Studies era, 1950-1980. *Educational Studies 56*(6), 599-618. https://doi.org/10.1080/00131946.2020.1837832

Perrotta, K.A. (2018a). Pedagogical conditions that promote historical empathy with "The Elizabeth Jennings Project." *Social Studies Research and Practice 13*(2), 129-146. https://doi.org/10.1108/SSRP-11-2017-0064

Perrotta, K.A. (2018b). A study of students' social identities and a historical empathy gap in middle and secondary social studies classes with the instructional unit "The Elizabeth Jennings Project." *Curriculum and Teaching Dialogue 20*(1&2), 53-69. https://www.proquest.com/docview/2097606392?pq-origsite=gscholar&fromopenview=true

Perrotta, K.A., & Bohan, C.H. (2018c). More than a feeling: Tracing the progressive era origins of historical empathy in the social studies curriculum, 1890s-1940s. *The Journal of Social Studies Research 42*(1), 27-37. https://doi.org/10.1016/j.jssr.2017.01.002

Rotherham, A.J., & Zhao, E. (2020). *74 Interview: Former Secretary of Education Arne Duncan Urges 'Empathetic Leadership' Through 'Brutal' Coronavirus Crisis and Toward a New Normal*. Retrieved from https://www.the74million.org/article/74-interview-former-secretary-of-education-arne-duncan-urges-empathetic-leadership-through-brutal-coronavirus-crisis-and-towards-a-new-normal/

Shakespeare, William, 1564-1616. (1958). *The tempest*. Harvard University Press.

Wineburg, S. (2001). *Historical thinking and other unnatural acts*. Temple University Press.

Yeager, E.A., & Foster, S.J. The role of empathy in the development of historical understanding, in Davis, O.L., Yeager, E.A., & Foster, S.J., Eds. *Historical empathy and perspective taking in the social studies.* Roman & Littlefield, pp. 13-20.

Yilmaz, K. (2007). *Historical empathy and its implications for classroom practices in schools. The History Teacher,* 40(3), 331–337.

CHAPTER 1

Literary Analysis

Brainstorming Activity

- What comes to mind when you think of the term *literature*?
- What works of literature are your favorites?
- How do you think you can use literature when promoting historical empathy in your teaching?

Introduction

The connection between the disciplines of English Language Arts (ELA) and Social Studies is a natural one; the former offers a narrative context through which the latter can be taught by highlighting the human element and presenting it from the distance that fiction affords. As well, there are numerous curricular standards and skills that support historical empathy in social studies that are complemented by the CCSSI standards, as well as the NCTE Standards. Katie remembers reading John Steinbeck's (1937) *Of Mice and Men* when she was high school and wondering how the backdrop of the Great Depression served as a literary device that was integral to telling the story of migrant workers and human suffering. Once she started teaching middle school social studies, Katie used excerpts from *Of Mice and Men*, as well as other works of literature such as Jose Marti's poem "To the Foreigner," Upton Sinclair's (1906) book *The Jungle*, and Remarque's All Quiet on the Western Front to engage students in how works of literature can provide historical and emotional insights to the experiences humans faced during ordinary and pivotal times in history.

Similarly, Jennifer's earliest favorite authors were novelists like Charles Dickens who offered the context of the time in which he lived in 19th century London and the social realities of that time as more than setting but as integral facets of his character's lives and situations. Later, writers like John Steinbeck, F. Scott Fitzgerald, Nella Larson, Richard Wright, James Baldwin, and Harper Lee would make similar impacts and as high school ELA teacher, the connection between history and literature would become a mainstay of literary analysis in her classroom. It may seem like a cliché to say that we understand the present by looking back at history, but Jennifer frequently found when teaching a novel like *Of Mice and Men* (Steinbeck, 1937) or a short story like "Sonny's Blues" (Baldwin, 1965) that the contextualized history represented in those works could become metaphors for present-day experiences that students could relate to, directly or indirectly.

This chapter presents approaches to teaching historical empathy through literary analysis, offering a template for cross-curriculum lessons that connect historical events and periods to literary works. The lessons employ literary analysis through the lens of historical empathy and offer approaches that are user-friendly to both the social studies teacher who has not used or taught literary analysis, and the ELA teacher unfamiliar with some historical contexts. Specifically, this chapter will start you on your journey in promoting historical empathy by exploring how applying literary analysis strategies for reading, research, and writing skills in social studies and ELA can support students' development of historical empathy from works of fiction and non-fiction literature.

What is Literary Analysis?

Literary analysis is typically thought of as reader interpretation through a close reading of text. Often, these close readings are accomplished through specific lenses such as power, gender, race, environment, philosophy, and science to name a few commonly employed. Deborah Appleman's (2023) work *Critical Encounters in Secondary English* is a valuable tool for ELA teachers to become acquainted with the process of historical empathy. Her book leans into how literary analysis and implementation of literary theories such as postcolonial, feminist, and critical race theories (CRT) supports how learners critically examine historical contexts of literature in order to glean diverse perspectives and voices of marginalized groups. Such cognitive or intellectual acts are integral for students to evoke reasoned affective responses to the stories and literature that they read, which can help them make sense of their world by making connections to historical content, and take informed action on issues facing their communities.

In ELA classes, close readings engage students in conversation with the text, asking them to make connections between what they are reading and other works, to other parts of the same text, to their own experiences, and to the world. The last of these connections, text to world, includes current and historic events. As many ELA teachers understand, these connections through close, critical readings, go beyond helping students to better understand the author's purpose or how themes emerge, they draw the reader into a context that may reflect their own experiences or introduce them to the experiences of others, thereby, offering opportunities for historical empathy.

Literary Analysis Approaches

Literary analysis theories are fascinating because they share deep commonalities with not only qualitative research methods, but also historical thinking and analysis strategies that social studies teacher use to engage students in inquiry and historical empathy. Qualitative research refers to how researchers, including historians and writers and teachers, study the experiences of humans to learn why a certain phenomenon exists, how people experience phenomena, and how they make meaning of phenomena in the world. *Phenomena* refers to anything that can be observed and examined. For instance, Jennifer and Katie could co-plan to teach a piece of American literature with historical documents from a particular time period as a phenomenon. Qualitative researchers seek to answer why something happens with data that comes from observations, interviews, reflections, writings, and any form of human expression. Since books and works of literature are products of phenomena, choosing a literary analysis approach or theory is important for students to examine a text through a particular lens in order to consider why an author wrote a something, and what that text means to the learner in a cognitive and affective way. Table 1.1. summarizes some of the major approaches to literary analysis:

The approaches to literary analysis are greatly impacted by not only the author of a text, but the theoretical perspective of the ELA teacher. As you read this table, we encourage you to take some time to think only about how you may implement these approaches, but which of these theories most speak to you when you are thinking about why you choose texts and strategies that engage students in analyzing the purpose, meaning, and message of literature and connect to the historical contexts and perspectives of a time when texts are written.

Connections to Social Studies

Literary analysis approaches can be very helpful and applicable to the social studies teacher who is using literature or other narrative texts in their instruction. Often, a misconception with teaching history, albeit just one content area of the social studies, is that historical research does not have a method or particular approach that historians follow. However, a historian's theoretical approach to how they view and interpret texts are similar to how the literary critic or teacher or student analyzes pieces of literature.

Traditional historical research, much like the Great Tradition approach to literary analysis, focuses on the collection of documents where the historian writes about the past based on evidence from an objective stance, thus asserting a truth about the past. Peter Novick (1988) wrote in his book *A Noble Truth* that the quest

Table 1.1 Major Approaches to Literary Analysis

Literary Analysis Approach	Explanation of Theory	Major Characteristics	Connections to Historical Empathy
The Great Tradition/ Modernism	Focus not on social context of when the text was written, but on how the art of writing is expressed	Essentialist view of learning from "classic" works of literature that stand the test of time, many of which of Western society.	Weak emphasis on historical context and multiple perspectives or voices. Focus on authors' expression of art and enduring message and truth
Reader Response	Focus on how connections between the reader and the texts impact perception of a text's meaning	Reading for explicit and implicit messages, meanings, foreshadowing; predicting what comes next, reacting to the author	Some focus on historical context, but mostly on the reader's connections to feelings, thoughts, experiences, prior knowledge to the text
Formalism	Focus on the form or structure of a text instead of the meaning of a text	Examination of an author's method on telling a story, use of literary devices, how information is conveyed	Some focus on historical context when analyzing text structure for literary devices and style that are popular at certain points in time
Structuralism	Focus on context and how texts construct meaning that is rooted in culture	Examination of patterns, themes, implicit meanings that are expressed in a text	Blended focus on historical contexts of social/cultural impacts on culture and construction of a text's meaning
Psychoanalysis	Focus on unconscious meanings and messages in a text	Examination of conflict, emotions or messages that may be glossed over or repressed and not explicitly stated in the text	Blended focus on historical contexts of social/cultural impacts on how transparent an author is when expressing an opinion, emotion, feeling, thought, or experience
Feminism	Focus on women's experiences and how those experiences are written about differently from men authors	Examination of power and oppression of women, traditional gender roles, and how women use literary devices differently from men	Focus on both the historical context of texts, the perspectives of women authors and characters who are marginalized or oppressed, considering connections to affective responses to power and gender

(Continued)

Table 1.1 (Continued)

Marxist/ Post-Colonial	Focus on the social contexts of the author and texts and the impact of power and oppression on the text and readers	Examination of how power and oppression marginalizes and impacts attitudes towards race, gender, and social class	Focus on both the historical context of texts, the perspectives of authors and characters who are marginalized or oppressed, considering connections to affective responses relating to race, ethnicity, social class, gender identity, etc.
Critical Race Theory	Focus on pervasiveness of racism in legal and social institutions and texts, and how addressing racial oppression can dismantle racism	Examination of social-political-economic contexts of racism, impact of institutionalized racism on texts and readers	Focus on historical contexts of racism in institutions, perspectives of racist and anti-racist views, amplifying counterstories of oppressed people to dismantle racism
Post-Modern Theory	Focus on individual narratives, perspectives, and subjective truth	Examination of how reality is explored and expressed in texts, no universal truth	Focus on perspectives and affective expression in texts, and how styles of writing, literary devices, and reflection are used in a non-rational or linear way
Genre Theory	Focus on the meaning of a text in relation to the genre or type of writing it belongs to	Examination of text for following or diverging from conventional rules or traditions of genres	Focus on historical contexts and perspectives of literary genres to gauge meaning of a text

for conducting historical research that highlights a universal truth to the past has always been at odds with progressive approaches to historical research, namely influenced by British philosopher R.G. Collingwood (see the works of Timothy Retz; we reference his book at the end of the chapter!), where the historian not only considers the diverse perspectives of people in the past, but also wrestles, reflects, and leans into how their own subjectivities impact historical interpretation. Kathleen Green and Anna Troup's book (2016) *The Houses of History* outline the major theoretical approaches to historical research and thinking, which do bear striking similarities to the literary analysis theories that we mentioned. Table 1.2, which we adapted from Allen Brizee and J. Case Tompkins' article for OWL Purdue, outlines these approaches to historical research and how they relate to not only historical empathy, but literary analysis approaches in ELA.

Table 1.2 Major Approaches to Historical Research

Historical Research Approach	Explanation of Theory	Characteristics of Theory	Connections to Literary Analysis	Connections to Historical Empathy
Empiricism	Focus on historical facts and truth	Analysis of historical documents and primary sources with minimal interpretation from the researcher	Grand Tradition/ Modernist	Focus on historical contexts and perspectives based on historical facts in primary sources, little to no affective connections
Marxist/ Critical	Focus on class struggles, power and oppression of capitalist system on history	Analysis of historical contexts and perspectives from primary sources that center the experiences of the working class, marginalized and oppressed groups, critiques elites in power	Critical/Post Colonial	Blended focus on historical contexts of capitalism how these historical contexts shaped perspectives of the classes, affective connections to power, oppression, and dismantling class struggle
Psychohistory	Focus on unconscious meanings, decisions, and actions of the past	Examination of historical facts and perspectives to determine why people in the past did what they did	Psychoanalysis	Blended focus on historical contexts, how historical contexts shaped perspectives in the past in order to analyze why past events and actions occurred

(*Continued*)

Table 1.2 (Continued)

Structuralism	Focus on the structure of language and cultures, and how structures impact actions	Analysis of primary sources for patterns in history about governmental, cultural, political, social, economic structures	Structuralism	Blended focus on how cultures, language, institutions, and structures impact historical contexts, how historical contexts shaped perspectives in the past in order to analyze how structures impact human behaviors and decisions
Post-Structuralism	Focus on the deconstruction of existing structures to challenge existence of objective knowledge	Examine primary sources and documents for different interpretations of power and historical facts	Post-Structuralism	Analysis of historical contexts and perspectives of power in systems and institutions and impact on how institutions and social structures impact action
Post-Modernism	Focus on multiple interpretations of the past; challenge historical fact	Examination of historical documents from multiple perspectives	Post-Modern	Focus on diverse perspectives and affective responses to historical contexts in past and present; no universal truth

(Continued)

Table 1.2 (Continued)

Gender History	Focus on how men and women experienced, witnessed the past	Examination of primary sources about power and oppression of women, gender minorities, impact of societal structures on gender roles	Feminist	Focus on both the historical context sources and impact on perspectives of women and gender minorities who are marginalized or oppressed, consider connections to affective responses to power and gender
Post-Colonial	Focus on the perspectives of colonized peoples and power dynamics between colonizers and the colonized	Critiques of the legacy of colonialism, post-colonialism at the dismantling of Western empires, amplification of marginalized racial, ethnic, religious groups	Marxist/ Post-Colonial	Focus on both the historical contexts and perspectives of marginalized or oppressed groups, consideration of connections to affective responses relating to race, ethnicity, social class, gender identity, etc.

These historical research approaches that Green and Troup outline are very similar to the literary analysis theories that ELA teachers use when doing close reading and critiques of literature. Even better, both historical research and literary analysis approaches to examining literature and primary sources can support historical empathy by engaging students in considering how the contexts in which texts are produced shape perspectives of authors, and how emotive responses to texts can elicit not only interdisciplinary connections between ELA and social studies, but also how students can apply what they learn to their lives through taking informed action on an issue.

Examples of Texts for Literary Analysis

Literary analysis is an approach to using fiction texts in ELA and social studies that can be used in a variety of ways that support student engagement in historical empathy. For example, drawing connections between themes in different works, understanding author's purpose, understanding the choices authors make with language, diction, syntax, imagery, and other literary devices. In terms of its use in social studies, students can examine the effect specific actions or events may have on groups or individuals. Additionally, when works of literature are analyzed through different lenses, students can develop more complex understandings of historic events.

Fiction

Fictional texts present human experiences in a large swath of historical, social, and emotional contexts. For the social studies teacher, employing literary analysis strategies can engage students who otherwise feel disconnected to the setting, and the culture, through a story that offers interesting characters and a captivating plot. Historical fiction, or realistic fiction set during a particular time period, can be impactful sources that can support students' development of historical empathy by reading these works and connecting literary style, narrative, prose, and themes to primary and secondary sources that provide context and perspective of people who lived in the past. ELA teachers who use historical fiction or realistic fiction can also build bridges between the analysis of literary style to how study of the socio-economic, political, and social contexts of the past impacted how and why authors wrote what they did.

Here are some of Jennifer and Katie's favorite classic novels that they used while teaching historical empathy skills in ELA and social studies! This is a limited list, so feel free to think about what you would add! You can also check out the Library of Congress' list of major books that shaped America from 1900-1950 here: https://www.loc.gov/exhibits/books-that-shaped-america/1900-to-1950.html

Henry David Thoreau (1845), *Walden & Civil Disobedience*
Upton Sinclair (1906), *The Jungle*
F. Scott Fitzgerald, (1925), *The Great Gatsby*
William Faulkner (1929), *The Sound and the Fury*
Zora Neale Hurston (1937), *Their Eyes were Watching God*

CHAPTER 1

> John Steinbeck (1939), *The Grapes of Wrath*
> Betty Smith (1943), *A Tree Grows in Brooklyn*
> George Orwell (1945), *Animal Farm*
> Ray Bradbury (1953), *Fahrenheit 451*
> Joseph Heller (1961), *Catch 22*
> Eugene Burdick & Harvey Wheeler (1962), *Fail Safe*
> Toni Morrison (1970), *The Bluest Eye*
> Sandra Cisneros (1984), *The House on Mango Street*

In Jennifer's American Literature class, she used short stories to introduce students to the variety of voices and perspectives that emerged in the American literary canon in the late 19th century. Rather than spend six weeks with one novel, studying the American Romanticism unit that encompasses the legends of James Fennimore Cooper, the Dark Romanticism of Edgar Allen Poe and Nathanial Hawthorn, to the Transcendental writings of Ralph Waldo Emerson and Henry David Thoreau, she offered her students a brief but substantive overview of these subgenres and placed more emphasis on the emerging literary voices of what was in the 19th century an increasingly pluralistic America. Her students would read Poe's "The Fall of the House of Usher" and Hawthorne's "The Minister's Black Veil" followed by Charlotte Perkin Gilman's "The Yellow Wallpaper" and Frances Ellen Watkins Harper's poem, "A Double Standard."

These works can also be seen as metaphors for a young country combatting its Puritan past and an increasingly complex present. Often cited as an important early feminist work, Gilman's story examines a woman suffering from post-partum depression whose choices as to how to cope and recover are taken from her by her husband and doctor, while Harper, a feminist and abolitionist, discusses not only privilege handed to men, but specifically, to white men, even in affairs of the heart. While there are scores of worthy novels to choose from, Jennifer felt her students deserved a broader swath to represent such a dynamic time in American literature. To help students implement literary analysis of Gilman's story in the context of westward expansion and spread of slavery during the mid-19th century, Jennifer offered some examples of differentiated strategies that can also engage students in historical empathy.

Young Adult Literature

While texts considered part of the American literary canon offer students insight into the contemporary events of the author, they frequently fail to engage students who are looking for characters who look like them, speak like them, and see bigger world events through their lens. Employing Young Adult Literature (YAL) in place of classic texts or alongside works like *The Crucible* can offer the engagement students desire and reflect cultural diversity. For example, Malinda Lo's National Book Award winning narrative *Last Night at the Telegraph Club* is set in the 1950's during the height of McCarthyism and focuses on an young Asian American protagonist whose family fears deportation despite their American citizenship. Both texts, *The Crucible* and *Last Night at the Telegraph Club*, deal with the themes of hysteria and otherness and offer opportunities for discussions around historic empathy and relevance in contemporary politics.

A great way to get students engaged in YAL is to build a class library. Jennifer wrote a grant proposal and used the received grant money to take her students "shopping." Her school's media center hosted a book fair that year, and Jennifer took each of her classes to the book fair and asked them to make lists of books they hoped to see in their new classroom library. Jennifer's students chose over 60 titles and many of these books' characters reflected the diversity of their school. Students were excited about independent reading, not only because they had a choice in what to read, but because they had voice in curating the library that offered that choice.

Table 1.3 Jennifer's Differentiated Instruction Strategies for Literary Analysis

Strategy	Task or Activity	Teacher Support	Assessment
Anticipation Guide	Before reading, students assess their prior knowledge of terms (ex: feminism, abolitionist, Puritanism, etc.) prior to, during, and after reading to support their acquisition of academic and disciplinary vocabulary. Students can reflect on any connections, thoughts, or feelings they have when they think of these terms.	Students can use scaffolding techniques such as the Frayer Model, word walls, and visuals from primary sources (i.e., engraving of the Seneca Falls Convention) to assist with academic language and vocabulary (see suggested resources).	Students self-assess by completing their Frayer Model, reflections on how historical contexts and perspectives highlight the difference between past and present, making connections to experiences and feelings and ideas for informed actions.

(Continued)

Table 1.3 (Continued)

Student-created questions.	During reading, students will keep Cornell notes (see suggested resources at the end!) to create a body of questions about the reading, the historical context, perspectives of characters in the story, and connections to current issues.	The teacher guides student with question stems, examples of literary analysis question from a feminist approach, and model writing a literary analysis question. Gradual release where students work together and individually on asking and answering questions.	Students assess one another in pair shares, small group, then large group, asking their questions and responding to classmate's questions. Connections can be made into big ideas and compelling questions that relate to literary analysis from a feminist lens concerning gender and power.
Socratic Seminar	After reading, students participate in small group or large group Socratic Seminar. Students develop open-ended questions in advance of the Socratic Seminar. Students use their copies of the texts, their questions, and their notes to participate in a literary analysis discussion using a feminist lens. Students take turns as participants in the discussion and observers and note-takers while citing textual evidence to support their findings.	The teacher is moderator, listening to students' questions, analysis, counterpoints, perspectives, experiential knowledge, and connections to the story.	The teacher assess the student's analysis by reading their questions, listening to responses, recording student's use of textual evidence, and overall participation. The teacher may want to ask students to turn in their questions at the end of the Socratic Seminar that involve reflection of how historical contexts and perspectives shape affective responses or ideas for informed action.

NCTE's "Build Your Stack" is a great resource for helping teachers begin and build your class library! There are many suggestions for both ELA and social studies classrooms!

https://ncte.org/build-your-stack/

Plays and Drama

Plays and drama are powerful texts that can foster historical empathy through analysis of historical contexts, perspectives, and connections to the contemporary world and lived experiences of students. For instance, the Pulitzer Prize winning drama *The Crucible*, by Arthur Miller meets these criteria. The drama is set in 1692 Salem, Massachusetts during the infamous Salem Witch trials. The drama offers insight into a period of American history when women were easy targets for suspicion and blame in a patriarchal theocracy seeped in fear of witchcraft. This work remains a standard in high school American Literature classes as a model of mid-century American theatre, its use of language that reflects both colonial and modern diction, syntax, and imagery, and the vivid characterization that Miller develops.

The play also offers an allegory to the McCarthy hearings of the early 1950's and a deep dive into the power of fear and hysteria when they take hold of people. Miller (1996) wrote years later for *The New Yorker*, "The Red Hunt, led by the House Committee on Un-American Activities and by McCarthy, was becoming a dominating fixation of the American psyche". This literary work offers a rare richness of resources for both the social studies and ELA teacher: The original work was written as an allegory and thus examines two historic events, the author wrote a reflective piece decades later that offers a secondary source for both the historical and literary contexts of the play, and Miller also wrote the screenplay for a film adaptation, offering another medium through which to teach the work.

Margaret Atwood's poem, "Half-Hanged Mary" offers a strong pairing with *The Crucible*. Based on a woman who actually survived her hanging after being accused of being a witch, the first-person voice emphasizes the bias against her gender and age.

Another approach to using plays and drama when employing literary analysis to promote historical empathy is examining how books were adapted for the stage. Lin Manuel-Miranda was inspired to write *Hamilton* after reading Ron Chernow's (2005) epic biography about Alexander Hamilton. *The Crucible* has been produced into both stage and film performances (more on film in Chapter 4!). Students can read excerpts from the texts that influenced the live performances of works of literature in order to examine the historical contexts that set the plot and setting of the story, the representation and depiction of perspectives in the story, analysis of how the performance and book are similar and different (which could lead to a discussion on creative license in art), and how these analyses of a piece of literature and a performance can elicit affective empathetic responses among students that can lead to taking informed action.

Perhaps understandably, some ELA and social studies teachers shy away from teaching Shakespeare. The characters are male-dominated, and after all, why do we continue to teach the works of one dead, white man whose work ended over 400 years ago? These questions are relevant and worthy of any discussion when considering middle school and high school curriculum. Works like *The Tempest* remain full of archetypal themes that can be found in more contemporary works. However, *The Tempest* by William Shakespeare, can be read through the lenses of power, gender, race, and environment while considering the realities of exploration during the Age of Discovery in which the play was written. *The Tempest* offers a playwright's (Shakespeare) imaginative reflection of exploration and colonization, giving the social studies teacher opportunities to convey outcomes of the latter through drama. Similarly, the ELA teacher is afforded opportunities for rich discussion and comparisons between real-world events and theatre that was contemporary to those events. In other words, literary analysis of fiction can offer opportunities for students to see the human element in historic contexts. Discussions around post-colonialism, injustice, imprisonment, and gender roles are omnipresent in YAL books such as *The Complete Persepolis* by Marjane Satrapi (2007), *Now is the Time for Running* by Michael Williams, and *The Deep Blue Between* by Ayesha Harruna Attah. These books can also be taught along with Shakespearean works for study of themes and connections to historic events.

Shakespeare can be challenging, and fun, when teaching about historical and literary time periods. Check out some of these sources for your ELA or social studies instruction if you're thinking about literary analysis as an approach to promoting historical empathy!

Northwest Evaluation Association: https://www.nwea.org/blog/2019/8-tips-bringing-shakespeare-to-life-students/

Digital Theater Plus:https://www.digitaltheatreplus.com/blog/5-practical-activities-to-engage-your-students-in-shakespeare

Edutopia: https://www.edutopia.org/article/set-stage-get-students-hooked-shakespeare/

Poetry

Poetry has an important role in not only studying human culture and history, but also ushering in some of the greatest literary works that were written down. There are so many poems that can the focus of literary analysis when teaching world and U.S. history, and ELA. For instance, the teacher of ancient world history and world literature teacher may be inclined to introduce students to the ancient works of Homer's *The Iliad* and *The Odyssey*, the Sumerian epic of *Gilgamesh*, Virgil's *The Aeneid*, *The Mahabharata* from the Gupta Dynasty in India (Deboy, 2015), the Old English work *Beowulf*, Chaucer's *The Canterbury Tales*, and *Shahnameh* by the Persian poet Ferdowsi. Epic poems are long, often in book format, that portray heroic journeys and battles between good and evil. Later epics that the world history teacher of early modern to post-1500 history may introduce students to Dante's (1321) *The Divine Comedy*, Milton's *Paradise Lost* (1667), *The Secret History of the Mongols* written in 1227 after the death of Genghis Khan, and Mircea Cărtărescu's (1990) *The Levant*. When couched in the historical context of when these epics were written, students can certainly engage in the process of historical empathy by considering the perspectives of the narrator and characters in the poem, and consider what emotive responses they may elicit when thinking about connections to why stories of good versus evil are consistent throughout human history, the function these stories have in societies, and why reading these texts are of significance today in the modern world.

The National Endowment of the Humanities provides lesson plans for teachers to engage students in considering compelling questions such as "what makes a poem epic?" that can promote historical empathy. You can check out that resource here!

https://edsitement.neh.gov/lesson-plans/story-epic-proportions-what-makes-poem-epic

There are extensive examples of poetry that the ELA and social studies teacher can use to not only teach about textual features, perspectives, and historical contexts, but also to engage students in historical empathy. For instance, the connections that can be drawn in an American literature class and a social studies class about the Harlem Renaissance are boundless. Students can apply literary analysis strategies to examine Langston Hughe's "I Too, Dream America" by examining how the social, economic, cultural, and political aspects of racial segregation and discrimination in the United States during the 1920s juxtaposed the "Jazz Age" image of fun, youth, and consumerism a decade after World War I. Analysis of the term "renaissance" as a big idea for a lesson or unit plan could be a powerful way to promote historical empathy in ELA and social studies regarding what the term means, and was the 1920s truly a time of "rebirth" of African American art, or a time when poetry, music, and other forms of Black culture were being accepted in mainstream white society.

Poetry can evoke emotion, spark imagination, make social commentary, inform people of important issues, and lead protest. Using Harlem Renaissance poetry such as Abel Meeropol's *Strange Fruit*, which Billie Holiday later sung (see Chapter 3), can be effective in engaging students in analysis of serious legal and moral issues of lynching through the historical contexts of the past, how the perspectives of the law and people changed concerning lynching through reading poems and other primary sources by activists such as Ida B. Wells, and how feelings and emotions about studying this issue can help inform how decisions concerning the justice system and race are arrived at in the contemporary world.

In the United States, the Poet Laureate is appointed by the head librarian of the U.S. Library of Congress. This position, established by Congress in 1985, is technically known as "The Poet Laureate Consultant in Poetry" where the poet consults with the Library of Congress on reviewing potential additions to the Library's collections, host lectures and events at the Library, and continue original creative and scholarly work. Although this is a relatively new position, there have been "Consultants in Poets" for the Library of Congress dating back to the 1930s that include Robert Frost. Many of the Poet Laureates, Consultants in Poets, and other prominent poets who speak at important events such as the Presidential Inauguration create works that speak to the climate and contexts of the times that we are living. For instance, Maya Angelou's poem "On the Pulse of Morning" at the Clinton Inauguration in 1993 struck a chord due to her message of unity over division in a sermon-esque style reminiscent to Martin Luther King, Jr.'s oratories. A more contemporary example of a consequential Presidential Inaugural poem was delivered by National Youth Poet Laureate Amanda Gorman at the Biden ceremony in 2021 where her poem "The Hill We Climb" was reminiscent of Angelou's message, yet powerful given the tumult leading up to the inauguration with the COVID-19 pandemic, January 6 capitol riots, and social justice movements of 2020. These are just a couple of the myriad of examples of important poetry that history and ELA teachers can certainly use to implement literary analysis of historical context, perspective, and narrative style when promoting the tenets of historical empathy.

> The Library of Congress' site for the Poet Laureate has several resources and information for students and educators about the position's history, upcoming events, and resources that can be used for the classroom!
>
> https://www.loc.gov/programs/poetry-and-literature/about-this-program/

Non-Fiction Texts

Non-fiction texts are special sources that can be used for literary analysis in ELA and social studies. Non-fiction texts can either be primary sources— documents such as journals, diaries, speeches, autobiographies, and memoirs that are produced by someone during a particular historical time period, or secondary sources— texts such as biographies, maps and atlases,[1] and historical monographs like the works by historians like Jill Lepore, Doris Kearns Goodwin, Stephen Ambrose, David McCollough, and Joseph Ellis. While these historians are prominent, we want to also emphasize that literary analysis can serve as a strategy to analyze works of non-fiction that also serve as primary sources that provided social commentary about the time in which the book was written. For example, W.E.B DuBois' (1903) seminal work *The Souls of Black Folks* is a staple of American literature and history during the time of the nadir of race relations where Black scholars who were part of the first generation of freedmen and women after the Civil War engaged in deep debate and discourse about whether African Americans were to accept an accommodationist perspective to racial segregation as laid out in Booker T. Washington's "Atlanta Compromise" speech or the more "radical" approach to protest for civil rights (also check out James Loewen's book *Sundown Towns*).

DuBois' book is not only an important piece of African American history and commentary about the state of the post-Reconstruction United States, but also a lyrical narrative that draws from religious songs and scripture. Literary analysis is a dynamic approach for students to engage in examining the historical contexts in which DuBois wrote this book, his perspectives on the inequities and hardships of Black people at the turn of the 20th century, and how their own affective connections to the prose and history support their understandings of race relations not only as a part of the past, but very much at the forefront of the present and future.

When implementing literary analysis for non-fiction texts, teachers need to engage students in not only examination of what the text is about, but also the thesis, position, and main arguments of the authors of the texts. In the history discipline, historiography refers to the study of how historians' interpretations of past events change over time. For example, implementing a historiographical approach to teaching the Civil War includes engaging students in examining how historians understood the people and events of the war during the time they wrote their books. An author writing about the Civil War in 1876, when the Reconstruction ended, differed greatly to an author writing about the same event in 1920. Teachers can use examples of "mint julep textbooks" that were published at the turn of the 20th century where the Civil War was explained as the "lost cause" and apologetic towards the South. Some further reading about these books can be found from the Thurgood Marshall Institute and the research article The mint julep consensus: An analysis of late 19th century Southern and Northern textbooks and their impact on the history curriculum, which was published in *"The Journal of Social Studies Research!"* We put the citations for these resources in the references list at the end of this chapter.

In ELA, nonfiction texts are examined much in the same way in which fictional texts are analyzed. The ELA standards include reading for fiction and reading for information. For the latter, Students often read many of the same documents they examine in their social studies class such as the Constitution of the United States and the Declaration of Independence. It is not uncommon for students to find that they are reading the same documents in two different classes but analyzing them for different reasons. For example, the U.S. History teacher may ask students to examine how Enlightenment writings by philosophers such as Locke, Rousseau, and Voltaire inspired the language used in the Declaration of Independence. Likewise, students' American Literature teacher may ask them to complete a close reading of the text for rhetorical devices. Together, students are engaged in a holistic experience of analyzing the historical contexts and perspectives expressed in the Declaration and can discuss and deliberate the extent to which those immortal words are relevant today. Jefferson employs a great deal of emotional in the twenty-seven complaints against Parliament and King George III that he includes in the Declaration of Independence. Through literary analysis, students can engage in historical empathy through scrutinizing the Declaration's historical significance, as well as the emotions of American colonists seeking liberty and independence from the British Empire.

LITERARY ANALYSIS

We tried to put together a list of suggested plays and films that were adapted from books that you can use to promote historical empathy through literary analysis. This is not exhaustive, and we hope that you add more to this list! We discuss the use of feature films and documentaries in Chapter 4, so keep this page bookmarked!

Biographies, Memoirs, and Autobiographies

Nonfiction works such as biographies, autobiographies, and memoirs are frequently read in ELA classes for their literary value. However, there are strong connections to how these literary pieces can be used in promote historical empathy in both ELA and social studies. To recap, a biography is a work of literature where an author writes about the life of someone else. Writing biographies comes with a lot of complexity and nuance. For one thing, the author must conduct historical research finding primary sources to construct the story of a person who is living or deceased. This is not an easy feat to accomplish for several reasons. First, authors must acknowledge their own motivations to write biographies, as well as their own feelings and biases about their biography topic. When Katie began writing about Elizabeth Jennings, she felt a great sense of closeness to a woman who she will never meet. She couldn't help but feel connected to Jennings because of the things they had in common, namely that they were both women teachers from New York City. This closeness could be a liability when writing a biography. If an author glosses over unflattering things about a person's life, the biography could be interpreted as being as a work of hero worship, or as a colleague cautioned me about her biographical research, a work of hagiography. However, if an author is overly critical of their subject, then issues could arise about the potential negative effects the work can have on the reputation of that person among the public and their family.

Table 1.4 Sample List of Plays or Films Adapted from Books

Play or Film	Book Author
To Kill a Mockingbird (1962)	Harper Lee (1960)
The Scarlet Letter (2015)	Nathaniel Hawthorne (1850)
All Quiet on the Western Front (2022)	Erich Maria Remarque (1929)
Last of the Mohicans (1992)	James Fenimore Cooper (1826)
A Raisin in the Sun (1961)	Lorraine Hansberry (1959)
The Color Purple (1985, 2023)	Alice Walker (1982)
Hidden Figures (2016)	Margot Lee Shetterly (2016)
The Grapes of Wrath (1940)	John Steinbeck (1939)
The Kite Runner (2007)	Khaled Hosseini (2003)
The Joy Luck Club (1993)	Amy Tan (1989)
Love in the Time of Cholera (2007)	Gabriel García Márquez (1985)

CHAPTER 1

Craig Kridel (2019), a scholar of biographical research in education, highlights the "primordial dilemmas" when doing this type of research stemming from not only how authors makes decisions on what sources they use to write about the facts of a person's life, but also the extent to which the author has the authority to make judgments on what experiences, actions, and events constitute a "definitive biography" of a person (p. 8, 10). Helen M. Hamilton's (2020) article about biography as life writing method is also a great resource that further highlights points to consider when writing or analyzing a biography, namely how the author or researcher balances their biases and feelings about the topic with the decisions they make on what details they focus on throughout the narrative. As a result, using biographies with close reading, annotation work, and reflection strategies when teaching to foster historical empathy involves not only literary analysis of the subject, but also the prose, narrative style, intentions, and perspectives of the author who wrote the text.

> The American National Biography site is a database of over 19,000 biographies of people who made significant cultural contributions to U.S. history. Check and see if your school, institution, or local public library subscribes!
>
> https://www.anb.org/page/about

Autobiographies and memoirs are important primary sources and literary works that are widely used in many social studies and ELA classrooms is *The Narrative of the Life of Frederick Douglass an American Slave* surveys the early years and young adulthood of the abolitionist and statesman. Douglass offers a stark and often painful reflection of his life as someone born into slavery. He delivers several narratives of events throughout his life as a slave, including the moment he was taken from his mother. He writes of witnessing the brutal punishment of his aunt by a slave owner. The language is bare and students are struck by its rawness, however, they are also struck by the significance of first person narrative; the words of one who experienced slavery, and not just the retelling of such events. William Lloyd Garrison offers the preface providing primary source information from two remarkable historic figures for students studying pre-Civil War American history.

Below are some of our favorite biographies and autobiographies that we have used to teach about historical contexts, literary devices, and perspective taking in ELA and social studies. Feel free to think of what you could add!

Memoirs and Autobiographies
- Malcolm X (1965), The Autobiography of Malcolm X
- James McBride (1995), The Color of Water
- Barack Obama (1995), Dreams from my Father
- Chanrithy Him (2000), When Broken Glass Floats
- Frank McCourt (1996), Angela's Ashes
- Malala Yousafzai (2013), I Am Malala

Biographies
- Annette Gordon-Read (2009). *The Hemingses of Monticello: An American Family.*
- Joseph J. Ellis (2000). *Founding Brothers: The Revolutionary Generation*
- Jeane Theoharis (2013). *The Rebellious Life of Mrs. Rosa Parks*
- David Waldstreicher (2023). *The Odyssey of Phillis Wheatley: A Poet's Journey through American Slavery and Independence.*

Literary analysis of autobiographies and memoirs can offer opportunities to engage students in historical empathy. The reader, after all, is invited into moments of an individual's life, but literary analysis requires a close study of language in all its contexts, asking the reader to question diction and syntactical choices that give clues to the significance of a text and the emotion behind it. That being said, we do not suggest that every historical document provides evidence of the writer's intent, nor do we imply that all fictional and nonfictional texts provide historic significance. Hopefully, though, this chapter offers suggestions and ways to think about literary analysis that builds connections between ELA and social studies in the teaching of historical empathy.

> **The National Council for the Social Studies and the Children's Book Council** has released its annual list of notable trade books for K-12 social studies instruction since 1972. The titles that are included on these lists are chosen based on literary quality, originality of topic or perspective on a known topic, and representation of diversity through its prose, research, and if applicable, illustrations. If you are a member of NCSS, you can access the most recent list. If you are not a member, you can access previous year's lists.
>
> NCSS Notable Trade Book List
>
> https://www.socialstudies.org/notable-trade-books

Connections to Standards

The process of literary analysis has a natural connection with the curricular and instructional aspects of historical empathy. When implementing literary analysis strategies, teachers strive to engage students in identifying the contexts in which a text or piece of literature was written, explaining the author's intent for writing the text, pinpointing the audience to whom the text is written for, discussing the author's perspectives that are expressed in the text, and drawing conclusions from the text about its cultural, political, and social significance. Although traditional historians strive to be objective in their analysis of texts, there has been an enduring call for historians, as well as students of history and literature, to examine their own backgrounds, subjectivities, views, and feelings that they experience from writing and analyzing texts. As you can see, literary analysis is a critical aspect of promoting historical empathy when implemented with the IDBM and the C3 Framework when teaching social studies or ELA.

An important point to note is that engaging students in literary analysis is not linear, but rather, a process, much like historical empathy. What this means is that students can circle back to initial inquiries and brainstormed ideas to find evidence from texts that can support responses to compelling questions and supporting questions to communicate conclusions about historical contexts, perspectives, and experiences in order to take informed action. We suggest using graphic organizers, such as the example below, as tools to support students' literary analysis of primary and secondary sources when engaging in inquiries that promote historical empathy:

Table 1.5 Graphic Organizer for Literary Analysis of Primary and Secondary Sources

Author, Date	Type of Source and Intended Audience	Historical Contexts of Source	Perspectives of Authors	Connections to Your Own Experiences	Connections to Experiences of Others	Connections to other Texts

Reflection: How can the information you learned from this source help you to take informed action on an issue facing your community?

Including a reflective piece with literary analysis procedures is important to tie the emotive aspects of historical empathy to the academic elements of historical empathy when being able to explain historical contexts and significance. Often, the reflection can tie back to the compelling question in order for students to contemplate how their views and responses may evolve or change throughout source analysis in the literary analysis inquiry. Best practice is to balance the intellectual and affective tenets of historical empathy in order to support students' historical research of historical contexts, how past and present differ, and various socio-economic and political factors shape perspectives of the past, while making reasoned connections to their feelings, beliefs, and experiences.

NCTE Standards and Literary Analysis in ELA

The National Council for Teachers of English (NCTE) is the oldest American organization dedicated to the teaching of English Language Arts. NCTE developed twelve standards for ELA instruction that, like the national Common Core standards, cover the strands of reading, writing, language, vocabulary, and speaking. The first and third NCTE standards focus specifically with reading texts through various contexts:

1. (NCTE ELA Standard 1) Students read a wide range of print and non-print texts to build an understanding of texts, of themselves, and of the cultures of the United States and the world; to acquire new information; to respond to the needs and demands of society and the workplace; and for personal fulfillment. Among these texts are fiction and nonfiction, classic and contemporary works.
2. (NCTE ELA Standard 3) Students apply a wide range of strategies to comprehend, interpret, evaluate, and appreciate texts. They draw on their prior experience, their interactions with other readers and writers, their knowledge of word meaning and of other texts, their word identification strategies, and their understanding of textual features (e.g., sound-letter correspondence, sentence structure, context, graphics)
3. (NCTE ELA Standard 2) Students read a wide range of literature from many periods in many genres to build an understanding of the many dimensions (e.g., philosophical, ethical, aesthetic) of human experience.

The first NCTE standard initially focuses on "understanding" of texts then extends this understanding to the student and cultures in "the United States and the world" (NCTE). While these are ELA standards, their focus extends to personal and cultural insight. The standard then recognizes the need to "acquire new information" (NCTE) for the purposes of living, working and enjoying broader understandings. The need and opportunity for teaching historical empathy can be understood in the language of these standards. NCTE recognizes the opportunity that literature possesses in teaching "broader understandings" through the experiences illustrated in both fictional and nonfictional works. The second and third NCTE standards also speak to "building understanding." Here, teachers are encouraged to provide texts and engaged lessons that offer students opportunities to explore other ways of thinking, other belief systems, and other ways of looking at the world. This standard, with its broad language invites teachers to include multiple genres across multiple foci to indulge the learning targets of understanding or empathizing with culturally diverse subjects.

Literary Analysis and the NCSS C3 Framework

Implementing literary analysis in ELA have deep parallels to the goals of the NCSS C3 Framework. Since its inception in 2013, the C3 Framework has been the model for states' creation of their social studies standards that aid in implementing the ELA literacy standards of the CCSI. The C3 Framework focuses on curricular skills that share literacy goals as outlined by the NCTE. Among the skills the C3 Framework outlines to promote inquiry, and historical empathy, include asking compelling questions, aligning source analysis and writing to content-area skills, and applying content and skills to communicating conclusions drawn from texts in order to take informed action. Basically, the C3 Framework encourages students to grapple with the age-old question, "why do I need to know this?" by emphasizing that this continuous cycle of questioning, analyzing, and communicating conclusions always circles back to how information from texts can be meaningful in students' lives and communities.

The C3 Framework includes its Inquiry Arc that has four dimensions that breaks down the process in which teachers can engage students in activating prior knowledge of content and skills to engage in literary analysis of primary and secondary sources in order to communicate conclusions, argue or explain historical significance, and deliberate ways in which content and skills can be applied to take informed action in their community. The four dimensions of the Inquiry Arc and their standards are included in Table 1.6.

Each dimension includes anchor standards derived from the ELA CCSS for elementary, middle, and secondary grades. Although too numerous to list here, we make connections to the standards in Dimension 2: Content Areas in our sample lesson plan because they were developed by NCSS specifically to address and promote literacy and inquiry within the core disciplines of social studies.

There are numerous examples of C3-aligned lesson plans in the NCSS publications and the C3teachers.org website https://c3teachers.org/inquiry-design-model/. What you may notice on the C3 Teachers site is that there are several examples of the Inquiry Design Model Blueprint IDBM. The IDBM is a template

Table 1.6 NCSS C3 Framework Inquiry Arc and Literary Analysis

Dimension	Description	Literary Analysis
1: Staging Inquiries	Creating compelling questions about enduring issues or concerns and supporting questions that focus on definitions, key terms, and descriptions of the social studies content areas that spark curiosity, discovery, and interpretation	Identifying types of texts being read, close reading for definitions, syntax, imagery, and literary devices; and preliminary connections that can be made to personal experiences or experiences of others
2: Content Areas	Applying disciplinary skills, concepts, and tools to engage in academic inquiry of the major disciplines of social studies—history, geography, economics, and civics, citizenship, and government	English language arts History Civics Humanities Social sciences
3: Evaluating Sources	Analyzing information from primary and secondary sources through gathering and evaluating evidence in order to support claims and make conclusions about an inquiry	Examining nonfiction or fiction texts for author point of view, setting, conflict, plot, connections to other readings or parts of the same text
4: Communicating Conclusions and Taking Informed Action	Applying disciplinary skills and content to communicate conclusions and take informed action	Analyzing connections to the world, personal experiences, and experiences of others

that teachers can adapt to meet the needs of their curricular and content goals when teaching social studies from an inquiry approach. A commonality between these templates are the basic components of the IDBM lesson plan template that engages students in all four of the dimensions of the C3 Framework Inquiry Arc that you can see in Table 1.7.

Literary analysis lives in each of these basic components of the IDBM lesson plan format and C3 Framework. However, to promote historical empathy with the IDBM, teachers need to be mindful that all aspects of an inquiry must be deliberately designed to evoke affective and academic responses from students. Historical empathy is not just imagining how a person in the past felt, but how evidence from sources supports the inquiry regarding student comprehension of how historical contexts of the past shaped the perspectives of people living during a particular time period. Therefore, when implementing the C3 Framework and IDBM lesson plan template as an interdisciplinary approach to promote

Table 1.7 IDBM Lesson Plan Alignment with the C3 Framework Inquiry Arc and Literary Analysis

IDBM Lesson Plan Component	Connection to the C3 Framework Inquiry Arc	Connections to Literary Analysis
Compelling Question Broad, open-ended questions that introduce the inquiry to students by connecting to students' prior knowledge and/or experiential knowledge that connects to the social studies content areas	Dimension 1: Staging Inquiries with Compelling Questions and Big Ideas	Examining nonfiction or fiction texts for information on author point of view, setting, conflict, plot, connections to other readings or parts of the same text
Standards and Practices Connections to discipline-specific curricular standards for history, economics, geography, and civics, citizenship, and government	Dimension 2: Content-Area Standards	NCTE Standards
Staging the Inquiry Begin the lesson by introducing the inquiry topic to students; can include the essential understandings or rationale for the inquiry, and lesson introductions by highlighting key concepts, key terms, and skills	Dimension 1: Staging Inquiries with Compelling Questions and Big Ideas Dimension 2: Content-Area Standards	Identifying types of texts being read, close reading for definitions, syntax, imagery, and literary devices; and preliminary connections that can be made to personal experiences or experiences of others
Supporting Questions Scaffolded questions that have definitive answers that support learning of disciplinary-specific skills, concepts, terms, and definitions that help students engage in the inquiry	Dimension 3: Evaluating Source Evidence	Scaffolded questions about the types of texts being read, definitions,, imagery, and literary devices in order to make connections to personal experiences or experiences of others
Featured Sources The primary and secondary sources and texts that provide insights and background information about the inquiry, and primary source documents that represent multiple perspectives of authors	Dimension 3: Evaluating Source Evidence	Classic pieces of literature Contemporary pieces of literature Nonfiction texts Fiction texts Primary sources

(Continued)

Table 1.7 (Continued)

Formative Performance Tasks The learning activities through direct teaching and structured practice where teachers model skills of identifying historical contexts, explaining perspectives of authors of texts, and students practice applying inquiry skills such as literary analysis to answer compelling and supporting questions	Dimension 3: Evaluating Source Evidence Dimension 4: Communicating Conclusions and Taking Informed Action	Analyzing featured sources for information on author point of view, setting, conflict, plot, connections to other readings or parts of the same text, connections to personal experiences or experiences of others
Summative Performance Task The final product where students demonstrate their skills and content knowledge through applying information learned from the inquiry through citing evidence from the featured sources to support their responses to the supporting questions and compelling question; extension tasks optional for remediation, reteaching, and/or supplementation	Dimension 3: Evaluating Source Evidence Dimension 4: Communicating Conclusions and Taking Informed Action	Applying evidence and information from featured sources to identify historical contexts of texts, perspectives of authors of texts, explaining connections to big ideas, deliberating answers to the compelling question
Taking Informed Action Deliberation on how students can apply what they learned from the inquiry to a real-world situation	Dimension 4: Communicating Conclusions and Taking Informed Action	Applying information from texts and reflections to explore other ways of thinking, other belief systems, and other ways of looking at the world

historical empathy with literary analysis, we must be aware that the questions, sources, and performance tasks assigned represent diverse perspectives and points of view to challenge students' biases, reflect students' experiences, and encourage students' demonstrations of content and skills proficiency through discussion of conclusions and taking informed action. Table 4 summarizes how

Sample Lesson Plan

As we noted, the IDBM template can be an entire example of an instructional unit that includes several days of lesson plans for students to analyze texts and engage inquiry in smaller chunks. The IDBM suggests that there should be 3-4 supporting questions, which alone could account for at least a week of instruction. Our sample lesson plan aligns with the C3 Framework that can be implemented into a single-day of instruction so that teachers can practice building inquiries that incorporate literary analysis as a way to engage students in demonstrating historical empathy in social studies and ELA.

Lesson Title: Examining the Complexities of the Women's Suffrage Movement

Grade Level: 11-12

Length of Time: 3-4 days

C3 Framework Inquiry Arc Dimension 1- Staging the Inquiry	
Big Idea	Equality
Compelling Question	Did all people experience equality at the end of the Civil War?
Essential Understandings/ Rationale	Although the end of the Civil War resulted in the abolition of slavery with the 13th Amendment to the U.S Constitution, African Americans were treated inequitably during the 12-year period after the war known as Reconstruction. Specifically, Black women were discriminated against when the 15th Amendment granted universal male suffrage, which excluded women from voting.
Learning Targets	• Students will be able to explain the 19th century roots of the early 20th century women's suffrage movement. • Students will be able to identify how major movements for racial and gender equality were supportive of the other, but also in contention • Students will be able to analyze the reasons why women of color who were fighting for enfranchisement did not possess the same leverage as white suffrage supporters.
Supporting Questions	• What does the term "suffrage" mean? • What were challenges to suffrage for Americans after the Civil War? • Why did people support and oppose universal suffrage after the Civil War? • What actions did Americans take to get the right to vote? • What rhetorical choices do Sojourner Truth, Elizabeth Cady Stanton, and Frederick Douglass make to persuade audiences? • What do these rhetorical choices indicate about each speaker's bias towards their subject? • What do these speeches convey about conflicts in these civil rights movements?

Lesson Materials	
Featured Secondary Sources	Anchor Text (fiction): *Saving Savannah* by Tonya Bolden
Featured Primary Sources	• "Ain't I a Woman" (1851) by Sojourner Truth. • Declaration of Sentiments (excerpt if necessary), Seneca Falls Convention (1848) https://www.nps.gov/wori/learn/historyculture/declaration-of-sentiments.htm • The Solitude of Self, Elizabeth Cady Stanton (1872) https://historymatters.gmu.edu/d/5315/ • "An Appeal to Colored Women to Vote and Do their Duty in Politics," Mary Church Terrell (1921) https://awpc.cattcenter.iastate.edu/2020/02/17/an-appeal-to-colored-women-to-vote-and-do-their-duty-in-politics-1921/ • "Is it a Crime to Vote?" Susan B. Anthony (1872) (excerpt if necessary) https://susanb.org/wp-content/uploads/2018/12/Susan-B-Anthony-1872-1873.pdf
Technology/Media Sources	Alfie Woodard delivers the "Ain't I a Woman" speech. Source: Voices of a People's History of the United States (2008).
Other Materials and Supports	Copies of speeches (digital and hardcopy) Pens, pencils, highlighters

C3 Framework Inquiry Arc Dimension 2- Standards Connections	
C3 Framework Content Standard	D2.Civ.8.9-12. Evaluate social and political systems in different contexts, times, and places, that promote civic virtues and enact democratic principles.
C3 Framework Content Standard	D2.Civ.14.9-12. Analyze historical, contemporary, and emerging means of changing societies, promoting the common good, and protecting rights.
C3 Framework Content Standard	D2.His.1.9-12. Evaluate how historical events and developments were shaped by unique circumstances of time and place as well as broader historical contexts.
C3 Framework Content Standard	D2.His.6.9-12. Analyze the ways in which the perspectives of those writing history shaped the history that they produced.
C3 Framework Content Standard	D2.His.9.9-12. Analyze the relationship between historical sources and the secondary interpretations made from them.

C3 Framework Inquiry Arc Dimension 2- Standards Connections	
NCTE Standard for ELA	Standard 2: Students read a wide range of literature from many periods in many genres to build an understanding of the many dimensions (e.g., philosophical, ethical, aesthetic) of human experience.
NCTE Standard for ELA	Standard 3: Students apply a wide range of strategies to comprehend, interpret, evaluate, and appreciate texts. They draw on their prior experience, their interactions with other readers and writers, their knowledge of word meaning and of other texts, their word identification strategies, and their understanding of textual features (e.g., sound-letter correspondence, sentence structure, context, graphics).
NCTE Standard for ELA	Standard 6: Students apply knowledge of language structure, language conventions (e.g., spelling and punctuation), media techniques, figurative language, and genre to create, critique, and discuss print and non-print texts.

C3 Framework Inquiry Arc Dimension 3- Analyzing Source Evidence	
Introduction/ Motivation	• Students are asked to complete a "quick write" about what they think the big idea "equality" means to them. After a few minutes, students can discuss their responses in a think-pair-share, or in a whole class discussion. • Next, the teacher can record on the board student responses to the question, "how does it feel if you are not treated equally?" Possible responses can include feeling sad, angry, confused, or aggrieved. • Finally, teacher asks students for examples in history when people were not treated equally and what they did to challenge inequality. Possible answers may include Rosa Parks, Martin Luther King, Jr., and that they engaged in non-violent protest, marches, speeches, etc.

LITERARY ANALYSIS

C3 Framework Inquiry Arc Dimension 3- **Analyzing Source Evidence**	
Teacher Direct Instruction	• After students completed list, the teacher leads a discussion on how diction, imagery, details, language, and syntax (DIDLS) not only helps an author of a text convey emotions and purpose but through analysis, but also to help the reader understand what the author/speaker wishes to convey. • Teacher asks students when they think the women's suffrage movement began and lists responses on the board. Responses may include the Seneca Falls Convention of 1848 and flappers of the 1920s. • Teacher leads a discussion on how women advocated for the right to vote since the American Revolution, and that many white suffragists supported the abolition of slavery. However, after the Civil War, the 15th amendment granted universal male suffrage, which led to white and Black women fighting for the right to vote. • Teacher can ask students whether they think that after the Civil War all suffragists agreed that Black and white women should be allowed to vote, and ask students why they think that. Some students may believe all women were united in granting suffrage, while some may highlight that some whites did not want Black women and men to vote (i.e., segregation, Jim Crow, literacy tests, poll taxes prevented Black men the vote after Reconstruction). • Students are given a copy of "Ain't I a Woman;" a speech delivered extemporaneously by Sojourner Truth (1851) at a women's convention in Akron, Ohio. Students are also given a DIDLS graphic organizer to aid them in their analysis of the speech:

Diction:	Imagery:	Details:
Language:		Syntax:
Tone:		
Mood:		
Theme:		

	C3 Framework Inquiry Arc Dimension 3- Analyzing Source Evidence
	• The teacher reviews the DIDLS chart to highlight the emotional language employed by students in their chart, how understanding how the historical context of the 1850s shaped Truth's use of language to convey her perspectives on suffrage, gender, and race. • Next, the teacher then can play a recording of the same speech performed by Alfie Woodard. Students listen to the actress's interpretation as they read the speech. • Students will record words that convey particular emotions, and respond to the question "What ideas, issues, or purpose does the speaker connect with emotional diction?" • As students share their responses, the teacher then asks students to examine imagery and detail the speaker offers, and think about how her perspectives and interpretations of the speech connects the audience to her personal experience and a woman of color. • Finally, the teacher asks students to identify the type of language used by the speaker (vernacular) and syntax (word order and phrasing). How do these affect the reader/audience? How do they support/strengthen the speaker's message?
Formative Performance Task/Student Structured Practice	• After completing a literary and rhetorical analysis of a text with the teacher's support and modeling, students will work in groups to analyze another speech. One group will analyze Susan B. Anthony's speech, one group will analyze the speech Elizabeth Cady Stanton, one group will analyze the Declaration of Sentiments, and one group will analyze the speech by Mary Church Terrell. • Students will complete a new DIDLS chart while analyzing the speech. • Next, students will explain in a presentation format of their choice (i.e., mind map, slide deck, speech, performance, etc.) about how historical context of the early and later 19th century impacted the author's views on equality relating to suffrage and race, and cite direct quotes that highlight what surprised them, what interested them, and what troubled them from reading the text.

C3 Framework Inquiry Arc Dimension 4- Communicating Conclusions and Taking Informed Action	
Student Share	In a jigsaw activity, students in each group will present their text analyses. Students in the audience will record notes about the historical contexts, perspectives, and group's quotes about what was surprising, interesting, and troubling regarding the complexities of the women's suffrage movement.
Closing	Students will reflect on the speeches and write a reflection as an exit ticket about whether they have personal experience, vicarious experiences of others, and/or knowledge current issues that relate to equality. Students will consider how these experiences make them feel, and how they could use the information that they learned from the speeches to address an issue relating to equality in their community.
Summative Performance Task/Extension	Students can share their reflections from the exit ticket, and brainstorm a list of ideas on how an issue relating to equality is impacting their community, and how they could take informed action by addressing this issue. For instance, if students raise the issue of voter registration, ideas for taking informed action can include creating posters or infographics with details on where and how to register to vote that can be distributed in their school or in approved public places.

Conclusion

We begin this book on how to promote historical empathy in ELA and social studies with literary analysis to frame how works of literature are natural companions to historical documents. History, at its core, is the narrative of the past; the stories of individuals caught up in remarkable times. While history offers the stories of the past, literature imbues those stories with characters that flesh out the human experiences during historic events. With literary analysis, teachers guide students through language dedicated to the promotion of curricular skills in ELA and social studies in order to support the human aspect in which students can make reasoned affective connections between texts to their lives, communities, and experiences of others.

Reflection

- What might be some pro's and con's when implementing literary analysis strategies to promote historical empathy?
- What kind of works of literature could you use to promote historical empathy with your students?
- What kind of primary sources could you use to support students' literary analysis?
- How can the dimensions of the C3 Framework Inquiry Arc support students' demonstration of historical empathy through the application of literary analysis?

Note

[1] Maps and paintings can be either primary or secondary sources depending upon the intent of the author. If a map produced in 1776 was showing the boundary lines of the British, French, and Spanish territories in North America, then that map is a primary source. However, if a map in 1920 was depicting the borders of the 13 British colonies, that map would be a secondary source because it was not produced during the colonial period.

Suggested Resources

Bohan, C.H., Baker, H.R. King, L., & Morris, W.H. (2022). *Teaching enslavement in American history: Lesson plans and primary sources*. Peter Lang.

Ditch That Textbook. (2019). *25 Free Google Drawing graphic organizers— and how to make your own*. Retrieved from https://ditchthattextbook.com/15-free-google-drawings-graphic-organizers-and-how-to-make-your-own/

Facing History and Ourselves. (n.d.). *Socratic Seminars*. Retrieved from https://www.facinghistory.org/resource-library/socratic-seminar

Foster, T. (2014). *How to read literature like a professor*. Harper Perennial.

Hughes, L. (1994). *The collected poems of Langston Hughes*. Random House.

Jolliffe, D. A., and Roskelly, H. (2014). *Writing American: Language and composition in context*. Pearson.

Loewen, J. (2005). *Sundown towns: A hidden dimension of American racism*. Touchstone.

McCall, A.L. (2004). Using poetry in social studies classes to teach about cultural diversity and social justice. *The Social Studies* 95(4), 172-176.

Miller, A. (1996). *Why I wrote "The Crucible:"* An artist's answer to politics. *Life & Letters, The New Yorker*. October 21 & 28, 1996.

O'Dell, C. (2002). *"Strange Fruit"- Billie Holliday, 1939, added to the national registry*. Library of Congress. Retrieved from https://www.loc.gov/static/programs/national-recording-preservation-board/documents/StrangeFruit.pdf

Retz, T. (2018). *Empathy and history: Historical understanding in re-enactment, hermeneutics, and education.* Berghahn.

Shea, R.H., Aufses, R.D., Scanlon, L., et al. (2022). *Literature and composition: Essential voices, essential skills for the AP Course.* Bedford, Freeman, and Worth.

Washington, B.T. (1908). *Booker T. Washington's narration of the "Atlanta Compromise Speech"* (with transcript). Library of Congress. Retrieved from https://www.loc.gov/exhibits/civil-rights-act/multimedia/booker-t-washington.html

Woodson, C.G. (2005; 1933). *The mis-education of the negro.* Dover Publications.

Chapter References

Anonymous. (1960). *The epic of Gilgamesh.* Penguin Classics.

Anonymous. (2010). *Beowulf.* Cricket House Books.

Angelou. M. (1993). *On the pulse of morning.* Retrieved from https://poets.org/poem/pulse-morning.

Appleman, D. (2023). *Critical encounters in secondary English: Teaching literacy theory to adolescents.* Teachers College Press.

Attah, A.H. (2022). *The deep blue between.* Carolrhoda Lab.

Atwood, M. *Half-hanged Mary.* Retrieved from https://woodlawnschool.pbworks.com/f/The+Crucible+-+Half+Hanged+Mary+Poem+PDF.pdf

Atwood, S. (2023). *The secret history of the Mongols.* Penguin Classics.

Baldwin, J. (1965). "Sonny's Blues." *Going to neet the nan.* Dial Press.

Bohan, C. H., Bradshaw, L. Y., & Morris Jr, W. H. (2020). The mint julep consensus: An analysis of late 19th century Southern and Northern textbooks and their impact on the history curriculum. *The Journal of Social Studies Research 44*(1), 139-149. https://doi.org/10.1016/j.jssr.2019.02.002

Brisbee, A., & Tompkins, J.C. (n.d.). *Literary theory and schools of criticism.* Retrieved from https://mseffie.com/assignments/heart_of_darkness/Purdue%20OWL%20Literary%20Theory.pdf

Chaucer, G. (2003). *The Canterbury tales.* Penguin Classics.

Cărtărescu. M. (2014, 1990) *The Levant.* POL.

Dante. (2014). *The divine comedy.* Penguin Classics.

Deboy, B. (2015). *The Mahabharata.* Penguin.

Douglass, F. (1858). *Narrative of the life of Frederick Douglass, An American slave.* Retrieved from https://www.gutenberg.org/ebooks/23

Ferdowsi. (2017). *Shahnameh.* Liverlight.

Gilman, C.P. (1892, 2018). *The yellow wallpaper.* Martino Fine Books.

Gorman, A. (2021). *The hill we climb: An inaugural poem for the country.* Viking Books.

Grant, S.G., Lee, J., & Swan, K. (2014). Inquiry design model at a glance. *C3Teachers.org.* Retrieved from https://c3teachers.org/wp-content/uploads/2019/08/Inquiry-Design-Model-at-a-glance.pdf

Green, A., & Troup, K. (2016). *The houses of history: A critical reader in history and theory, second edition.* Manchester University Press.

Hamilton, H.M. (2020). Balance in writing life: Some issues in biography. *Collegian 27*(6), 585-588. https://doi.org/10.1016/j.colegn.2020.07.001

Harper, E.W. (1992). *A double standard.* Retrieved from https://www.poetryfoundation.org/poems/52449/a-double-standard

Hawthorne, N. (1836). *The minister's black veil.*

Homer. (2024). *The Iliad* and *The Odyssey.* Fingerprint Publishing.

Kridel, C. (2019). Thoughts for the field: A personal epilogue for educational biographers. *Vitae Scholasticae: The Journal of Educational Biography 36*(1), 6-11.

Lo, M. (2021). *Last night at the telegraph club.* Dutton Books.

Marti, J. (1997). "To the Foreigner" (Al extranjero). *Versos Sencillos.* Monthly Review Press.

Milton, J. (2003). *Paradise lost.* Penguin Classics.

C3 Teachers. (2025). Inquiry design model. Retrieved from https://c3teachers.org/idm/

National Council for the Social Studies. (2013). *The college, career, and civic life framework for social studies standards.* National Council for the Social Studies. Retrieved from https://www.socialstudies.org/sites/default/files/c3/c3-framework-for-social-studies-rev0617.pdf

Novick, P. (1988). *That noble dream: The 'objectivity question' and the American historical profession.* Cambridge University Press.

Poe, E.A. (2003, 1839). *Fall of the house of usher and other writings: Poems, essays, tales, and reviews.* Penguin.

Remarque, E. M. (1989). *All quiet on the western front.* Atlantic Books.

Satrapi, M. (2007). *The complete Persepolis.* Pantheon.

Shakespeare, W. (2019). *The tempest: A Norton critical edition, second edition.* W.W. Norton & Co.

Sinclair, U. (1906). *The jungle.* Doubleday, Page, & Co.

Steinbeck, J. (1937). *Of mice and men.* Penguin Books.

Virgil. (2008). *The Aneid.* Penguin Classics

Wells, I.B. (1892). *Southern horrors Lynch laws in all its phases.* Retrieved from https://www.gutenberg.org/files/14975/14975-h/14975-h.htm

Williams, M. (2013). *Now is the time for running.* Little Brown Books.

CHAPTER 2

Digital Media

Brainstorming Activity

- How do you define *media*?
- How would you describe *digital media*?
- What kinds of media, digital or non-digital, do you use daily?
- What are your favorite examples of digital media that you can use when promoting historical empathy in your teaching?

Introduction

Media comes in all shapes and sizes, and is certainly not a 21st-century phenomenon. Katie and Jennifer went to school as kids during the mid to late 20th century where the fanciest technology schools had to support using different types of media for teaching included VCR machines, cassette and record players, mimeograph machines (look that up!), and *Weekly Reader* magazines.[1] When we started teaching in the early 2000s, we used clunky Smartboards that we rolled into the classroom, hopefully connected to a computer, that could be used as projectors for presentation slides, notetaking, and connecting to the internet for videos, images, and other forms of visuals. Smartphones were not around yet, so using laptop carts was a novel approach to teach students how to access digital tools to conduct research and create their own modes of media that demonstrated what they were learning. However, the use of electronic or digital technology was not the only form, and is still not the only form, of media that teachers in ELA and social studies can use to promote historical empathy with their students.

Media refers to diverse modes of mass communication of information that includes, but is not limited to, news, entertainment, and research, that is disseminated to large groups of people. Jukka Korti's (2019) book *Media in History* is a comprehensive examination of how the evolution of modern-day media has its roots in the first forms of human communication of pictures, letters, numbers, and words on clay, stone, and papyrus. As technology revolutionized how communications were shared and distributed, particularly with the printing press in the 15th century, *multimedia* emerged where the use of visuals, texts, and orations in religious services, dramatic performances, political debates, print news, and other public events grew.

Today, we are surrounded by media in various forms on television, internet streaming, and applications to instantaneously stream shows, sports, news, concerts, and content created by ordinary people. Specifically, *digital media* refers to the distribution of information through electronic devices that are enabled with Smartphones, tablets, and the internet. Digital media has a huge influence on how we interact and view the world because of how it has become a common part of our daily lives. From the way we dress, how we speak, where we eat, where we shop, how we vote, what we read, how we get information, and who we spend time with, digital media is impacting the ways we teach, as well as who we teach. However, digital media content can also serve as ways in which people document lived experiences, global events, and other phenomena that become part of the historical record or inspiration for works of literature. Because children and adults are surrounded by 24/7 modes of mass communications, we focus on digital media in this chapter by sharing some examples, strategies, and skills that can be implemented when using texts, visuals, and other internet-based materials to promote historical empathy in ELA and social studies.

Types of Digital Media for Promoting Historical Empathy

Listing the various types of digital media that we can use when we plan our instruction to promote historical empathy can be exhaustive. From websites, graphic arts, video games, movies, electronic books (e-books), news broadcasts, television shows, formal presentations, and audio-visuals in the form of the spoken word, films, or music, it is easy to get overwhelmed when trying to vet and find resources that can support historical empathy during ELA and social studies instruction. Over the years, we've observed how digital technologies have evolved and changed. For example, when Katie began teaching in 2006, the most state-of-the-art technology she had in her classroom was a bulky Smartboard on wheels that was hooked up to a Dell desktop computer with spotty internet connectivity. Now, many schools are equipped with faster Wifi, projectors and swivel screens, document cameras, tablets, laptops, and software that can enable students to create sophisticated research and creative projects. As a result, we need to have an idea about what kind of digital media we can use not only to teach standards and learning objectives, but also to engage students in the process of historical empathy through inquiry, critical thinking, and application to civic life in a democratic society. In this chapter, we focus on digital media that is distributed by news outlets, social media, archives, and organizations. We will specifically examine documentaries and films, music, and images in our later chapters in more detail.

The News Media

Often, the media and 24/7 news cycle is equated to digital media. However, the news media has its own distinction. The *news media* refers to the press—journalists and reporters who work for newspapers, television outlets, radio broadcasters, and other outlets that reach broad audiences—that provide information, news, and other forms of communication with the goal of highlighting critical issues, events, and happenings in a community. The media consists of coverage of a wide variety of topics spanning from sports, education, entertainment, politics, fashion, local issues, and global events. The traditional news media in which materials were published in print or real-time broadcast at certain times during the day are rapidly expanding their digital presence, making their stories and perspectives instantly available on their specific websites and on social media platforms. Instead of waiting for breaking news to be printed and sold on newsstands the next day, newspapers, television, and internet-based news outlets release information instantaneously on websites and as push notifications on Smartphones and tablets.

There are so many digital news outlets to access news from that target certain audiences based on age, race, and gender demographics, as well as political affiliations. As a result, it's incumbent upon teachers to be aware of what content they use from digital media outlets that are appropriate and geared specifically towards children and young adult audiences, especially when engaging students in the process of historical empathy by examining historical and contemporary contexts and perspectives. The reality is that some pertinent news that can be used to support teaching ELA and social studies content can be troubling for students, particularly when content deals with current issues such as war, drug use, sex, and gun violence. Still, teachers can use digital media to engage students in historical empathy by analyzing patterns of cause and effect and how historical events can bear significance and relevance to current events.

News articles that are published in print or digital media can be considered as primary sources because they capture the issues and perspectives of people and groups at a particular point in time. News articles provide insights into the patterns, landscapes, and trends of the socio-economic and political climate of a local town, country, and world that provide insight into the contexts and perspectives of people at a particular point in time. The print media was critical for the American patriots to disseminate information throughout the 13 colonies during the American Revolution. Pulitzer and Hearst's penchant for yellow journalism influenced national perceptions of global crises, such as the Cuban revolution and Spanish-American War. Moreover, the muckrakers of the Gilded Age and Progressive Era such as Jacob Riis, Upton Sinclair, Ida Tarbell, Lincoln Steffens, and Ida B. Wells exposed the myriad of social, economic, and political issues stemming from the racial trauma Reconstruction, laissez-faire capitalism, urban poverty, and the horrific working conditions in food processing plants and factories. These sources can be effective historical documents that foster historical empathy with students by engaging them in analysis of how socio-economic and political problems in the past were experienced, addressed, and still relevant to the modern world.

Print and digital media also includes advertisements and commercials that can be important primary sources when promoting historical empathy. The ads and commercials in newspapers, magazines, and websites provide a wealth of information on cultural, social, economic, and political values and views of a society. The power of advertisements cannot be understated, particularly when teaching about time periods such as the Cold War during the 1950s where modern appliances such as refrigerators, vacuum cleaners, soda, and televisions were used to not only promote consumerism, but also to fight the growing threat of communism and the Soviet Union. Today, the advertisements that we consume come in the form of television commercials, internet pop-up ads, emails, and text messages can provide insights to the how consumers can spend their money on things that are conveniences, solutions to problems, and make life better.

Ads and commercials also function as ways to influence or convince the public to support or oppose positions. Jennifer uses commercials to teach the rhetorical triangle and the three appeals— pathos, logos, and ethos—to engage students in analyzing how appeals are used to sway or persuade audiences. Politicians have used the media since the birth of this country to argue for certain positions convince voters for support. The feuds between Alexander Hamilton and Thomas Jefferson through their writings in the newspapers during the 1790s and early 1800s were infamous for mudslinging and garnering political support on establishing the national bank. The Lincoln-Douglas debates for the Illinois U.S. Senate race in 1858 epitomized the growing national crisis over slavery, which later influenced the outcome of the 1860 Presidential election. Theodore Roosevelt took the American tradition of the local "stump speech" when campaigning to the bully pulpit, most notably by establishing the White House Press Secretary. Later, President Calvin Coolidge became the first president to give a national radio address.

Franklin D. Roosevelt capitalized on the popularity of radio's influence on mass media to give his fireside chats during the Great Depression. Movie reels were forerunners of television news and commercials, as mass media companies featured celebrities, public figures, and events such as the Hindenburg disaster and footage of FDR and Truman dealing with World War II in the movie theater. As television rose as a major source of mass communication, political candidates such as Dwight D. Eisenhower and Adalai Stevenson produced commercials during the 1952 presidential election that were advertised to millions of potential voters on television.

The 1960 televised Kennedy-Nixon debate further encapsulated television's mark on modern-day politics and how public officials can reach constituents for votes and supporting their agendas with soundbites, ads, and televised debates and townhall meetings.

The Museum of the Moving Image has digitally archived Presidential television campaign commercials from 1952! Check out their digital archive of these videos that can support your historical empathy teaching of the historical contexts and perspectives of 20th and 21st century elections!!

http://www.livingroomcandidate.org/

It should come as no surprise that when the internet was introduced in the early 1990s, the use and consumption of digital media for personal, professional, and public purposes proliferated. President George H.W. Bush became the first president to send an email; in 1994, the website www.whitehouse.gov was established during the Clinton administration and refined during the George W. Bush administration. President Obama was the first President to actively use social media for not only campaigning, but for his administration to distribute press releases. President Trump's use of X, formerly Twitter, normalized how elected officials use social media, but also how news outlets harness the power of social media to deliver content and coverage of events to millions of people around the world. Consequently, the popularization of the internet has changed how information is created, consumed, and interpreted for academic and leisurely purposes.

Social Media

Not long after the internet became ubiquitous in daily life, social media arose as a type of digital media where people can post written texts, images, videos, audio, and engage in real-time communication with others. Katie remembers creating a MySpace page in her later high school years, then a Facebook page in college— and barely used it. When she got married in 2010, upon returning from her honeymoon, she received texts from friends and family encouraging her to share the photos that were posted on her Facebook page from the wedding. From that point, Katie realized how her peers were using social media to keep in touch, share updates on their lives, and to share information ranging from news articles, clips from Youtube, funny memes and cartoons, and family photos. Maybe it was a case of FOMO (fear of missing out), but she entered the world of posting and reposting content on social media where ordinary photos and words she shared actually memorialized points in time that could give insights to what life was like for a something? millennial teacher before, during, and after the Great Recession of 2008.

Social media can serve as a repository where digital primary sources are created and shared that can be used for historical empathy instruction and research. Official communications from elected officials such as the President of the United States are considered primary sources as their words reflect their positions on issues facing the nation and the world at particular points in time. For example, Katie facilitated a local history research project with high school students about the COVID-19 pandemic where they looked back on social media posts for videos, texts, stories, photographs, and illustrations that the kids or people they knew created and shared about their experiences during the pandemic. These posts ended up being primary sources that the students examined poems, pictures of being masked at school events, and notices sent out by their schools about social distancing for historical context of life during the start of the pandemic in 2020, the perspectives expressed in these posts, and how their reflections of their experiences compare and contrast to how they feel about the pandemic today. Katie shares more about this project in Chapter 6.

Social media can also be utilized as a roadmap of sorts that can direct students, teachers, researchers, and the public to the official websites of brick-and-mortar archives, libraries, museums, and other places to gather information. In many ways, social media has become crucial in providing access to places that people may otherwise would not due to distance, finances, and other obstacles. News outlets, entertainment companies, political parties, schools, stores, government agencies, museums, historical societies, and research institutes large and small use social media to advertise what they have to offer educators and the public that include digital exhibits, professional development webinars, and virtual field trips that are often offered for free. For instance, the National Women's History Museum offers an array of digital media including biographies, lesson plans, and professional development sessions on how to promote historical empathy when teaching topics relating to women's history. National organizations such as NCTE and NCSS also use social media to highlight their services to its members and the public at large that include professional development, curricular materials, and conference opportunities that focus on how to implement historical empathy strategies with K-12 students.

By and large, social media platforms function as online gathering places of archival materials, pedagogical resources, and interpersonal communications around the world that can support historical empathy through the examination of the contexts in which digital content is created and for what purpose, the perspectives expressed by the content creators and those who follow these posts, in order to make reasoned affective connections to how and why social media content can be a conduit of sharing information in order to promote interconnectedness and civic discourse among people around the world.

> Jennifer Gonzalez's podcast and blog *Cult of Pedagogy* is a tremendous resource of digital media aimed at K-12 teachers with instructional suggestions on how to use these sources to promote critical thinking, engagement, and historical empathy!
>
> https://www.cultofpedagogy.com/

Caution with Social Media

All of these uses of social media show how this technology can be harnessed for positive educational outcomes for teachers and students. However, we'd be remiss to not highlight that social media must be used with discretion. Like vetting the reliability and credibility of digital media that is published by reputable and amateur outlets, teachers need to exercise caution when using social media to find materials for teaching, as well as posting theirs or their students' content on the internet. In recent years, issues related to social media use including the spread of misinformation, inappropriate content, privacy breaches, and bullying have resulted in severe mental, emotional, and physical health conditions for youth. The American Psychological Association (the APA) recommends that "adult role models can work together with teens to understand the pitfalls of technology and establish boundaries to protect them from dangerous content and excessive screen time" (Weir, 2023). Therefore, some guidelines are needed for teachers, should they choose, to model how to use social media to conduct research to engage students in historical empathy. The use of personal profiles on sites such as Facebook, Instagram, TikTok, and Twitter should be limited, or not used at all in the classroom, to ensure the privacy of teachers and students, especially when complying with privacy laws such as FERPA and community standards for ethics or moral turpitude in a state or district where you teach. You should check into your district and state's social media policies, as well as any guidance your professional organization or union has about this.

These cautions do not mean that social media cannot be used in the classroom by teachers and students. Instead, search for teachers who have their own professional social media sites that relate to teaching strategies or content pertinent to the classroom could be used. Consider creating a separate social media profile if you are thinking about posting curricular ideas, literature citations, links to primary and secondary sources, and other materials that can be helpful in fostering historical empathy and digital literacy with students. For example, an impactful exercise to plan and teach can involve showing students the social media handles and profile locations of news and reputable digital media outlets on social media can be beneficial in helping kids navigate social media platforms when using the tools for academic or research purposes. A teacher could share with the class the @POTUS Twitter (X) handle, and let students know that they can follow official updates from the United States President that are written and verified with a blue check by White House staff. Moreover, students can examine the accounts that are titled with seemingly official names for verifications in the form of check marks or verified badges to discern whether a social media account is credible and verifiably associated with a legitimate organization, agency, company, or person.

There are many appropriate examples of social media tools that teachers can incorporate in their classrooms to promote historical empathy and engaged learning. The use of blogs can be useful for teachers to formatively assess students' inquiry and critical thinking when teaching with literature and primary sources to engage learners in identifying historical contexts in which sources were created, explaining how contexts shape different perspectives of people during a particular time, and express affective responses to what they are learning by making connections to prior knowledge, life experiences, feelings, and experiences of others. Some blog sites that are effective for classroom use include EduBlogs, websites created by Weebly, Word Press, or Google Sites, or blog or digital discussion tools on learning management programs such as Canvas. Students can practice citation, using evidence to support positions on topics, and respond to either the teacher and classmates to keep textual discussion going with replies, questions, and comments to other posts.

Additionally, video-based blogs, or vlogs, can enhance classroom community and engagement by pairing written materials by students with recordings that they can make explaining what they learned, what questions they have, and providing their own perspectives on issues or topics of study. In addition to including vlogs in the above examples of text-based blogs, teachers and students can use applications such as Kami and Classtime to provide more personalized instruction. One thing to check out is if you need a subscription to use these tools to access their full potential in engaging students using social media.

Digitized Archives

Perhaps the most consequential aspect of the use of social media, the internet, and digital technologies for promoting historical empathy in social studies and ELA are how places such as museums, cultural institutions, and historical societies have made physical documents and artifacts available for view on the internet. Before, the only way to access public records, historical artifacts, films, audio recordings, personal writings, and other types of primary sources needed for research or for curriculum development was to travel to a brick-and-mortar hall of records, libraries, archives, and museums. The archive is the place where the work of the historian, the journalist, the writer, the curator takes place. Katie's first time at an archive to conduct research for her Master's thesis was overwhelming — she had to make an appointment to schedule the visit, fill out forms to indicate which documents she wanted to research, and had to abide by strict rules concerning photocopying and photographing documents, touching and handling old documents, and of course, not taking anything out of the archive. A visit to the archive is not like a casual trip to the library where you can just browse through boxes of documents and artifacts. You must plan ahead and be very intentional about what you want to find. If you realized that you needed more materials, you had to ask an archivist for their assistance, or possibly return for another visit.

Allison Lindsey said in a 2014 article in *Medium* that "traditional notions of archives are not changing, but expanding." This is true, particularly as more and more repositories of primary sources have digitized their collections for research and public use. They use computer and artificial intelligence (AI) technologies to perform archival and preservation tasks such as scanning images and texts, and converting vinyl records, cassette tapes, film reels, and compact discs (CDs) into digital audio-video files that are readily accessible to people all over the world. Moreover, they use social media platforms to direct potential students, teachers, and scholars to their materials and to the various services and programming they offer.

Digital archiving, although being the wave of the future, is not a substitute for the physical archive. The materials that archives digitize need to be organized, preserved, and stored somewhere. Not every artifact is in the condition to be handled by humans to be uploaded onto a digital platform. Physical objects can be photographed and posted online, but a student of history or art or literature or anthropology may need to analyze the object in person. Sometimes, issues concerning funding to pay for archivists, support staff, and equipment to archive materials, either digitally or physically, are scarce. Also, archivists play a tremendous role in making decisions about what they accept for preservation and whether a primary source or artifact bears historical significance or collective remembrance. Therefore, researchers, students, teachers, and the public need to remember that just because something that they are looking for isn't in a particular repository does not mean the source does not exist. As a result, the work of archivists not only involves historical preservation and making primary sources accessible to the public, but also to engage stakeholders in examining which historical contexts and perspectives are expressed, or not, in their collections. Analyzing aspects of what are missing and present in archives can be an impactful pedagogical strategy to promote historical empathy with students.

In the United States, the Library of Congress (LOC), National Archives (NARA), and Smithsonian Institution are the bastions of scholarship and historical preservation. The LOC was founded in 1800 and burned during the War of 1812; Thomas Jefferson's expansive personal library at his home in Monticello was sold to Congress to rebuild its collections. Now, the LOC extends to three buildings on Capitol Hill in Washington D.C. that "is an unparalleled world resource. The collection includes millions cataloged books and other print materials in 470 languages; millions of manuscripts; the largest rare book collection in North America; and the world's largest collection of legal materials, films, maps, sheet music and sound recordings" (Library of Congress, n.d.). The LOC has dedicated physical exhibits and digital collections that include Chronicling America, a repository of historical newspapers from across the country, Civil War maps and glass negatives of deuragoatypes, the National Photo Company Collection, and the Historical American Buildings Survey.

To navigate the LOC's website to find primary sources to use for promoting historical empathy can be a challenge because of its expansive collections, research aids, and holdings. Therefore, accessing the LOC's Teaching Resources is invaluable to access lesson plans, primary source sets, reusable materials that are not subject to copyright approvals, and blogs, videos, and articles that provide tertiary information to support primary source analyses for students.

Here are some Teacher Resources at the Library of Congress that have primary documents and other media that you can use to promote historical empathy with your students!

- Teaching with the Library of Congress Blog: https://www.loc.gov/about/general-information/
- Primary Source Sets: https://www.loc.gov/classroom-materials/?fa=partof_type:primary+source+set
- Free to Use Materials: https://www.loc.gov/free-to-use/
- Teacher Guides for Analyzing Primary Sources: https://www.loc.gov/programs/teachers/getting-started-with-primary-sources/guides/
- Lesson Plans: https://www.loc.gov/programs/teachers/classroom-materials/lesson-plans/

Additionally, the LOC provides expansive professional development opportunities for teachers to refine, hone, and learn new skills when teaching with primary sources—even when using documents to promote historical empathy. Educators at the LOC host webinars and person workshops during the summer for K-12 teachers to apply for, self-paced modules on how to analyze primary sources for multiple perspectives, and ready-made materials for a teacher or qualified history educator to facilitate with groups in local settings. In order to learn more about professional development provided not only by the LOC in Washington D.C., but by regional partners who receive grants to fund workshops and projects using the LOC's collections with teachers and students, check out the LOC's Regional Partners site. The LOC's regions are organized into three regions — Eastern Region, Midwest Region, and the Western Region. You can browse the each region's websites to see what kind of programs teachers, museums, professors, and other educators developed that focus on the use of primary sources from the LOC to promote historical empathy with teachers and students.

The National Archives and Records Administration (NARA) is another pivotal government institution that is charged with keeping the nation's official records. According to NARA's home page, although its building was constructed in 1934 during the Franklin D. Roosevelt administration, the nation's records have been kept since 1775. The NARA keeps not only the official documents of the United States government, most notably the Declaration of Independence and Constitution, but also ship manifests, treaties, enlistment records, films, photographs, and naturalization papers. NARA's holdings include documents that are required by law to be turned over for review and preservation, such as when a presidential administration ends, and materials donated by private citizens. As mentioned previously, archives cannot keep everything, and NARA only keeps from 2-5% of documents from federal agencies. However, over the years, NARA contains millions of texts, maps, films, illustrations, photographs, recordings, as well as "837 terabytes of electronic data" (NARA, 2024) deemed valuable to citizens and the continuity of American government.

Like the LOC, navigating the NARA website can be daunting, which is why their Educator Resources, specifically DocsTeach, are designed to support teachers with user-friendly materials for students to engage in historical empathy by analyzing digitized primary sources. Among their resources include distance learning opportunities with free student programs that focus on civics and literacy, lesson plans and activities that span primary source analysis through major time periods in U.S. history, and worksheets designed for primary source analysis of various types of digital media. DocsTeach is a repository of teacher-created lesson plans and document-based activities that educators can search by grade level or time-period. Teachers can download printable worksheets for source analysis, or create a log-in to create their own web-based DocsTeach activity.

Ready-made activities created by teachers and the NARA education team connect to essential skills of historical thinking and inquiry that align with Bloom's Taxonomy that can guide teachers when engaging students in historical empathy when examining primary sources for context and perspectives, and making affective connections to content. For instance, the "Deborah Sampson: A Woman Soldier in the Revolutionary War" activity, which is designed for grades 9-12, engages students in document analysis of Gannett's testimony regarding her application for her federal pension, discuss what they learned about her service during the American Revolution, and to consider "What would motivate a woman in the 18th century to join the army disguised as a man? (National Archives Education Team, n.d.)." To answer that question as a vehicle to promote historical empathy, students would need to grasp not only the causes of the war and role of civilians in the fight against the British, but also examine the conditions and societal expectations of women during the Revolutionary Era. Teachers can utilize the primary and secondary sources on DocsTeach to support students' acquisition of foundational knowledge of the social-political contexts of the American Revolution to discuss Gannett's motivations that can, hopefully, lead to consideration of how experiential knowledge or affective responses connect to what students learned about this person from the American Revolution.

The Presidential Libraries and Museums (PLM) are another NARA branch that provides primary sources and instructional resources that can be used to promote historical empathy. PLMs are "bringing together the documents and artifacts of a President and his administration and presenting them to the public for study and discussion without regard for political considerations or affiliations. Presidential Libraries and Museums, like their holdings, belong to the American people" (NARA, n.d). The PLMs are repositories of print texts, film, audio and video recordings, electronic data, photographs, and almost 100,000 physical objects that not only pertain to specific presidencies, but the histories of the states where the presidents; libraries are located. There are 15 PLMs with websites that contain digitized archival materials, as well as educational programming, materials, and standards-based lesson plans. For example, the Herbert Hoover library in Iowa contains numerous virtual and physical exhibits and educational resources about the Girl Scouts, Laura Ingalls Wilder, and the Great Depression that can provide important insights about the historical contexts in which events occurred and the perspectives of those involved that can be used to engage students in considering their own feelings, thoughts, and reflections on potential connections to these historical topics.

Here are some quick links to NARA and PLM education resources that can get you started using digital media and primary sources to promote historical empathy!

- Civics for All of Us: https://civics.archives.gov/
- DocsTeach: https://docsteach.org/
- Teaching with Documents: https://www.archives.gov/education/teaching-with-documents
- Civics for All of Us programming: https://civics.archives.gov/
- Milestone Documents (Transcribed): https://www.archives.gov/milestone-documents/list
- Situation Room Experiences: https://situationroom.archives.gov/
- White House Decision Center: https://www.trumanlibrary.gov/education/white-house-decision-center
- Advise the President Series: https://www.archives.gov/presidential-libraries/education/advise-the-president

Social Justice Organizations

Many non-profits, such as museums and historical societies that we will examine in greater detail in Chapter 6, also provide powerful digital media resources and curricular materials that can be used to promote historical empathy in social studies and ELA. Facing History and Ourselves (FHAO), which began in 1976, is an organization that connects middle and high school teachers across the United States and around the world in preparing "students to participate in civic life—using intellect, empathy, ethics, and choice to stand up to bigotry and hate in their own lives, communities, and schools." FHAO offers extensive curricular materials and professional development for history, social studies, and ELA teachers that focus on how to teach about current events, controversial issues, and difficult topics in history with pedagogical approaches such as facilitating book clubs, document-based lesson plans, and implementation of the C3 Framework. While some lesson plans and curricular materials require a login, their FHAO website offers extensive free digital media materials that emphasize implementing tenets of historical empathy in ELA and social studies instruction. For example, over 300 videos and images are available in their Resource Library for teachers to use when exploring topics such as

> Jane Elliot's groundbreaking lesson in 1968 demonstrating the effects of racial discrimination in an elementary classroom based on eye color is one of the videos FHAO features in its Resource Library. "A Class Divided" was originally aired as a PBS special in 1983. Using this video with pre-service teachers or during professional learning can be a powerful way to demonstrate implementing historical empathy strategies when teaching about difficult issues and hard histories:
>
> https://www.facinghistory.org/resource-library/class-divided

what is an American identity, definitions of freedom, antisemitism, and racism in the media that can serve as big ideas or compelling questions when staging inquiries that engage students in historical empathy.

Learning for Justice (LFJ), which is formerly Teaching Tolerance, is an initiative of the Southern Poverty Law Center that was founded in 1991 with the goal of being "a catalyst for racial justice in the South and beyond, working in partnership with communities to dismantle white supremacy, strengthen intersectional movements and advance the human rights of all people". LFJ offers numerous free resources such as virtual workshops, lesson plans, teaching strategies, curricular frameworks, podcasts, and resource kits to educators who are teaching topics pertaining to the civil rights movement, hard histories, digital literacy, and social justice matters. Specifically, its Classroom Resources includes student texts that can be used by teachers to engage students in multimedia primary and secondary research about historical contexts and contemporary events. For instance, the "Build a Learning Plan" feature is extremely helpful for teachers who are browsing through the list of primary sources that include government reports, photographs, audio, and literature such as Zora Neale Hurston's *Barracoon*. By signing up with your email address, teachers can create a learning plan by selecting a text, developing a title, choosing a grade level, connecting to a content area, selecting suggested essential questions, and selecting from LFJ's student tasks and teacher strategies to formulate a lesson plan. The only aspect of the learning plan is that state standards are not included. Common Core standards for ELA/History are included in the lesson plans that are already provided by LFJ. Therefore, teachers must connect their respective standards when they build a custom learning plan when using the student texts on the LFJ site.

Teaching for Change (TFC): Building Social Justice in the Classroom is a national organization whose mission is to promote democracy by providing teachers, schools, and communities with "participatory lessons that go beyond a hero's version of history and a curriculum that helps students become active citizens rather than passive consumers." Among the social justice topics that they provide include civil rights, anti-bias education, and Black Lives Matter. Additionally, TFC collaborates with Rethinking Schools, another social justice education organization, on the Zinn Education Project (ZEP), which is named after Howard Zinn who authored the seminal book *A People's History of the United States*. This partnership aims at teaching social justice, counternarratives, and multicultural education in schools through the use of primary sources, social justice literature, and digital media such as documentary films. Teachers can access lesson plans on the TFC and ZEP sites, as well as sign up for magazine subscriptions and webinar offering from Rethinking Schools. Teacher webinars are also offered by these non-profits to engage educators in how to teach social justice in history, such as the Reconstruction, and to analyze contemporary issues such as voting rights and climate change. Taking a critical approach to engaging students in historical empathy in ELA and social studies through examining historical and contemporary issues of power, oppression, and marginalization with counternarratives and primary sources of underrepresented people and groups can be a powerful way to implement inquiry strategies of the C3 Framework that can lead to students taking informed action on topics and issues facing their communities.

You can access these educational materials if you are interested in digital media resources to promote historical empathy by teaching matters of social justice:

- Teaching for Change: https://www.teachingforchange.org/educator-resources
- Rethinking Schools: https://rethinkingschools.org
- Zinn Education Project: https://www.zinnedproject.org/materials/

These organizations are examples of non-profits that grew out of grassroots teacher,
librarian, and community activism regarding teaching hard histories, controversial issues, and current events that have structural and historical roots in social justice issues such as racism. The reality of the political climate today is that there are at least six states with anti-divisive concepts laws that have impacted what teachers can teach regarding race, gender, identity, and bias, particularly in ELA and socials studies, which includes the types of fiction and non-fiction literature that can be used in K-12 schools. However, there are several states that have passed legislation to include cultural competency standards. When using these resources, or any primary or secondary source for that matter, to promote historical empathy, we advise that presenting multiple perspectives on issues such as race be aligned to your state's standards to protect your employment and reputation in case you work in a state with anti-divisive concepts legislations can result in your termination. We do not advocate for the "both sides" argument regarding universally condemned human rights atrocities such as chattel enslavement; but we do support the intentional selection of digital media, literature, and historical documents that can engage students in historical empathy where they can grapple with how and why historical contexts shaped perspectives in the past, and how their reasoned affective connections to content can lead to civil discourse on difficult topics and informed civic engagement in schools and communities.

Simulations and Games

Educational non-profit organizations have grown to be valuable repositories of digital media such as interactive games and simulations for teachers to use when promoting historical empathy. iCivics was founded by Sandra Day O'Connor in 2006 after she retired as the first woman justice on the Supreme Court. iCivics is a one-stop shop for standards-based digital media inclusive of games, simulations, videos, and DBQ and webquests for students to engage in learning about the branches of government, the Constitution, and major turning points, people, and court cases in U.S. history relating to civil rights. iCivics includes a scope and sequence for elementary, middle, and high school civics that are available in English and in Spanish. So many of iCivics' digital media can be used to promote historical empathy. For instance, among the learning objectives for the DBQuest about the Nashville sit-ins include "Use evidence from informational texts to support analysis and answer questions; Identify an author's point of view or purpose; Integrate visual information with other information in print and digital texts (iCivics Teachers Guide, 2018). This lesson plan includes primary sources such as interview transcripts and photographs of key figures involved in these sit-ins, as well as graphic organizers for students to examine the intent and purpose of the sources, as well as to ask questions and explain any reactions they had to reading these sources.

The simulations and games also have teacher guides and tools to connect to state standards that also engage students in inquiry and historical empathy in a variety of ways. For example, the *Neighborhood Good* teacher guide features several inquiry questions to consider when starting the simulation by asking "what does perspective mean?" and "what are multiple examples?" to set the foundation for the processes in which community stakeholders address an issue or need (iCivics, 2023). Moreover, the National Endowment of the Humanities (NEH) funds many non-profits that provide resources and professional development for teachers who are interested in digital media to promote the emotive and cognitive aspects of historical empathy. For example, the NEH'S EdSitement provides an incredible amount of lesson plans, teacher guides, interactive timelines, and digital media resources to support teaching topics in civics, history, and ELA. The list of lesson plan topics that teachers can choose from on EdSitement include poetry, poetry, theatre, and literature and language arts where historical contexts and perspectives can be analyzed and discussed in connection to students' affective responses. For instance, a lesson plan on Lois Weber and early women filmmakers in Hollywood engages students in analysis of the film 1916 *Shoes* to examine the role of women in society, and how to raise awareness of underrepresented narratives and history of women in the filmmaking industry. This lesson plan connects to historical empathy goals by engaging students in considering the state of women's rights in 1916, three years prior to the ratification of the 19th amendment, Weber's experiences and perspectives entering a male-dominated field, and how her experiences connect to students' experiences, prior knowledge, and affective responses to matters concerning women's rights.

Additionally, Mission U.S., another NEH funded initiative, contains "serious history" and "serious games" for teaching "complex topics in American history," including seven missions that students can select when learning about topics such as the American Revolution, Westward Expansion, the antebellum era, immigration, Japanese incarceration during World War II, and the Civil Rights Movement. Each mission includes videos, character introductions, background information, and primary sources for the topic of study where students are asked to consider the perspectives and experiences of diverse people during different time periods. The mission "For Crown or Colony?" highlights the decisions a teenager must make when deciding to support the Loyalists or Patriots during the American Revolution. In "A Cheyenne Odyssey," students are asked to consider the perspectives of a Cheyenne boy whose community faces challenges for survival with the construction of the transcontinental railroad. These games are in tune with the goals of historical empathy as students analyze videos and secondary and primary sources to identify the historical contexts and perspectives of people in the past to make informed and reasoned affective connections to the present. Teachers and students can create a free login with username and password to access these resources.

The New American History Project, which is a project based out of the University of Richmond, is a comprehensive one-stop-shop for various types of digital media that teachers can use for free when planning instruction to promote historical empathy. Among the resources the NAHP offers include, but are not limited to, documentary films, podcasts, panoramic maps, and namely, its BUNK History Project (https://www.bunkhistory.org/how) that serves as a "connection engine" of contemporary news and stories that address topics from the past. Learning resources can be customized based on reading level, curricular topics, state standards, and type of social studies learning activity such as critical thinking prompts or graphic organizers. There are 72 ready-made educational resources that teachers can access that include a wide variety of topics from mock elections, the Chinese Exclusion Act, Confederate monuments, spotting fake news. Between EdSitement, Mission 250, and NAHP (the links are in the Suggested Resources at the end of this chapter), teachers have access to a vast array of digital media resources that can support historical empathy through engagement in primary and secondary source analysis.

Weighing the Use of Digital Media

Sometimes, if we use a tool frequently, we take for granted these how these tools need to be properly vetted before use for teaching. According to a Common Sense Media (2023) report, 43% of children ages 8-12 have smartphones, and between 88-95% of teens ages 13-18 have smartphones, which leaves youth exposed to app use, marketing, and notifications that can impact behavior regarding socialization, sleep, and learning (p. 1). The risks of overexposure and overuse of digital media, especially social media, has been the subject of Congressional hearings regarding the dangers of cyberbullying, sexual exploitation, and other behavior issues that children who use these internet-based apps are exposed to. As a result, we as educators cannot assume that students know how to use digital media tools, apps, and other web-based programs for academic use. Therefore, we need to do our homework when choosing which digital media to use when promoting historical empathy in social studies and ELA, as well as teaching students skills to identify the purpose, intent, accuracy, and reliability of digital media.

The U.S Department of Education's Office of Educational Technology (2021) recommends that teachers evaluate digital media, and all technology for that matter, based on four goals for classroom use that include 1) empowering students with skills to use technology as responsible digital citizens, 2) choosing digital media that meets the needs of students, 3) engaging families in the decision-making process when selecting digital media, and 4) engaging in regular professional development to stay abreast of trends and new research in using education technology (p. 5). Common Sense Media, in partnership with Harvard University, has a repository of lesson plans for grades K-12 that focus on topics such as privacy and security, well-being, relationships, and digital literacy. Specific to digital literacy, the lesson plans address how students can evaluate digital media sources for credibility, confirmation bias, and how to distinguish from real versus fake news. These lessons are useful tools when teaching skills about how to use digital media; however, empathy is not a curricular goal in these standards. However, the skills outlined in these lessons are helpful in designing lessons that promote historical empathy through analysis of contexts in which sources are created, how different perspectives are expressed, and the ways in which students can make affective connections to content learned.

Additionally, Common Sense Media connects its lesson plans to the International Society for Technology in Education (ISTE) standards. ISTE provides standards for students, educators, education leaders, and coaches that are aligned with the United Nations Educational, Scientific, and Cultural Organizations' (UNSECO) Sustainable Development Goals for the world's most pressing issues. Similar to Common Sense Media's lesson plans, the ISTE standards focus on building the skills of students, teachers, and educational leadership of using the internet and e-learning tools to promote digital literacy and citizenship. Although the term *empathy* does not appear in the ISTE (2018) standards, the term perspectives appears five times in the full document for educator, leader, coach, and student standards, referring to how the use of digital media can foster culturally-relevant learning that "incorporates and values unique perspectives" (p.11).

> Laurel Aguilar and Karalee Nakatsuka's book *Bring Civics and History to Life* highlights technological sources and strategies to teach historical empathy and civics that align to ISTE standards!
>
> https://iste.org/products/a1w1U000003ggCEQAY/Bring-History-and-Civics-to-Life

The resources provided by the institutions, non-profits, educational organizations, and digital archives include materials that support the promotion of historical empathy with pedagogical approaches for evaluating sources. The LOC's teacher guide for using their primary source analysis tool is connected to its process of observing details in a document, reflecting on the contexts and perspectives of the document, and asking additional questions for further investigations. The NARA also has document analysis resources that teachers can download as worksheets to support students in engaging in the historical empathy process through identifying what kind of document is being examined, observing its parts, make sense of what the document means, and to consider how to use the source as historical evidence.

> Teachers can download the Library of Congress' primary source analysis tools, which include digital materials, as printable worksheets or to be directly typed into on their website!
>
> https://www.loc.gov/static/programs/teachers/getting-started-with-primary-sources/documents/Primary_Source_Analysis_Tool_LOC.pdf

When weighing the use of digital media to promote historical empathy, practitioners must be aware of influence of *presentism*. Presentism refers to when practitioners and students of history impose their present-day beliefs on their interpretations and understandings of the past. NCHE offers specific guidance on how to analyze primary sources for historical contexts and multiple perspectives to make reasoned affective connections with its ten HHM. Specifically, the historical empathy as outlined in the HHM emphasizes that using current events should be done with "caution" to avoid "applying our current views to historical people's experiences." Therefore, historical empathy is an important habit of the mind because of the purpose of discerning how the past and present differ.

Now, inquiries and source analyses about the historical contexts of the past should not lead to sympathizing or condoning atrocities, poor decisions, crimes against humanity, and any form of oppression and marginalization. In fact, employing historical empathy as a habit of the mind invites the researcher, teacher, and student to grasp why certain actions, beliefs, or attitudes in the past were prevalent to further support why some actions in the past were wrong then as they are now. As a result, when engaging students in using digital media, historical empathy can and should be mindfully implemented so that analysis of the past, and contemporary matters, is done through examination of the context in which a source is created and the perspectives and intent of the content creators of digital media sources in order to discern not only how the past and present differ, but how historical investigation of digital media sources can support informed action by students in the present.

Connections to Standards

There are so many ways teachers can use digital media when teaching to promote historical empathy in social studies and ELA. For example, a civics lesson about function of the Electoral College with use of simulations such as "Winning the White House" from iCivics can lead to discussions about how and why voter turnout and the popular vote are influential on the outcomes of Presidential elections. Surely a history lesson about the Electoral College, such as in 1824 when there was no majority winner in the Electoral College, connects to the issue of the popular vote and role of Congress where John Quincy Adams won the presidency over Andrew Jackson in a "corrupt bargain." Using NARA's digital archival sources, Mary Frances Greene's (2023) lesson about the House of Representative's tally sheet can engage students in historical empathy when considering why the election of 1824 was contentious, why representatives from the states voted the way they did, and to deliberate on the role of ordinary citizens in deciding the outcome of Presidential elections.

As such, reading fiction and non-fiction literature relating to voting for high school students in ELA can support development of historical empathy because of the connections that can be built between content knowledge of social studies and experiential knowledge of real-life events like elections. For instance, the Denver Public Library (DPL) provides a comprehensive list of fiction and non-fiction books about voting for teenagers. The non-fiction suggestions include books about the suffrage movement, African American voting rights, the origins of the Constitution, and contemporary issues facing democracy. Elizabeth Rusch's (2020) book *You Call This Democracy?* breaks down issues facing American democracy such as gerrymandering and provides examples from young adults who took informed action to address these issues in their communities. Although not featured on the DPL list, Representative John Lewis' graphic novel series *March* is also an excellent example of non-fiction literature that can complement examinations of voting and civil rights when promoting historical empathy in social studies and ELA. The DPL fiction recommendations include books that revolve around elections and the lives of high school and college-bound teens who face a myriad of real-life situations such as gender identity, falling in love, and working with people with different opinions and backgrounds. These books can be vital tools in promoting historical empathy in ELA and social studies because of the ways the topic of the Electoral College and voting is framed to be relevant to kids' lives while demonstrating how historically the system works, the changes to the system that resulted in changes in legal and social perspectives on voting rights, and the role citizens play in elections and securing the right to vote.

> For a complete list of the DPL's recommended fiction and non-fiction books about voting for high school students, check out their website:
>
> https://www.denverlibrary.org/teen/list/voting-books-teens

NCTE Standards and Digital Media

The NCTE Standards for ELA address and support the use of digital media to teach historical empathy in ELA in several important ways. According to NCTE (2020), introducing students to a variety of texts and "technological resources" such as political documents "gives students a new perspective on their own experience and enables them to discover how literature can capture the richness and complexity of human life" (p. 11). Major NCTE standards that align with the use of digital media to promote and support historical empathy in ELA and social studies are located in Table 2.1.

These selected standards address the use of digital media and contemporary forms of texts that can foster historical empathy by couching students' affective responses to content learned through analysis of the historical contexts in which texts are created and the perspectives of the authors who produce these texts.

Table 2.1 NCTE ELA Standards Connections to Digital Media and Historical Empathy

Standard	Description
1	Students read a wide range of print and nonprint texts to build an understanding of texts, of themselves, and of the cultures of the United States and the world; to acquire new information; to respond to the needs and demands of society and the workplace; and for personal fulfillment. Among these texts are fiction and nonfiction, classic and contemporary works (p. 19).
4	Students adjust their use of spoken, written, and visual language (e.g., conventions, style, vocabulary) to communicate effectively with a variety of audiences and for different purposes (p. 24).
5	Students employ a wide range of strategies as they write and use different writing process elements appropriately to communicate with different audiences for a variety of purposes (p. 25).
6	Students apply knowledge of language structure, language conventions (e.g., spelling and punctuation), media techniques, figurative language, and genre to create, critique, and discuss print and nonprint texts (p. 26).
8	Students use a variety of technological and informational resources (e.g., libraries, databases, computer networks, video) to gather and synthesize information and to create and communicate knowledge (p. 28).

C3 Framework and Digital Media

The C3 Framework is not as explicit as the NCTE standards regarding the role of digital media and technology when introducing students to primary and secondary source analyses with the goal of promoting historical empathy. The term *digital media* yielded zero results in the C3 Framework; however, the term *media* was used 17 times referring to forms of governmental and non-governmental communications that are in print or internet based. Specifically, Dimension 2: Content Standards highlights how media, such as articles, can be used as primary sources when studying topics such as the Great Depression (p. 96). Dimension 3: Evaluating Sources provides guidance on the importance of analyzing multiple sources for perspective, credibility, and reliability of evidence in documents that can support claims. Additionally, Dimension 4: Communicating Conclusions and Taking Informed Action is where many standards connections with using digital media is located, namely outlining ways students can "represent their ideas in a variety of forms and communicate their conclusions to a range of audiences" (NCSS, 2013, p. 60). The suggested standards from the C3 Framework are implicit to the use of digital media to promote historical empathy.

Table 2.2 C3 Framework Connections to Digital Media and Historical Empathy

Inquiry Arc Dimension	Standard
1	**D1.5.9-12.** Determine the kinds of sources that will be helpful in answering compelling and supporting questions, taking into consideration multiple points of view represented in the sources, the types of sources available, and the potential uses of the sources.
2	**D2.Civ.5.9-12.** Evaluate citizens' and institutions' effectiveness in addressing social and political problems at the local, state, tribal, national, and/or international level.
2	**D2.Geo.2.9-12.** Use maps, satellite images, photographs, and other representations to explain relationships between the locations of places and regions and their political, cultural, and economic dynamics.
2	**D2.Eco.10.9-12.** Use current data to explain the influence of changes in spending, production, and the money supply on various economic conditions.
2	**D2.His.6.9-12.** Analyze the ways in which the perspectives of those writing history shaped the history that they produced.
3	**D3.1.9-12.** Gather relevant information from multiple sources representing a wide range of views while using the origin, authority, structure, context, and corroborative value of the sources to guide the selection.
3	**D3.3.9-12.** Identify evidence that draws information directly and substantively from multiple sources to detect inconsistencies in evidence in order to revise or strengthen claims.
4	**D4.3.9-12.** Present adaptations of arguments and explanations that feature evocative ideas and perspectives on issues and topics to reach a range of audiences and venues outside the classroom using print and oral technologies (e.g., posters, essays, letters, debates, speeches, reports, and maps) and digital technologies (e.g., Internet, social media, and digital documentary).

Sample Lesson Plan

In Chapter 1, we explored how the IDBM template can be used for an entire instructional unit that includes several days of lesson plans with at least three to four supporting questions or adapted for a single-day lesson. Our sample lesson plan is aligned with the C3 Framework that can be adapted for one or multiple days of instruction so that teachers can practice building inquiries that engage students in using and examining digital media as a way to promote historical empathy in social studies and ELA.

DIGITAL MEDIA

Lesson Title: The Long Road to Freedom

Grade Level: 9-12

Length of Time: 3-4 days

C3 Framework Inquiry Arc Dimension 1- Staging the Inquiry	
Big Idea	Freedom
Compelling Question	What does voting have to do with freedom?
Essential Understandings/ Rationale	The purpose of this lesson is to engage students in examining how Jim Crow segregation and voter suppression led to violence against African Americans in the Southeast, and how community and national activists who organized the Selma March influenced the passage of the Voting Rights Act of 1965.
Learning Targets	Students will be able to: • Explain the socio-economic and political causes for the Bloody Sunday violence • Identify major people, places, and groups involved in supporting and opposing desegregation, civil rights, and African American voting rights • Analyze the socio-economic and political ramifications of the Selma March
Supporting Questions	• What caused the Bloody Sunday violence in Selma, Alabama in 1965? • What was the community and national response to the violence in Selma on Bloody Sunday? • How did the Selma March impact the passage of continued civil rights legislations during the 1960s? • Why was there opposition to Black voting after the Civil Rights Act of 1965? • Who were some of the major organizations and people involved with the marches in Selma? • What was the outcome of the marches? • What is the historical significance and legacy of Bloody Sunday and the Selma marches on the US today?

Lesson Materials	
Featured Secondary Sources	U.S. Civil Rights Trail "The Movement" https://civilrightstrail.com/experience/marching-for-the-right-to-vote/

Lesson Materials	
Featured Primary Sources	Lynda Blackmon Lowery, *Turning 15 on the Road to Freedom* Universal News Reel, National Archives https://docsteach.org/documents/document/selma-story John Lewis Testimony after March 7, 1965 https://www.archives.gov/exhibits/eyewitness/html.php?section=2 Georgia Governor Responds to Voting Rights Act https://dp.la/primary-source-sets/voting-rights-act-of-1965/sources/1392
Technology/Media Sources	Library of Congress video, Lynda Blackmon Lowery https://www.loc.gov/item/2021689634/ Mission 250 Simulation, No Turning Back Google Slides Flip Book Template
Other Materials and Supports	SQ3R Chart

C3 Framework Inquiry Arc Dimension 2- Standards Connections	
C3 Framework Content Standard	**D2.His.6.9-12.** Analyze the ways in which the perspectives of those writing history shaped the history that they produced.
C3 Framework Content Standard	**D3.1.9-12.** Gather relevant information from multiple sources representing a wide range of views while using the origin, authority, structure, context, and corroborative value of the sources to guide the selection.
C3 Framework Content Standard	**D3.3.9-12.** Identify evidence that draws information directly and substantively from multiple sources to detect inconsistencies in evidence in order to revise or strengthen claims.
C3 Framework Content Standard	**D2.Civ.5.9-12.** Evaluate citizens' and institutions' effectiveness in addressing social and political problems at the local, state, tribal, national, and/or international level.
NCTE Standard 1 for ELA	Students read a wide range of print and nonprint texts to build an understanding of texts, of themselves, and of the cultures of the United States and the world; to acquire new information; to respond to the needs and demands of society and the workplace; and for personal fulfillment. Among these texts are fiction and nonfiction, classic and contemporary works (p. 19).
NCTE Standard 5 for ELA	Students employ a wide range of strategies as they write and use different writing process elements appropriately to communicate with different audiences for a variety of purposes (p. 25).
NCTE Standard 8 for ELA	Students use a variety of technological and informational resources (e.g., libraries, databases, computer networks, video) to gather and synthesize information and to create and communicate knowledge (p. 28).

DIGITAL MEDIA

C3 Framework Inquiry Arc Dimension 3- Analyzing Source Evidence	
Introduction/ Motivation	Teacher can start with students in small groups or pairs to brainstorm what the term "freedom" means to them. They can list their ideas or create a mind map. After students share their responses, teacher can ask students what voting has to do with freedom? Potential answers can include choosing representatives to make decisions on our behalf, being treated equally in society, etc.
Teacher Direct Instruction	Teacher will share a mini-lecture how the Civil Rights Act of 1964 had its limitations dating back to the Reconstruction Era, and ask students what those limitations were, including restrictions on Black voting in the South that included literacy tests, poll taxes, and violent intimidation preventing voter registration. Teacher will ask why voter registration is important. Answers can include to represent the people, make good choices for communities, etc. Next, teacher will highlight the role of SCLC and SNCC in going to Alabama to register voters in February 1965, and how a planned march from Selma to Montgomery to support voting rights legislation led to violence on "Bloody Sunday" when marchers were beaten by law enforcement and youth pastor Jimmy Jackson was killed. Teacher will show the newsreel of Bloody Sunday from docsteach (to 3:49) and ask students to reflect on the following: what did the marchers experience? How does this make you feel? What were some political, social, and economic issues happening in 1965 that led to these events in Selma?
Formative Performance Task/Student Structured Practice	Students will work in small groups and read Lynda Blackmon Lowery's memoir *Turning 15 on the Road to Freedom*. Students will complete an SQ3R chart to annotate the text for answers to the above questions using the graphic organizer below:
	Survey- write the chapter titles and provide main ideas for each
	Questions • Why was there opposition to Black voting after the Civil Rights Act of 1964 was passed? • What caused the violence on Bloody Sunday in Selma, Alabama on March 7, 1965? • Who were some of the major organizations and people who supported and opposed the marches in Selma? • What was the outcome of the marches? • What is the historical significance and legacy of Bloody Sunday and the Selma marches on the US today?
	Read- find evidence from the text to answer each question. Include direct quotes and page numbers
	Recite- summarize the main points of the text that highlight the most important information about the Selma marches

C3 Framework Inquiry Arc Dimension 3- Analyzing Source Evidence

Review- Reflect and answer the compelling question, "What does voting have to do with freedom?" List some additional questions you have about the Selma marches.

Next, students will research digital archives for primary sources to answer their review and reflection questions from the SQ3R chart. Some suggested digital archives include:

- John Lewis on the National Archives Eyewitness site: https://www.archives.gov/exhibits/eyewitness/html.php?section=2
- Library of Congress video, Lynda Blackmon Lowery https://www.loc.gov/item/2021689634/
- Digital Public Library of America: https://dp.la/primary-source-sets/voting-rights-act-of-1965/sources/1391
- President Obama Presidential Library https://obamawhitehouse.archives.gov/issues/civil-rights/selma
- Impact of Selma, DocsTeach: https://www.docsteach.org/activities/teacher/the-impact-of-bloody-sunday-in-selma
- US Civil Rights Trail: https://civilrightstrail.com/experience/marching-for-the-right-to-vote/

Next, students will use the primary source evidence that they researched to answer their questions to create a digital flipbook using Google Slides (scan the QR code for template example and directions).

Each page will include the question and answers from last section of the SQ3R chart with cited evidence and images or video from the digital archives. Student groups can delegate roles- digital designer of the flipbook, researcher of images and video for the pages, writer types the responses to the questions citing primary source evidence, and reporter will present the flipbook to the class.

C3 Framework Inquiry Arc Dimension 4- Communicating Conclusions and Taking Informed Action	
Student Share	Student groups will present their digital flipbook to the class by explaining why they chose their questions, what evidence they found to support their answers, and their overall conclusion about the compelling question, "what does voting have to do with freedom?"
Closing	Students will individually submit an exit ticket responding to the following prompts: how did learning about Lynda Blackmon and Selma make you feel? How can learning about Selma connect to an issue facing your community today, and what can you do about it?
Summative Performance Task/ Extension	Extension activities can include student deliberation on action steps on how to address an issue facing their community that relates to their research about Selma. For example, students can research how to get involved in local voting registration events and create infographics to raise awareness on how voters can register to participate in elections.
	Another extension activity can be using the Mission 250 Simulation "No Turning Back" about sit-ins and demonstrations challenging racial segregation in Mississippi. Students can do the simulation individually or in small groups, then reflect on their experience engaging in perspective taking about youth experiences during the 1960s civil rights movements and how those experiences connect to what they learned about Selma and what voting has to do with freedom.

Conclusion

Digital media is all around us. The choices for using digital modalities of primary and secondary sources can be overwhelming because of the vast archival and secondary source materials that are at our fingertips thanks to the internet. When using digital medial to promote historical empathy, we encourage teachers to be discerning about what types of sources they want to use, how to be clear about the content and skills those sources can be used to teach, and empowering students to conduct their own research when answering compelling questions and considering how to take informed action. Digital media has the potential to open new worlds up for students using archives, games and simulations, collaborative apps, and accessing rich texts that can spark emotion, imagination, and historical inquiry.

This chapter highlights the significance of media in teaching historical empathy and teaching in general. As Katie and Jennifer have experienced, like most teachers, media literacy is double-edged sword. As we discuss later in Chapter 4, teachers in all disciplines bare responsibilities in teaching media literacy. As teachers committed to teaching historical empathy to a generation of students who do not remember a time when they could not access multiple forms of digital media, it is incumbent upon educators to help their students navigate their choices. That being said, teachers can feel overwhelmed. Most of us are not media specialists and are not digital natives like our students. As a result, we offer in this chapter and the rest of this book, resources and lesson plans to support teachers in promoting historical empathy that we hope can lead to connections with your school's media specialists so that through strong collaboration, we can all support our students in learning how to safely navigate and use digital media.

Reflection

- What are some benefits and limitations to using digital media resources to promote historical empathy?
- What kind of digital media resources could you use to promote historical empathy with your students?
- How can your use of digital media engage your students in interdisciplinary engagement of historical empathy through source analyses in ELA and social studies?

Note

1. *The Weekly Reader* magazine began in 1928 and was a staple for teachers who taught current events in 28 different content areas. In 2012, Scholastic bought The Weekly Reader and incorporated the magazine with its broader Scholastic News publications. Check out Jason Tomassinni's article in Education Week to learn more: https://marketbrief.edweek.org/strategy-operations/longstanding-classroom-magazine-weekly-reader-stops-printing/2012/07

Suggested Digital Media Resources

Common Sense Media Lesson Plans, K-12. Retrieved from https://www.commonsense.org/education/digital-citizenship
EdSitement (https://edsitement.neh.gov)
Facing History and Ourselves. https://www.facinghistory.org/about
iCivics. Winning the White House. (https://www.icivics.org/games/win-white-house?check_logged_in=1

International Society for Technology in Education Standards. Retrieved from https://iste.org/standards
Learning for Justice. https://www.learningforjustice.org/about
Mission 250 (https://www.mission-us.org)
National Archives Education. www.archives.gov/education
National Archives DocsTeach: www.docsteach.org
New American History: (https://www.newamericanhistory.org
Teaching for Change. https://www.teachingforchange.org/about/history

Chapter References

Beale, J., Clothier, S., Stamp, S. (2023). In her shoes: Lois Weber and the female filmmakers who shaped early Hollywood. *EDSITEment!* Retrieved from https://edsitement.neh.gov/lesson-plans/her-shoes-lois-weber-and-female-filmmakers-who-shaped-early-hollywood

Common Sense Media. (2023). *Constant companion: A week in the life of a young person's smartphone use.* Retrieved from https://www.commonsensemedia.org/sites/default/files/research/report/2023-cs-smartphone-research-report_final-for-web.pdf

Greene, M. F. (2023). *Tally of the 1824 Electoral College Vote.* Retrieved from the National Archives. https://www.archives.gov/education/lessons/electoral-tally

iCivics. (2023). *Good neighbor teacher's guide.* Retrieved from https://www.icivics.org/sites/default/files/2024-01/Neighborhood%20Good%20Extension%20Pack%20with%20Supports%20for%20ELs_MLs.pdf

iCivics. (2018). *Nashville sit-in teacher's guide.* Retrieved from https://www.icivics.org/sites/default/files/Nashville_DBQuest%20Teacher%20%26%20Student%20Materials.pdf)

Korti, J. (2019). *Media in history: An introduction to the meanings and transformations of communication over time.* Springer.

Lewis, J. & Aydin, A. (2013). *March: Book one.* Penguin Books.

Library of Congress. (n.d.). General information. Retrieved from https://www.loc.gov/about/general-information/

Lindsey, A. (2014). Tradition versus digital in archives. *Medium.* Retrieved from https://medium.com/archives-records/tradition-versus-digital-in-archives-80919121b9c8

National Archives Presidential Libraries and Museums. (n.d.) *About page.* Retrieved from https://www.archives.gov/presidential-libraries/about.

National Archives and Records Administration. (n.d.). *General information leaflet, number 1.* Retrieved from https://www.archives.gov/publications/general-info-leaflets/1-about-archives.html

National Council for History Education. (n.d.). *History's habits of the mind: Historical empathy.* Retrieved from https://ncheteach.org/conference/history-of-habits-of-mind/#:~:text=History's%20Habits%20of%20Mind%20articulates,productive%20learning%20and%20active%20citizenship.&text=

Grasp%20the%20significance%20of%20the%20past%20in%20shaping%20the%20present.

National Council for Teachers of English. (1996). *Standards for the English language arts*. Retrieved from https://cdn.ncte.org/nctefiles/resources/books/sample/standardsdoc.pdf

National Council for the Social Studies. (2013). *The college, career, and civic life framework for social studies standards*. National Council for the Social Studies. Retrieved from https://www.socialstudies.org/sites/default/files/c3/c3-framework-for-social-studies-rev0617.pdf

National Women's History Museum. *Digital classroom resources*. Retrieved from https://www.womenshistory.org/students-educators/digital-classroom-resources

Rusch, E. (2020). *You call this democracy? How to fix our government and deliver power to the people*. Clarion Books.

United States Department of Education Office of Educational Technology. (2021). *Teacher digital learning guide*. Retrieved from https://tech.ed.gov/files/2021/01/Teacher-Digital-Learning-Guide.pdf

Weir, K. (2023). Social media brings benefits and risks to teens. Psychology can help identify a path forward. *Monitor on Psychology 54*(6), p. 46. Retrieved from https://www.apa.org/monitor/2023/09/protecting-teens-on-social-media

CHAPTER 3

Music and Recording Arts

Brainstorming Activity

- What role has music played in your life?
- How have you used music in previous lessons?
- How might music help promote historical empathy with your students?

Introduction

Katie and Jennifer love music both on a pedagogical and personal level. Katie grew up listening to a lot of classic rock from the 1960s and 1970s, so it should come as no surprise that she won first prize for the Staten Island borough-wide social studies fair for her research about The Beatles when she was in fourth grade. Growing up during the mid-20th century, Jennifer and Katie were influenced, inspired, and moved by the diverse genres of music that makes up the fiber of human culture, and the unique American history and experience. From country music to 80s new wave to alternative rock to hip hop to classical symphonies, music is a very powerful tool that teachers can use to promote historical empathy with their students. The aesthetics, composition, and lyrics that comprise songs and music are intrinsically linked to the human experience. Music contextualizes and memorializes the events most important to us such as weddings and funerals, historical events such as presidential inaugurations and remembrances, and national celebrations such as the Fourth of July.

Some songs and genres have become historically connected to specific events either because they were written for the events or because popular culture responds to those events with music that conveys the common feelings of the moment. During World War I, popular songs reflected a mix of emotions from patriotism to disillusionment. "Over There" by George M. Cohan (1917) is an upbeat march that asserts, "The Yanks are coming! The Yanks are coming! ...And we won't come back 'till it's over until it's over, over there!," while

"I Didn't Raise My Boy to be a Soldier" (1915) reflects the anti-war movement of the time. Similarly, songs underpinned a national sense of patriotism after the United States joined the allies during World War II. The popular music genre of the period was Jazz and artists such as Glen Miller and the Andrew Sisters combined common sentiment with the genre of Swing. Young people danced the Jitter Bug to songs like "Bugle Call Rag" (1945) and "Boogie Woogie Bugle Boy" (1941) while more sentimental songs conveyed the national acceptance that while Americans were separated from loved ones, the separation was temporary and for a greater good "Sentimental Journey" (1944) and "I'll be Seeing You" (1944).

Historically, beyond sentiment and patriotism, music has underscored protest and social unrest. In the 1960's, the music of artists such as Nina Simone, the Staple Singers, Creedence Clearwater Revival, and Bob Dylan voiced the frustration and determination of those in the Civil Rights movement and protest against the Vietnam War. Popular songs reflected the feelings of those fighting for racial equity and the long years leading up to the demand for change. Sam Cook's "A Change is Gonna Come" (1964), "Freedom Highway" (1965) by the Staple Singers, and "We Shall Overcome," a hymn revitalized in the 1960's by Pete Seeger and recorded by folk artists such as Joan Baez, became the soundtrack for marches and protests led by Civil Rights leaders including Dr. Martin Luther King. Paralleling the Civil Rights movement was the anti-war movement. Unlike the two World Wars, the Vietnam War lasted over a decade and drew protests from artists across all genres. Artists from Johnny Cash, "What is Truth?" (1971), Chad Mitchell Trio, "Business as Usual" (1965), Crosby, Stills, and Nash "Wooden Ships" (1969), and Marvin Gaye, "What's Going On?" (1971) voiced the feelings of a generation called into a war they did not support and questioning the government that supported that war. Music represents not only artistic genres of country, rock, folk, R&B, and pop; music has a powerful effect in representing the feelings, perspectives, and societal landscapes throughout a nation.

Contemporary pop music remains a constant of social commentary. In 2015, Kendrick Lamar's song "Alright" became part of the unofficial sound behind the Black Lives Matter movement, along with J. Cole's "Be Free" (2014). The Me-Too movement inspired artists such as Kesha who released "Praying" (2022). Stella Donnelly's "Boys Will be Boys" (2015), Margo Price's "Pay Gap" (2017), and Childish Gambino's (2018) "This is America" found new audiences during the movement. During the summer of 2024, Vice-President Kamala Harris' presidential campaign was invigorated on social media by pop singer Charli XCX's post likening her to the concept of being a "brat" on her namesake album *Brat*. These songs, like so many written over decades, touch the emotions of people and provide words and, through the music, an energy that complements their own feelings about events and societal change.

In this chapter, we offer ideas and lesson plan templates for ELA and social studies to use music as a tool for promoting inquiry that supports historical empathy. Besides offering soundtracks to historical events, music, with its themes, repetition, metaphors, and narratives, provides text to text connections that teachers can offer their students to compliment other readings. Music is a common connection for adolescents who cannot always articulate their ideas in the ways curriculum and the traditional rules of writing dictates. Giving students a musical lens through which to examine historical events can provide students with connections to events they might not make otherwise. The selected time periods that we focus on are examples of how music can be used as primary sources to engage students in historical empathy.

Great Depression Songs

Music played a big role in how Americans, and people around the world, coped with the devastation of the Great Depression. Jennifer has a very strong connection to the Dust Bowl because she grew up in Oklahoma. In the United States, folk music became an outlet for people to express their sorrow as they suffered through unemployment, poverty, and economic insecurity. When Katie taught about the Great Depression, she would bring in three examples of songs during the 1930s for students to listen to for historical context, perspectives expressed, and how they felt. The songs were Bernard "Slim" Smith's *Bread Line Blues* and Woody Guthrie's *Talking Dust Bowl Blues*. I made a two-column chart and asked students to write down how they felt and what images came to their mind while they listened to each song. Next, students reflected on how these songs depicted changes in the U.S. economy and society from the end of World War I through 1929.

For example, you can search YouTube or the Library of Congress' site of Great Depression and Dust Bowl Music. Katie used to play "Breadline Blues" and "Talking Dust Bowl Blues" when she taught about the 1930s with her eighth graders. Students would record imagery and feelings they had while listening to both songs, then compare the messages of the songs to examine how the economic and political climate of the Great Depression impacted people's perspectives and experiences during this time in history. The graphic organizer in Figure 1. is a chart that Katie developed to support her students' analysis of these songs.

Also, the lyrics can be provided for students to annotate for historical context and perspective, as well as for literary analysis of language, imagery, and intent for the song. For instance, the verse in "Breadline Blues" that refers to political parties can be a compelling example of how music can be analyzed for historical significance, artistic expression, and relevance to students' experiences, emotions, and connections to current events.

> He elephant said, 'You long-eared mule
> Well, you shut your mouth, you never been to school'
> The mule said, 'Elephant, it ain't no joke
> 'We've got to do something or we're all gonna croak
> 'We ain't got nothing but a carload of tax
> 'And the doggone load is just a-breaking our backs
> 'We've got the blues, the breadline blues' (Smith, 1931)

Teachers can ask students to highlight or circle lyrics that they believe refer to the political climate of 1931, what the personification of the mule and elephant represents, what perspective is expressed in the verse, and what images, feelings, and connections students can make to the song to their lives or contemporary issues. Additionally, playing these songs alongside photographs documenting the migrant and urban plight of the Great Depression (see Chapter 5!) generated deep discussions among the kids about individuals and families were impacted by the stock market crash, environmental disaster in the Midwest, and politics of the 1932 election. The students also examined songs and other primary sources from the Brooklyn Public Library to research about how contemporary economic issues like the 2008-2009 Great Recession shared similarities and differences to the challenges Americans faced during the Great Depression, with a focus on their neighborhood in Brooklyn.

20th-21st Century Protest Songs

Protest songs have been a part of musical creation, political engagement, and individual expression throughout human history. The First Amendment Museum has a great digital exhibit of protest songs spanning the 20th and 21st century (see the suggested resources at the end of the chapter!). However, the popularization of rock and roll during the 1950s-1960s with album sales, radio DJs, and televised performances of groups such as the Jefferson Airplane, the Rolling Stones, Creedence Clearwater Revival, and the Beatles on programs such as The Ed Sullivan show allowed for protest songs to enter mainstream American and western culture. These songs were written and performed during the tumultuous times of the Cold War, the civil rights movement, and the Vietnam War. For example, using The Beatles music from 1963 through 1970 can be an audio-visual journey for students to observe their evolution from the suited mop-top group of the British Invasion to the psychedelic *Sgt. Pepper's Lonely Hearts Club Band* to the bearded virtuosos of *Abbey Road* and *Let it Be*. Songs on the 1968 *White Album* such as "Helter Skelter," "Revolution," and "Blackbird" comment on the political and racial turmoil in the U.S. and around the world. Noticing the lyrical and visual changes of The Beatles can be in many ways a literary and historical timeline of how the 1960s started out as hopeful and exciting with Camelot and youth (i.e., "I want to hold your hand") to dark and dismal with

Name: _____ Course and Section #: _____ Date: _____	
The Great Depression in Song, 1929-1933	
Directions: Listen to the songs *Breadline Blues* and *Talking Dust Bowl Blues*. List how you feel and any imagery that you think depicts what Americans faced during the Great Depression from 1929-1933?	
Breadline Blues	**Talking Dust Storm Blues**

How do you think these two songs depicted changes in the American economy and society from the end of World War I in 1919 and the beginning of the Great Depression in 1929?

FIGURE 3.1 Great Depression Song Analysis Worksheet, by Katherine Perrotta

assassinations, race riots, and ongoing war (i.e., "You say you want a revolution. Well you know, we all want to change the world"). Inspired by the Civil Rights Movement, specifically, The Little Rock Nine, a group of Black students who enrolled in Central High School in Little Rock, Arkansas after the Supreme Court ruled that segregated schools were unconstitutional, Paul McCartney wrote "Black Bird." Nearly 60 years later, Beyoncé covered "Black Bird" on her

Cowboy Carter (2024). Both versions could be offered to students to compare and contrast the political and social contexts for the original 1968 release by the Beatles and the 2024 of the Beyoncé version.

There is no shortage of popular music and television performances that teachers can use in ELA or social studies. The creation of hip hop during the 1970s and rise of contemporary pop and alternative rock music since the 1980s have marked not only how music continues to be a vehicle of personal expression, but also commentary of current events at particular points in time. When using music to promote historical empathy strategies, students must consider when a song was written and recorded in order to glean the perspectives of the artist and whose voices or points of view are expressed. Students can make connections to how they feel not only about a piece of literature or historical topic when listening to a song (or watching a performance or music video), but also consider popular music today that resonates with their lives, feelings, and experiences.

Some songs that Katie used when teaching about the role of protest songs and popular music during the 20th and 21st century are included below where students listened to the songs and watched the accompanying videos and recorded in a chart the tone, imagery, and message of each song.

You can hear both versions of "Black Bird" by searching YouTube:

https://www.youtube.com/watch?v=Man4Xw8Xypo Remastered Beatles version.

https://www.youtube.com/watch?v=xhempeEjGUA Official Beyoncé version.

Students concluded the activity with discussion about how the music represented perspectives of historic times, and what those songs mean to students in both affective and cognitive ways. Social studies and ELA teachers can also engage students in analysis about the concept of *multi-perspectivity* when engrossed in the process of historical empathy. According to researchers Wansink, Akkerman, Zuiker, and Wubbels (2018), *multi-perspectivity* involves how the lens or approach in which we examine historical contexts impacts how we understand perspectives of the past. To put it simply, songs can be analyzed in the context of the time when it was written, or completely in the present. We discussed being careful with presentism in Chapter Two regarding the caution of judging the past solely on today's terms. However, the authors of this study advise teachers

Centuries of Songs and Protests

Name: _____ **Course and Section #:** _____ **Date:** _____

Directions: Listen and pay attention to the music video or performance for each song. Write down what you think the tone, imagery, and message of each song are. Next, answer the reflection question at the end. Be ready to share!

Song	Tone	Imagery	Message
"Strange Fruit," by Billie Holliday			
"Eve of Destruction," by Barry Maguire			
"Fortunate Son," by Creedence Clearwater Revival			
"Ohio," by Crosby, Stills, Nash, and Young			
"Born in the USA," by Bruce Springsteen			
"Buffalo Soldier," by Bob Marley and the Wailers			
"Video Killed the Radio Star," by the Buggles			
"Changes," by Tupac Shakur			
"Icky Thump," by the White Stripes			
"American Idiot," by Green Day			

Reflection: How did events happening around the country and world shape the perspectives that are expressed in these songs? How do these songs make you feel? What connections can you make to these songs?

FIGURE 3.2 20th-21st Century Protest Song Analysis Worksheet, by Katherine Perrotta

to implement "informed reflexivity" with students as an important aspect of teaching multiperspectivity and historical empathy because of the subjective nature of how perspectives, past and present, are subjective and personal (Zuiker, and Wubbels, 2019, p. 499).

CHAPTER 3

Music Videos and Visual Albums

In 1981, the launch of "Music TV" or MTV, on cable television ushered in the mainstream mode of musicians creating videos to accompany the messages, aesthetics, and composition of their songs. Music videos existed prior to MTV. The earliest video recordings of musical and dance performance date back to 1895 with Thomas Edison's kinetophone machine. The advent of "talkies" or movies with recorded sound ushered in the production of films with soundtracks. Live-action movies and cartoons were accompanied with symphonic music, singing, and the "bouncing ball" that led audiences in sing-alongs in a theatre. As television became mainstream in American households during the 1950s and 1960s, variety shows like the Ed Sullivan Show featured Broadway performers and popular artists such as Elvis Presley, The Beatles, and The Rolling Stones that played their music live to audiences in studio and in their homes. The success of The Beatles' first Ed Sullivan appearance led to the first "feature length" music movie with "A Hard Day's Night" in 1964 where the band's music on that album was featured along with the story in the film. This is equivalent to "going viral" in the 21st century! From there, major pop stars, musicians, actors, and dancers utilized television shows such as The Monkees, Dick Clark's American Bandstand, Soul Train, and even the musical guests on Saturday Night Live to showcase their performances in visual formats.

MTV was pioneering because artists could create videos for specific songs that could be rerun multiple times instead of once during a live performance. Additionally, MTV became a vehicle to launch and propel careers of artists such as Michael Jackson, whose 1983 "Thriller" video was among the first music videos that were technically short films. The MTV Music Video Awards, also known as the VMAs, were first held in 1984 that is infamous for Madonna's risqué performance of her hit song "Like a Virgin." While showing these examples may not exactly align with your teaching standards, there are music videos that can be used when engaging students in various aspects of literary analysis (Chapter 1 shoutout!) and historical inquiry that can foster demonstration of historical empathy by examining historical contexts when music videos are created, the perspectives expressed by the artists, and affective responses they may have. These responses can be varied from liking the imagery and message of a video to suggesting different ways to use visual and fine arts to accompany a song.

> Billy Joel's (1989) *We Didn't Start the Fire* is a staple in social studies classrooms to play when teaching about major Cold War people and events. Fall Out Boy (2023) released an updated version of the song with events spanning the 21st

century. Britannica's online encyclopedia has an article explaining all of the events in Billy Joel's song that you can highlight for students when examining perspectives and historical contexts of the 20th century:

https://www.britannica.com/list/all-119-references-in-we-didnt-start-the-fire-explained

Music videos have grown more sophisticated with the advancement of digital technologies for music production, recording, and dissemination on the internet and other "smart" devices. Beyoncé's visual albums have been groundbreaking artistic achievements with original videos for each song that blur and recreate musical genres of dance, pop, R&B, and country to evoke powerful messages about Blackness, feminism, and human relationships. NPR has a great transcript of dialogue discussing Beyoncé's (2022) visual album *Renaissance* that we highly encourage teachers to read for not only historical empathy purposes, but also for literary analysis. The article is in our chapter references.

Musicals

Musicals can also be powerful mediums of music, performance, and art that can be used to teach content and promote historical empathy. We mentioned *Hamilton* in Chapter 1 when highlighting how literary analysis strategies can be implemented to examine how plays and dramas are often adapted from works of fiction and non-fiction. Musicals like *Hamilton* that are based on historical events and people have the potential for supporting historical empathy by engaging students in not only researching the historical contexts and perspectives of historical figures, but also how music can be part of the story that illustrates human emotion, experiences, and feelings. There are so many great examples of musicals, both as plays and feature films (see Chapter 4!), that ELA and social studies teachers can use to foster historical empathy through primary and secondary source research and literary analysis of works of textual and performing arts.

The Sound of Music is an interesting musical that is both a play and movie. Indeed, the music is beautiful and catchy. Julie Andrews' singing is phenomenal and iconic. The overall story is compelling with its themes of love and loss through grieving the death of the Von Trapp wife, harnessing the seven kids' musical talents, finding one's purpose in life (i.e., Maria figuring out she was not cut out to be a nun), marriage and family, and bravery, freedom, and independence when the Captain and his family escape his pending conscription into the Nazi military by escaping Austria by climbing the Alps. A social studies teacher could use scenes from the musical as a tool when teaching about the German Anschluss, particularly asking students to consider why the Captain tore up the Nazi flag, why the family left everything they had, and even why the daughter's love interest became a Nazi soldier. There is a lot of caution here to not ask students to sympathize with Nazis. Absolutely not. However, indoctrinating youth was a major Nazi strategy and audiences see that impact through the evolution of the character Rolfe from being a love-sick delivery boy to a Nazi snitch. Students can debate and deliberate through reading primary sources about the experiences of ordinary people living in pre-World War II Europe about the fears of the Third Reich by considering big ideas and compelling questions relating to why people leave everything behind to go to another country, namely the United States.

Both the social studies and ELA teacher can also use *The Sound of Music* to critically examine how the movie, albeit a work of art, diverged from the actual experiences of the Von Trapp family. For instance, Maria Von Trapp and daughter Agathe wrote memoirs about their lives before and after immigrating to the United States. Students can read these non-fiction works and compare and contrast the perspectives of these women in their books and the movie. Moreover, students can analyze reasons why book adaptations are changed for stage performances and films, as many details such as the number of children there were in the family, the portrayal of Captain Von Trapp as cold, and the family's actual journey to the United States which was actually uneventful and anti-climatic (they did not really climb the Alps). While all of these suggestions seem to diverge from using music to promote historical empathy, we want to highlight how using musicals can be catalysts for students to engage in historical inquiry through determining what primary and secondary sources were used in order to examine whether the portrayals of past people and events are accurate or dramatized. Additionally, having students pay attention to the music- both melodies and lyrics- can be powerful in connecting to their affective responses to the topics of study, in this case World War II, and how their emotive responses can lead to consideration of historical significance and potential ways to take informed action.

> The National Archives has many of the Von Trapp documents that are accessible on their website. Check out this article about the "true" story of *The Sound of Music* if you are interested in engaging students in historical empathy strategies through examining how the movie differs from the primary sources by the family on the NARA site:
>
> https://www.archives.gov/publications/prologue/2005/winter/von-trapps-html

Musicals can be fun or serious. Katie showed the scene from *1776* where the Continental Congress sang "sit down John" when John Adams was making his arguments about declaring independence from England. This scene was effective when Katie taught the American Revolution to seventh graders because the kids had to consider why wasn't there a unanimous decision on separating from England. She connected that scene to the case of Caesar Rodney, who made an epic trip from Delaware to Philadelphia to cast the tie-breaking vote for the Delaware delegation voting in favor of independence. Discussion often tied back to Thomas Paine's *Common Sense* and reading the Declaration itself regarding the document's structure and the risk that all the signers faced by essentially committing treason from Great Britain.

Another time, Katie took one of her seventh grade classes to see *West Side Story* at a Broadway matinee performance for school groups. She remembers how the kids hung to every spoken and sung word, not only chatting about issues of immigration and prejudice in the play, but also how this version of Leonard Bernstein's masterpiece included Spanish lyrics of songs such as "I Feel Pretty." As they sang the songs on the subway back to the school, Katie asked the kids what they liked the best from the play. She will never forget one boy saying to her, "wow, Maria and Tony really had things rough." Social studies and ELA teachers could use the musical *West Side Story* to engage students in literary analysis by examining how the setting of Shakespeare's *Romeo and Juliet* is similar and different to the setting of the 1961 musical, and how those contexts shaped the characters' perspectives, emotions, and even the feelings that students feel watching the musical. Musicals have the power to humanize historical figures by evoking humor, suspense, sadness, outrage, and other emotions that play a big role in how students can demonstrate the intellectual and emotive aspects of historical empathy in social studies and ELA.

> We made a list of our favorite musicals to use when teaching to promote historical empathy. This isn't an exhaustive list, and we hope that you can add your own preferences and ideas!
>
> Hamilton
> 1776
> West Side Story
> Porgy and Bess
> Oklahoma
> Meet Me in St. Louis
> The Scottsboro Boys
> Assassins

Connections to Historical Empathy

Similar to our discussion of literary analysis in Chapter 1, music not only has implications for effective social studies and ELA instruction, but as interdisciplinary tools that can spark inquiry, empathy, and care across content areas and subjects. Musical lyrics are poetry, and incorporating the recording arts into curriculum and teaching can support students' engagement in historical empathy through examining the historical contexts of when a song was written, the perspectives expressed in the song, and reflecting on the affective connections that are experienced by the listener. According to Janet Revell Barrett (2022), "cataclysmic moments in the 20th century United States history" have been accompanied by music, art, literature, and poetry (p. 135). Music has can foster historical empathy by tapping into students' interests, feelings, emotions, and prior knowledge of other content areas. As seen throughout this chapter, adding music not as an extra to studying the Great Depression or Vietnam War but as primary sources that documented these points in history can promote historical empathy among students.

Even the scores and soundtracks to films and documentaries, as we will discuss in Chapter 4, can be part of source analysis for historical context and plot, perspectives of characters, and evoke affective connections as the music often becomes part of a story that connects to the audience's engagement and emotions (Gilbert & Harris, 2017). Imagine a film like *Saving Private Ryan* without the music. Would that storyline and portrayal of the events leading up to and following D-Day have as wide an impact without the film score? Probably not. Music, whether instrumental, or featuring vocals, or performed by a solo artist or a group has the power to humanize social studies and ELA by touching the creative and emotive aspects of people's lives through considering the expression of a moment in time or a personal experience from another's perspective.

Instrumentals

Instrumental music, whether in the form of classical symphonies, jazz improvision, reggae, flamenco, bluegrass, gospel, mariachi, Gregorian chants, and electronic dance beats can be just as effective in evoking cognitive and affective aspects of historical empathy when used to teach ELA and social studies. Whether instrumentals were composed for religious purposes, propaganda, entertainment, or personal expression, music without lyrics can set the tone or mood to a classroom, but also a soundtrack to studying a historical period. For instance, symphonic music is very much related to western literary and artistic movements. The timeline in Figure 3.3. shows how major time periods in western art history go hand in hand with the evolution and creation of symphonic music. Much of the music during medieval and Renaissance periods included both parochial and secular music.

Using recordings of Gregorian chants, named after Pope Gregory, can accompany an ELA lesson when teaching about the epic works of literature after the fall of western Rome and rise of the early Christian church (see Chapter 1 and 3!) and for the social studies lesson to illustrate the socio-economic and political contexts of European kingdoms after 476 A.D. Both medieval and Renaissance art (see Chapter 4) can be shown as visuals that demonstrate perspectives of people living in western societies during and after the outbreak of the bubonic plague, and how music can highlight how people might have felt during a time of "rebirth" of faith, economics, and political stability. The music of the baroque period can serve as a backdrop to opulence of divine right monarchies in Europe (think gold, big dresses, and white wigs), which ultimately were destabilized with notions of natural rights as a result of the Enlightenment. The classical period saw a time of continued operas and dramatic works, as well as airy tunes like Mozart's Minuet in G were popular. The technological changes of the 19th century that derive from industrialization in Europe and around the world influenced the music of the Romantic period with more dramatic orchestral arrangements.

In addition to considering the historical contexts of the artistic influences on these instrumentals, students can also discuss who listened to these songs, how they listened to these songs, and why. Obviously today we can listen to music at the touch of an app on our smartphones, but 400 years ago, everyday things, such as books, that we use for entertainment were luxuries that only a few people had access to. Attending a live performance of an opera or symphony was something that elites in society most likely had access to doing. As a result, another angle to implement historical empathy strategies when listening to music can involve examining how the composition, performance, and distribution of music evolved from something only certain segments of society consumed to a popular form of entertainment and artistic expression that people of diverse social strata or backgrounds could enjoy.

The 20th and 21st centuries, which can be analyzed as modernist and postmodernist, are a time of continued innovation of instruments, arrangements, rhythms, and dissonance such as Gustav Holst's *The Planets Suite*, which was composed between 1914 and 1917, is a powerful cacophony of chaotic melodies throughout seven movements that very much echoed the confusion, terror, and horrors people were experiencing during World War I in Europe. According to Karla Walker (2018), "many composers were touched by World War I" such as Benjamin Britten, Enrique Granados, and Igor Stravinsky whose orchestral works include marching rhythms, dramatic crescendos, and thundering percussions that mirrored the climate of uncertainty and despair during and after a war

CHAPTER 3

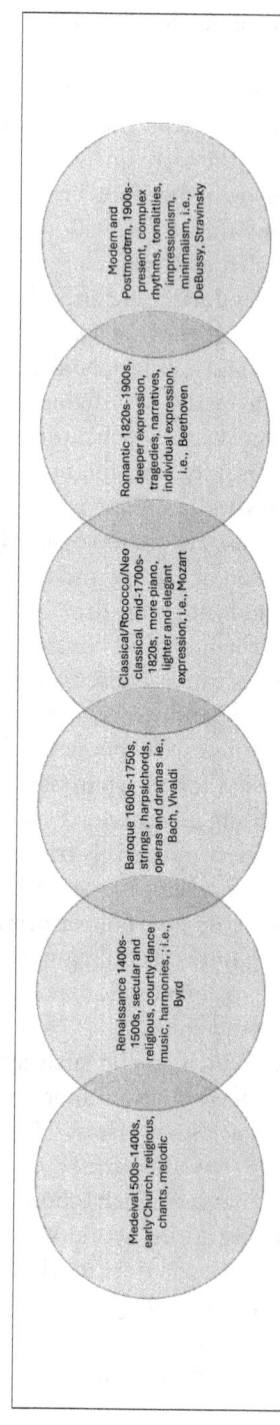

FIGURE 3.3 Timeline of Western Art History and Classical Music

that was supposed to end all wars. Examining how the contexts of World War I, whether directly or indirectly, influenced Holst's suite can engage students in historical empathy by investigating the causes of the war in Europe, how the Allied and Central Powers were dragged into a war that led very quickly into a stalemate, and how the end of the war led to deep economic depression and political instability that led to other catastrophic events throughout the 20th and 21st centuries.

Western-style classical music is not the only type of instrumentals that can be used to promote historical empathy. Centering non-Western compositions when teaching topics pertaining to U.S. and world history and literature can be extremely impactful when engaging students in perspective taking of marginalized people and groups through studies of topics in ELA and social studies such as ancient dynasties, imperialism, and decolonization. For example, music from Africa not only serves as historical context and perspectives of diverse people across the continent before European enslavement, but also how music served as a vehicle of resistance against racial oppression and slavery as traditional beats, rhythms, and songs endured throughout European colonies in Latin America and North America. Genres such as rhumba, salsa, calypso, mambo, samba, merengue, and the Chacha are deeply influenced by African and indigenous roots. Listening to the instrumentals of music from Southern and Eastern Asia, particularly India, China, Japan, and South Korea can engage students in historical empathy through examination of the historical contexts of the rise and influence of the socio-economic and political systems and dynasties that shaped the development of these empires before and after European colonization, and how that legacy of imperialism continues to impact the people of these nations today.

PBS Learning Media's site has lesson plans and resources to teach about world cultures and societies through music. These materials may be a great place to start when using music to promote historical empathy with your students!

https://gpb.pbslearningmedia.org/collection/social-studies-and-world-history-through-music-and-dance/

American jazz, bluegrass, and country music were born from traditional African folk tunes and gospel spirituals, which can lead to critical inquiry about how songs that were written and performed by Black artists only became popular when white artists such as Elvis Presley covered their music. Examination of "race records" from the early to mid-20th century by listening to the different versions of songs performed by white and Black artists can be a sobering experience for students to examine how the historical contexts of Jim Crow segregation impacted perspectives about what kind of music would be "preferable" to mainstream white audiences, and how the success of white artists like The Beatles helped and hindered the amplification of Black musicians and artists. You can learn more about this history from George Mason University's *Hearing the Americas* project that is funded by the National Endowment of the Humanities (the reference is at the end of the chapter!).

Connections to Standards

Richard Henry Stoddard (1882) wrote in a biography about poet Henry Wadsworth Longfellow that "thanks to his beautiful gift of his poetry—in a succession of exquisite melodies...flow on and along to a music of their own making" (p. 161). Longfellow is credited with saying that "music is the universal language of mankind" because every human society has a form of musical expression that tells stories, evokes emotions, entertains, and serves as personal expression. Music can be instrumental or poetic, melodic or dissonant (we could not find the 1835 poem, but found that Stoddard's perspective of Longfellow's poems were relevant to role of music when promoting historical empathy). According to Janet Revell Barrett (2022), music is the "humanistic foundation" of the arts and culture of human societies (p. 136). As such, we show how the following standards connections highlight how music can be incorporated in ELA and social studies to promote historical empathy.

NCTE Standards and Music Literacy

NCTE recognizes music as part of a multimodal approach to literacy (2021). In Table 3.1, we have provided a list of NCTE ELA standards that align employing music to promote historical empathy.

C3 Framework and Music

The C3 Framework does not mention music in the Inquiry Arc. However, the use of music as a primary or secondary source is supported throughout the C3 Framework where "practicing the arts and habits of civic life" are essential for growth and development as active and engaged citizens (NCSS, 2013, p. 6). As seen in Chapter 2, Dimension 3: Evaluating Sources stresses the importance of analyzing multiple sources for perspective, credibility, and reliability of evidence in documents that can support claims. Music can certainly be powerful literary and historical documents that elicit emotion, critical thinking, and empathetic

Table 3.1 NCTE ELA standards that align employing music to promote historical empathy.

Standard	Statement	Connection to Historical Empathy
1.	Students read a wide range of print and non-print texts to build an understanding of texts, of themselves, and of the cultures of the United States and the world; to acquire new information; to respond to the needs and demands of society and the workplace; and for personal fulfillment. Among these texts are fiction and nonfiction, classic and contemporary works.	This standard supports the reading of a wide range of texts to help inform students' analysis of the historical contexts of music, the perspectives that are expressed in music, how multiperspectivity of music analysis in its historical context or present time can impact how students discern how the past and present differ, as well as how they can make connections to feelings, experiences, and prior knowledge in order to communicate conclusions and discover ways to take informed action in the present.
2.	Students read a wide range of literature from many periods in many genres to build an understanding of the many dimensions (e.g., philosophical, ethical, aesthetic) of human experience.	Like the previous standard, a connection is made between reading diverse texts and cultural fluency to support student "understanding of the many dimensions of human experience" (NCTE).
3.	Students apply a wide range of strategies to comprehend, interpret, evaluate, and appreciate texts. They draw on their prior experience, their interactions with other readers and writers, their knowledge of word meaning and of other texts, their word identification strategies, and their understanding of textual features (e.g., sound-letter correspondence, sentence structure, context, graphics).	The use of music as a strategy to promote historical empathy, as suggested in this chapter's introduction, aligns with NCTE's standard 3, offering opportunities for students to draw on prior knowledge and experiences with other texts through primary source analysis of music, lyrics, poetry, videos, and other sources through literary analysis of text features, purpose, voice, prose, and perspective.
9.	Students develop an understanding of and respect for diversity in language use, patterns, and dialects across cultures, ethnic groups, geographic regions, and social roles.	Music, like poetry, offers a "diversity in language use, patters" (NCTE) through metaphors, rhyme, repetition, use of vernacular, and slang that reaches across cultural and social roles, generations and values, place and beliefs.

(Continued)

Table 3.1 (Continued)

10.	Students whose first language is not English make use of their first language to develop competency in the English language arts and to develop understanding of content across the curriculum.	Many adolescents whose first language is not English, learn some of their words in English through television, videos, and music. Music can offer differentiated instruction to promote historic empathy among students who may still struggle with the classroom dominate language.
11.	Students participate as knowledgeable, reflective, creative, and critical members of a variety of literacy communities.	Again, as with poetry, the use of music to promote historical empathy offers opportunities to encourage creative reflection and critical thinking, such as asking students to create a soundtrack to an historical event.
12.	Students use spoken, written, and visual language to accomplish their own purposes (e.g., for learning, enjoyment, persuasion, and the exchange of information)	This standard encourages student choice of multimodal literacies to meet learning targets as well as support personal goals. NCTE recognizes music on their list of multimodal literacies (NCTE, 2005).

responses to the experiences of others in the past and present. Dimension 4: Communicating Conclusions and Taking Informed Action is a natural place where students can use music, either existing songs or creating original compositions, to "represent their ideas in a variety of forms and communicate their conclusions to a range of audiences" (NCSS, 2013, p. 60). The suggested standards from the C3 Framework are implicit to the use of music to promote historical empathy.

Sample Lesson Plan

This lesson plan, created in the IDBM template, emphasizes the use of music to promote historical empathy. Teachers are encouraged to adapt the lesson to best fit the needs of their students and classroom schedule. As with subsequent chapters on documentaries and film, and photographs and visual arts, this chapter relies on different forms of technology to support the lesson. Teachers should use their discretion in allowing students to choose music for the soundtrack activity as well as how to meet school expectations on student technology use. As with other chapters, this lesson can be recreated within the time frame of one or two days or expanded for a full unit study that could take place over the course of several days. The sample lesson plan is very complex as we designed

Table 3.2 C3 Framework Connections to Digital Media and Historical Empathy

Inquiry Arc Dimension	Standard
1	**D1.5.9-12.** Determine the kinds of sources that will be helpful in answering compelling and supporting questions, taking into consideration multiple points of view represented in the sources, the types of sources available, and the potential uses of the sources.
2	**D2.Civ.5.9-12.** Evaluate citizens' and institutions' effectiveness in addressing social and political problems at the local, state, tribal, national, and/or international level.
2	**D2.His.6.9-12.** Analyze the ways in which the perspectives of those writing history shaped the history that they produced.
3	**D3.1.9-12.** Gather relevant information from multiple sources representing a wide range of views while using the origin, authority, structure, context, and corroborative value of the sources to guide the selection.
3	**D3.3.9-12.** Identify evidence that draws information directly and substantively from multiple sources to detect inconsistencies in evidence in order to revise or strengthen claims.
4	**D4.3.9-12.** Present adaptations of arguments and explanations that feature evocative ideas and perspectives on issues and topics to reach a range of audiences and venues outside the classroom using print and oral technologies (e.g., posters, essays, letters, debates, speeches, reports, and maps) and digital technologies (e.g., Internet, social media, and digital documentary).

the activities to complement listening to music and examining historical documents with literary analysis by connecting primary sources about the Russian Revolution and Soviet Union to George Orwell's book *Animal Farm*. This lesson plan in its entirety may take several days to complete. However, teachers are welcome to pick and choose which activities may work best for truncated instruction when using music to promote historical empathy in ELA and social studies when teaching about the historical contexts and perspectives of the impact of the Russian Revolution on U.S. and world history.

Lesson Title: Animal Farm: What Does Rebellion Sound Like?

Grade Level: 9-12

Length of Time: 5-10 days

C3 Framework Inquiry Arc Dimension 1- Staging the Inquiry	
Big Idea	Rebellion
Compelling Question	What does rebellion sound like?
Essential Understandings/ Rationale	The big idea and compelling question will support students' analysis of how language, specifically propaganda, has been and can be used to persuade others, especially during times of major socio-economic and political change or rebellion. Students will examine language and distinguish between persuasion and propaganda while using the Russian Revolution and aftermath during Lenin and Stalin as historical context. Music will be used as support texts for students to analyze and use as examples of language, in its many forms and uses, can engender feelings that underpin people's opinions and beliefs, especially regarding rebellion.
Learning Targets	Students will be able to: 1. Identify major causes and people involved with the founding of the Soviet Union 2. Explain major causes of the Cold War 3. Distinguish between persuasive language and propaganda. 4. Draw from primary and secondary sources for textual evidence. 5. Analyze how persuasive language can be used for positive outcomes versus how propaganda can be used to turn one group against another.
Supporting Questions	• What was the historical context at the time when Orwell published *Animal Farm*? • How does the Russian Revolution set the historical backdrop of this book? • Where do we see examples of propaganda in *Animal Farm*? • Why do you think the author, George Orwell, creates an allegory to tell this story?

Lesson Materials	
Featured Secondary Sources	• *Animal Farm* by George Orwell • National Geographic, The October Revolution https://education.nationalgeographic.org/resource/october-revolution/
Featured Primary Sources	• Speech by Stalin, On the Industrialization of Russia, https://people.uncw.edu/townendp/stalinspeech.htm • Emma Goldman, excerpts from "My Disillusionment in Russia"
Technology/ Media Sources	• Le Internationale, by Geyter, 1888, https://www.youtube.com/watch?v=Eqm9iSoHBdU • March of the Defenders of Moscow, Mokrousov, 1941 https://www.youtube.com/watch?v=qWiqDtWywmI • Pigs (Three Different Ones) by Pink Floyd, 1977 https://www.youtube.com/watch?v=gOqblSqx_VI

MUSIC AND RECORDING ARTS

Lesson Materials	
Other Materials and Supports	Notebooks, pens, pencils, *Animal Farm* text, post-notes

C3 Framework Inquiry Arc Dimension 2- Standards Connections	
NCTE Standard 2 for ELA	1. Students read a wide range of literature from many periods in many genres to build an understanding of the many dimensions (e.g., philosophical, ethical, aesthetic) of human experience.
NCTE Standard 3 for ELA	3. Students apply a wide range of strategies to comprehend, interpret, evaluate, and appreciate texts. They draw on their prior experience, their interactions with other readers and writers, their knowledge of word meaning and of other texts, their word identification strategies, and their understanding of textual features (e.g., sound-letter correspondence, sentence structure, context, graphics).
NCTE Standard 12 for ELA	12. Students use spoken, written, and visual language to accomplish their own purposes (e.g., for learning, enjoyment, persuasion, and the exchange of information).
C3 Framework Content Standard, History	D2.His.4.9-12. Analyze complex and interacting factors that influenced the perspectives of people during different historical eras. (p. 47)
C3 Framework Content Standard History	D2.His.9.9-12. Analyze the relationship between historical sources and the secondary interpretations made from them. D2.His.5.9-12. Analyze how historical contexts shaped and continue to shape people's perspectives.
C3 Framework Content Standard History	D2.His.9.9-12. Analyze the relationship between historical sources and the secondary interpretations made from them.

C3 Framework Inquiry Arc Dimension 3- Analyzing Source Evidence	
Introduction/ Motivation	• Students begin by doing a gallery walk of propaganda posters from the 1917 Russian Revolution (i.e., the University of California Berkeley has a website of propaganda posters with English translations of the Russian writing https://exhibits.lib.berkeley.edu/spotlight/russian-revolution/feature/propaganda). • Students will put post-it notes on the images that highlight examples of how persuasive language and propaganda are being used.

CHAPTER 3

C3 Framework Inquiry Arc Dimension 3- Analyzing Source Evidence	
Teacher Direct Instruction	**Day 1** • Teacher will ask students to define propaganda, and discuss why propaganda was important during and after the Russian Revolution. Possible answers include to persuade workers to join the fight in overthrowing the government, resisting absolute rule of the czar, and to support Soviet principles of economic equality for the working class. Students can read in small groups or pairs about the October Revolution from National Geographic and explain the historical context for the Russian Revolution and perspectives of Lenin, Trotsky, and others who were opposed and supportive of the czar. • Teacher will then ask students what problems arose in the Soviet under Lenin and Stalin during the 1920s-1940s. Possible answers include poverty, political oppression, and inequities. Teacher can split the class into halves, having one side read Stalin's speech On Industrialization and the other excerpts from Emma Goldman's book My Disillusionment in Russia. Both sides will explain what perspectives their documents revealed about the Soviet Union, and how they think the propaganda they saw in the gallery walk impacted those perspectives. **Day 2** • Next, the teacher will lead discussion with students about the context of when Orwell wrote *Animal Farm* in 1945 and ask what were the reasons for the start of the Cold War? Answers can include nuclear weapons, both US and Soviet Union becoming superpowers, and critiques of communisms as a political and economic system versus capitalism and democracy in the west. • The teacher will introduce *Animal Farm* to students, explaining that Orwell wrote the book as an allegory for the Russian Revolution and its aftermath. understanding the allegory, a comparison chart can be used. • The teacher will distribute copies of *Animal Farm* (Teacher preference on how to schedule the reading. Depending on the publisher, the book is approximately 92-144 pages with fairly short chapters.) • As a pre-reading exercise, students will survey the book and reflect on the following in a dialogue journal: • How do you think the historical context of the rise of the Soviet Union and start of the Cold War will impact this story? • What kind of perspectives do you think will be expressed in this book? • What are some of your thoughts/feelings/questions before you start reading?

MUSIC AND RECORDING ARTS

C3 Framework Inquiry Arc Dimension 3- Analyzing Source Evidence

Formative Performance Task/Student Structured Practice	**Days 3-10** • During the beginning chapters of the book, play for students the Soviet anthem "The Internationale." Students will record in their dialogue journal comparisons to the characters in the book with historical figures during the Russian Revolution and make notes about how they think the music supports the message of these chapters, specifically the song in Chapter 1 "The Beasts of England." Students can annotate the chapters for evidence of historical contexts and the dynamics of the characters, and predict what they think will happen next. • During the middle chapters of the book, teacher can play for students Soviet marching songs such as "The Song of the Soviet Army." Students will continue to record in their dialogue journal comparisons to the characters in the book with historical figures during the Russian Revolution and make notes about how they think the music supports the message of these chapters once the farm comes under Napoleon's control. Students can continue to annotate in the chapters for evidence of historical contexts and how and why the dynamics of the characters, and predict what they think will happen next. • During the final chapters of the book, teacher can play "Pigs" by Pink Floyd. Students will complete their dialogue journal by making final comparisons between characters in the book with historical figures during the Russian Revolution and make notes about the overall message of the book. • Once the book is read, groups of four students will discuss how the big idea of "rebellion" and compelling question "what does rebellion sound like?" relate to the historical context of the rise of the Soviet Union and start of the Cold War. Student groups will then create a poem, song, or an illustration that expresses a perspective from *Animal Farm* and how that perspective connects to a topic or issue that is relevant to today.

C3 Framework Inquiry Arc Dimension 4- Communicating Conclusions and Taking Informed Action

Student Share	• Student groups will share their poem, song, or illustration and explain how the perspectives expressed from *Animal Farm* connects to a topic or issue that is relevant today.
Closing	• The teacher will ask students to complete a quick write in which they explain how they distinguish between persuasive language and propaganda. Students will be asked to discuss how they feel after reading *Animal Farm* and what they think rebellion sounds like to them.

C3 Framework Inquiry Arc Dimension 4- Communicating Conclusions and Taking Informed Action	
Summative Performance Task/ Extension	• Students will research protest songs, both past and present, looking for themes that are reflected in the novel. Students will create a soundtrack for the novel *Animal Farm*. Students will choose a minimum of five songs (The teacher can add or subtract the number of required songs to adapt to the needs of her students.) • Students will choose three characters who represent different ideas or positions in the novel and choose songs that reflect these ideas or positions. The teacher may also wish to add a creative element and allow students to write their own protest songs based on the topic or issue they connected their analysis of *Animal Farm* to in the structured practice section of the lesson.

Conclusion

Humans possess an affinity for music. Music provides a means of connection to people, places, ideas, emotions, and beliefs. It is difficult to find a young person who is not tuned in to their favorite artist through ever-present earbuds or headphones, so offering music as a mode of literacy to students can provide engagement and access. In the lesson provided in this chapter, students are given opportunities to examine songs that express the strong resistance to war, the passion of patriotism, calls for equality, and the lament of the lack of equality. Through these examinations, students may understand that an art form they engage with on a daily basis possesses a dynamic and irrefutable place in history. Through the task of creating a soundtrack to a novel about rebellion, students analyze the language of song lyrics through the lens of persuasion and protest. Finally, students may see that beyond the ability to entertain, music has the potential to provide a vehicle for change.

Reflection

- How have you used music in your classroom?
- What are some of the benefits and challenges in using music in the classroom?
- How might music be used as a differentiation strategy?
- How might music be used in a cross-curriculum lesson plan?

Suggested Music Resources

American Music Research Center- University of Colorado Boulder. https://www.colorado.edu/amrc/

Breadline Blues: https://www.youtube.com/watch?v=1YwyW8ppbyA

Black Gospel and Listening Archive, Baylor University: https://library.web.baylor.edu/gospel

Ed Sullivan Show: https://www.edsullivan.com/all-artists/

The First Amendment Museum: https://firstamendmentmuseum.org/teacher-resources/

Goering, C.Z., & Burenheide, B.J. (2010). Exploring the role of music in secondary English and history classrooms through personal practice theory. *SRATE Journal 19*(2), 44-51.

Hearing the Americas Project: https://hearingtheamericas.org/s/the-americas/page/race-records

Kreps, D. (2016). Paul McCartney meets women who inspired Beatles' "Blackbird." *Rolling Stone Magazine*. Retrieved from https://www.rollingstone.com/music/music-news/paul-mccartney-meets-women-who-inspired-beatles-blackbird-57076/

Library of Congress Great Depression Resources: https://www.loc.gov/item/ihas.200197402

Mangram, J.A., & Weber, R.L. (2012). Incorporating music into the social studies classroom: A qualitative study of secondary social studies teachers. *The Journal of Social Studies Research 36*(1), 3-21.

Rock and Roll Hall of Fame: Holla if you Hear Me- Hip Hop at 50: https://rockhall.com/exhibitions/hip-hop-50/

Society of American Music K-12 Teacher Resources: https://www.american-music.org/page/K12Resources

Society of American Music Database of Libraries, Archives, and Research Centers: https://www.american-music.org/page/Libraries

Soden, G.J., & Castro, A.J. (2013). Using contemporary music to teach critical perspectives of war. *Social Studies Research & Practice 8*(2), 55-67.

Talking Dust Bowl Blues: https://www.youtube.com/watch?v=dkAxuqrVNBM

Thorpe, C. (2024). Cowboy Carter: Why Beyonce's cover of The Beatles' Blackbird is they key to the new album. *The BBC*. Retrieved from https://www.bbc.com/culture/article/20240329-beyonce-cowboy-carter-the-beatles-blackbird

Chapter References

2Pac (1998). Changes [Song]. On *Greatest Hits*. Amaru.

Armstrong, B.J. (2004). American Idiot. [Song]. On *American Idiot*.

Barrett, J. R. (2022). Fostering historical empathy through music, art, and poetry, in Abril, C.R., & Gault, B.M., (Eds). *General music: Dimensions of practice*. 134-151: Oxford University Press.

Brown, Les; Green, Bud; and Homer, 'Sentimental Journey' (1944). Vocal Popular Sheet Music Collection.

The Beatles. (1968). "Blackbird." [Song]. *The Beatles (White Album)*. Apple Records.

Beyonce. (2024). "Blackbird." [Song]. *Cowboy Carter*. Columbia Records.

Cash, J. (1970). *What is Truth*. Columbia Records.

Christensen, L. (2009). *Teaching for joy and justice. Re-imagining the language arts classroom*. Rethinking Schools.

Cleveland, A., Benson, R. and Gaye, M. (1971). What's Going On [Song]. *What's Going On*. Tamla.

Cohan, G. M. (1917). Over There [Song]. William Jerome Publishing Corporation.

Cole, J. (2014). *Be Free*. Apple Music.

Cooke, Sam (1963). A Change is Gonna Come [Song]. *Ain't That Good News*. RCA Victor.

Crosby, D. Kanter, P. and Stills, S. (1969). Wooden Ships [Song] *Crosby, Stills & Nash*. Atlantic Records.

Donnelly, S. (2019). Boys will be Boys [Song]. *Beware of the Dogs*. Secretly Canadian.

Duckworth, K., Williams, P., and Spears, M. (2015). Alright [Song]. *To Pimp a Butterfly*. Top Dawg Records.

Fain, S. and Kahal, I. (1938) I'll be seeing you [Song].

Gilbert, L., & Harris, M. W. (2017). Film music as a tool for fostering critical thinking and historical empathy, in Russell, W.B.III & Waters, S. (Eds). (2017). *Cinematic social studies: A resource for teaching and learning social studies with film*. 79-101: Information Age Publishing.

History.com Staff. (2023). *The music video, before music television: From Thomas Edison to MTV, the music video's long history*. Retrieved from https://www.history.com/news/the-music-video-before-music-television

Lennon, J. and McCartney, P. (1963). I want to hold your hand [Song]. Parlaphone (UK) Capitol (US).

Lennon, J. and McCartney, P. (1968). Revolution 1 [Song]. On The Beatles. EMI.

Lovy A., & Calker, D.. (1941). Boogie Woogie Bugle Boy of Company "B." Retrieved from https://www.loc.gov/item/ihas.200000021/

Marley, B. and Williams, N. (1983). Buffalo Soldiers [Song]. On *Confrontation*. Tuff Gong.

Meeropol, A. (1939). Strange fruit [Song]. Commadore.

Matthias, M. (2023). All 119 references in "We Didn't Start the Fire," explained. *Encyclopedia Britannica*. Retrieved from https://www.britannica.com/list/all-119-references-in-we-didnt-start-the-fire-explained

NCTE (2021). *Statement on Multimodal Literacies*. Retrieved from https://ncte.org/blog/2021/08/music-literacy-history/#:~:text=NCTE's%20Summary%20Statement%20on%20Multimodal,drama%2C%20which%20should%20not%20be

Pettis, J. (1922). *Bugle Call Rag*. Columbia Records. Retrieved from https://www.loc.gov/item/jukebox-670424/

Piantadosi, A. & Bryan, A. (1915). I didn't raise my boy to be a soldier [Song]. Retrieved from https://www.loc.gov/item/2002600251/

Powers, A., King, J., & Harris, L. (2022). Revolutionary fun: Why we can't stop talking about Beyoncé's Renaissance. *NPR Music*. Retrieved from https://

www.npr.org/2022/08/01/1114499960/revolutionary-fun-beyonce-renaissance-review-roundtable

Price, M. (2017). Pay Gap [Song]. *All American Made*. Third Man Records.

Orwell, G. (1945). *Animal Farm*. Secker and Warburg.

Seeger, Pete, 1919-2014 performer. (1989). We shall overcome: the complete Carnegie Hall concert: historic recording of June 8, 1963. Columbia.

Serbert, K, & Andrew, J. (2017). Praying [Song]. *Rainbow*. RCA.

Sloan, P.F. (1965). Eve of destruction [Song]. Dunhill.

Springsteen, B. (1984). Born in the U.S.A. [Song]. On *Born in the U.S.A*. Columbia.

The Staple Singers (1965). Freedom Highway [Song]. *Freedom Highway*. Epic Records.

Stoddard, R.H. (1882). *Henry Wadsworth Longfellow: A medley in prose and verse*. George W. Harlan & Co. Publishers. Retrieved from https://ia801307.us.archive.org/cors_get.php?path=/9/items/cu31924022036473/cu31924022036473.pdf

White, J. (2007). Icky thump. [Song]. On *Icky Thump*. Warner Brothers.

Wilson Center (2024). Stalin, Joseph [Biography]. Wilsoncenter.org.

Young, N. (1970). Ohio [Song]. Atlantic.

Films and Documentaries

Brainstorming Activity

- Do you have a favorite documentary or film? If so, why?
- How have you used documentaries or films in previous lessons?
- How can films and documentaries help promote historical empathy?

Introduction

When it comes to drawing adolescent learners into historical context, books alone do not always engage students. Even when reading the greatest writers of history and fiction, students may get lost in a wall of words they do not understand or struggle to make connections with cultures and settings outside of their own. Katie remembers when she saw *Glory* for the first time when she was in middle school. Seeing this movie was an eye-opener for her because she did not realize the discrimination and inequities that Black soldiers faced fighting for the Union during the Civil War. The scene about getting the troops shoes was particularly impactful to Katie, and she used that clip when teaching about the complexities of race and abolition in the North when she taught the Civil War with her eighth graders.

Much of Jennifer's childhood memories are centered around watching movies with her family, old westerns with her grandmothers, classic comedies with her brothers, and family holiday favorites like *It's a Wonderful Life* and *The Bishop's Wife* (her mother's favorite). She remembers sitting in... hospital room watching Ken Burns' documentary *The Dust Bowl* and each shedding quiet tears. These films are intrinsically linked to memories with her family because there is... something so visceral about watching movies and documentaries. Forgive the cliché, but film takes viewers to other places and other times. The images and sounds can stay with us like a beloved memory or haunt us like a deep regret.

In this way, movies and documentaries have the potential to inform historical empathy in students that other modes of literacy cannot.

The visual arts, especially films, include action, sound, and of course images that touch the senses and ignite the imagination in unique ways as compared to reading a text. In an interview with the American Film Institute (2020), filmmaker, writer, director, and actor Spike Lee recalls that he chose the title for his 1989 film, *Do the Right Thing* before he knew what the movie would be about. He notes that the words in the title mean different things to different people and the film sparked debate across the country and begged questions regarding race, culture, and communities' relationships with the police. So why do films like Lee's invoke public conversation in volume and across political and social perspectives that books cannot always match? In part, it is because on screen, our imaginations come to life and the events that are read about become real people who lived, or are living, real lives just as we are. Using film and television in the classroom is not a new concept. Some of us are old enough to remember televisions wheeled into our elementary classrooms to see astronauts leave the earth with all the sound and imagery of the rockets blasting into space. How we use this medium, though, is what matters. How educators use film to elicit empathy and start conversations in the classroom takes planning, just like any good resource does. This chapter offers suggestions and examples of using film and documentaries to ignite conversations among our students and draw them closer to history and current events that will become historical.

Documentaries

Documentaries were once relegated to the tastes of history buffs and regular viewers of PBS. The genre more recently has gained popularity through streaming services such as Max, Curiosity Stream, Netflix, Magellan TV, and of course, PBS. Documentaries, however, are not created equally and some discernment is required by educators to find films that are both educational and worthy of the classroom. For instance, while Ken Burns' documentaries are a standard-bearer for the genre, his films are not without critique. His iconic *Civil War* documentary that featured writer Shelby Foote came under scrutiny due to the production team's all-White staff that did not include professional historians of the Civil War and Reconstruction such as Eric Foner (Merritt, 2019). Despite these shortcomings, his documentaries can be useful tools to promote historical empathy when engaging students into examining the film's purpose, whose voices are featured, whose are not, and who the film's target audience is. Jennifer particularly loves Burns' documentaries on *The Dust Bowl* and *Baseball* because of his use of primary sources, narrative prose, and stunning images and music that engage and educate audiences about pivotal times throughout U.S. history.

The list of documentaries that ELA and social studies teachers can use to teach content and promote historical empathy would be very long and exhaustive. We highlight three documentaries with sample lesson plans to show how this genre of film can be impactful when promoting historical inquiry and historical empathy. We chose these documentaries because of the topics and social issues they addressed, and how they connect to Chapter 1 about Literary Analysis when using texts that were adapted for films.

The first on our list is *John Lewis: Good Trouble* by Time Films. The documentary opens with Congressman John Lewis sitting on a stool in a blue suit in front of cameras and stage lights. An assistant straightens his tie. Behind the congressman's profile is a blown up black and white image of a young Lewis and others, arms locked in solidarity, as they march. He looks into the camera and says, "I feel lucky and blessed that I'm serving in Congress, but there are forces today that are trying to take us back to another time and another dark period. We've come so far, and we've made so much progress, but as a nation and as a people, we are not there yet. We have miles to go" (Time Films, 2020). He speaks calmly, but there is sadness in eyes. The scene cuts to black and white images of Lewis and others marching in protest, black and white film of a younger Lewis speaking at the Washington Monument, another black and white photograph, this time of Congressman Lewis embracing a young President Barac Obama. Music plays, the beat of a drum in a march cadence. The words "freedom" and "march" move across the screen and credits appear. The effect is at once nostalgic and haunting for those who know these images well. For younger viewers it ties the images of the past to a man who lived that history. This documentary ties past to present.

The documentary, *John Lewis: Good Trouble* was released July 3, 2020, only fourteen days prior to Congressman Lewis' death at the age of eighty. It includes interviews with the family of the late congressman, friends, and those who marched with him and served with him. The film offers unique access to the Civil Rights Movement through one of its leaders who ties that period with current issues, recognizing the advancements while voicing the work still left

Table 4.1 Documentaries and suggested companion texts

John Lewis: Good Trouble	March (2013) by John Lewis, Andrew Aydin, and Nate Powell For further reading, March is book one of a three-book series. Thoreau, H.D. (1849). Civil disobedience.
He Named Me Malala	Yousafzai, M. and Lamb, C. (2015). *I am Malala*. Back Bay Books.
Writing with Fire	Kroeger, B. (2023). *Undaunted: How women changed American journalism*. Penguin Random House. (Chapters and passages can be given to students to read).

to do. The following lesson sample employs the NCSS C3 Framework Inquiry Arc and Literary Analysis.

Lesson Title: Reflecting on the Civil Rights Movement and its implications for today.

Grade Level: 11-12

Length of Time: 5-6 days

C3 Framework Inquiry Arc Dimension 1 – Staging the Inquiry	
Big Idea	Equality
Compelling Question	Why do challenges concerning the right to vote still exist?
Essential Understandings/ Rationale	In 1965, the Voting Rights Act passed by Congress. Enfranchising minority voters. The Voting Rights Act of 2006 enacted by congress through broad bipartisan support, reauthorized the 1965 law. However, in 2013, the Supreme Court ruled in favor of the prosecution in *Shelby v. Holder* which allows for individual states to pass laws making it harder for some to vote.
Learning Targets	• Students will be able to explain the socio-economic and political significance of the 1965 Voting Rights Act. • Students will be able to explain how the national voting rights law has been affected by local and state laws. • Students will be able to analyze and synthesize film and autobiographical text to identify how past events inform present voting rights in the United States.
Supporting Questions	• What caused the 1965 "Bloody Sunday" events in Selma, Alabama? • How did the events in Selma, Alabama impact the passage of the Voting Rights Act of 1965? • What does the Voting Rights Act of 1965 do? • What are some existing challenges to vote today?

Lesson Materials	
Featured Secondary Source	Porter, D. (2020). *John Lewis: Good trouble*. Magnolia Films.
Featured Primary Source	Lewis, J., Aydin, A. and Powell, N. (2013). *March*. Top Shelf Publications.
Technology/Media Sources	Porter, D. (2020). *John Lewis: Good trouble*. Magnolia Films.
Other Materials and Supports	Copies of *March* (2024), chart paper, pens, pencils, laptops with internet connection to apps such as Canva, and graphic organizers, markers.

C3 Framework Inquiry Arc Dimension 2 – **Standards Connections**	
NCTE Standard for ELA	3. Students read a wide range of print and non-print texts to build an understanding of texts, of themselves, and of the cultures of the United States and the world; to acquire new information; to respond to the needs and demands of society and the workplace; and for personal fulfillment. Among these texts are fiction and nonfiction, classic and contemporary works.
NCTE Standard for ELA	6. Students apply knowledge of language structure, language conventions (e.g., spelling and punctuation), media techniques, figurative language, and genre to create, critique, and discuss print and non-print texts.
NCTE Standard for ELA	7. Students conduct research on issues and interests by generating ideas and questions, and by posing problems. They gather, evaluate, and synthesize data from a variety of sources (e.g., print, and non-print texts, artifacts, people) to communicate their ideas.
C3 Framework Content Standard	D2.Civ.8.9-12. Evaluate social and political systems in different contexts, times, and places, that promote civic virtues and enact democratic principles.
C3 Framework Content Standard	D2.Civ.14.9-12. Analyze historical, contemporary, and emerging means of changing societies, promoting the common good, and protecting rights.

C3 Framework Inquiry Arc Dimension 3 – **Analyzing Source Evidence**	
Introduction/ Motivation	• Students will complete a gallery walk of common/well-known images from the Civil Rights era such as the Little Rock 9, Rosa Parks' arrest photo, Martin Luther King, Jr.'s delivery of his "I Have a Dream" speech, the police riots of protestors in Selma, and John Lewis and MLK Jr. marching. As they view the images, they will write down one-word responses about what they think the historical context of the image is, the perspectives expressed in the image, and what connections/thoughts/questions/feelings they have from examining the image.
Teacher Direct Instruction	1. After students have finished their gallery walk, the teacher will invite them to share their responses to the images. 2. The teacher will record student responses' in a three-column chart of "historical contexts," "perspectives in the images" and "thoughts/ connections/feelings." 3. The teacher then asks the students what they think the images have to do with voting, and record answers on the board below the three-column chart.
	Historical Contexts Perspectives in Images Feelings/ Thoughts/ Connections

	C3 Framework Inquiry Arc Dimension 3 – Analyzing Source Evidence
	What do you think these images have to do with voting?
	4. The teacher then introduces the documentary, *John Lewis: Good Trouble*, connecting Lewis with their previous discussion about Civil Rights images. The teacher explains that the class will view the documentary over three class periods. The teacher then hands out a graphic organizer for students to use while watching the documentary. The graphic organizer identifies four note-taking categories: images, autobiographical/biographical perspectives or anecdotes, historical event(s), and emotional/responses. The teacher models how students will use the graphic organizer. Students are to note images (example: John Lewis walking together with President Obama across the Edmund Pettus Bridge in Selma, Alabama), then a brief annotation of the autobiographical/biographical information offered during the image segment, the historical context, and the students emotional response.
	Images Autobiographical/Biographical Perspectives or Anecdotes
	Historical Events Emotions/Responses/Feelings
	5. After watching the first 25 minutes of the documentary, *John Lewis: Good Trouble*, students will record in their journals their responses to the images in the documentary. What they noticed, what they heard, and what they learned.
	6. Students will respond to the question, what is meant in the film by "good trouble," and how that relates to matters of voting and equality.
Formative Performance Task/ Student Structured Practice	7. After completing the film, the teacher introduces the graphic novel, *March*, by John Lewis, Andrew Aydin, and Nate Powell.
	8. Students will be placed in small groups. Two days (potentially three depending on class period length) to read the graphic novel. The teacher will assign pages for the day's reading then students will engage in small groups discuss the novel's historical contexts, perspectives expressed, and emotive responses/connections/feelings from reading the book, and similarities/differences to how events in Selma are portrayed in the book and film.
	9. Each group will examine their notes from the documentary and the graphic novel to construct a timeline of major events, people, and dates leading to the passage of the Voting Rights Act on chart paper. They can also use computer apps such as Canva to present their timeline to the class. Students will explain why these events were significant, and what they learned from the book and film to support their answers.

FILMS AND DOCUMENTARIES

C3 Framework Inquiry Arc Dimension 4 – Communicating Conclusions and Taking Informed Action	
Student Share	After completing the graphic novel *March*, students present their timelines and then engage in a whole-class Socratic Seminar to discuss how their analysis of Selma and the Voting Rights Act connects to issues impacting voting today. Students will be encouraged to cite information from the film and the book to support their ideas, and how learning about these events make them feel about issues about voting today.
Closing	After each lesson, the teacher will ask students to complete a quick reflection about their personal responses to the film and book, and to record further questions they have about the John Lewis, voting, and other issues that they connect to this lesson.
Summative Performance/ Extension	Students can research the causes and outcomes of the 2013 *Shelby v. Holder* case, and outline possible ways to address challenges to voting in their community through examination of newspaper articles, research articles, and other digital media or archives pertaining to legal decisions and court cases (see examples in Chapter 2!)

The second documentary we suggest is ***He Named Me Malala*** (2015), the story of Malala Yousafzai, the young Pakastani woman who at the age of 15 was shot by Taliban soldiers for her outspoken support of education for girls and women. The "He" in the film's title is Malala's father, Ziauddin Yousafzai, who, Malala explains in the film's opening, named her after the heroine of an Afghan folktale. In the folktale, Malalai Maiwand, the heroine, is shot and killed while leading her people in rebellion. The name, "Malalai" is associated with freedom in Afghanistan.

The documentary is narrated by Malala herself and explores the impact of her shooting not only on her but her family, particularly her parents. Students watching this film will see a young woman, not so different from themselves and peers, joking with siblings, playfully arguing with her parents, and talking about her plans. Underpinning this intimate view of Malala's circumstances, however, are the stark realities that face young women in parts of the world where education is not a promise but something that is fought for and a great risk. To underscore these realities, moments with her family cut to visits to the hospital for her rehabilitation. She is told that some muscles in her face will never recover as a dramatized flashback to the day of her shooting appears on the screen. Images of the Taliban flag and girls riding on a bus with books in their hands flash across the screen like flashes of memory for Malala. This film offers educators the opportunity to open discussion and build activities around topics including education, the education of girls and women, freedom/oppression,

CHAPTER 4

and courage. Suggestions for companion texts and activities can be found in Table 1 at the end of the chapter.

Lesson Title: Girl against the Taliban: Rights and freedoms for girls and women.

Grade Level: 8-10

Length of Time: 5-6 days

C3 Framework Inquiry Arc Dimension 1 – Staging the Inquiry	
Big Idea	Education
Compelling Question	Is education a right?
Essential Understandings/ Rationale	Only 49% of countries have achieved gender parity in education in elementary education and only 42% in secondary education (UNICEF). Although gender inequities exist in the United States, students will be able to analyze how these inequities in other parts of the world have serious consequences for girls and boys, and how ordinary citizens can take a stand against these inequities.
Learning Targets	• Students will be able to identify general examples of inequities between girls and boys in education. • Students will be able to identify countries where there is a lack of gender parity in education. • Students will be able to explain how the socio-economic-and political contexts of Afghanistan contributed to educational inequities for girls and women. • Students will be able to analyze and synthesize film and autobiographical text to discuss the role education for girls and women impact the global economy.
Supporting Questions	• What were the socio-economic and political conditions that led to laws prohibiting girls from receiving an education in Pakistan? • What effect do the images and film of Malala and her family have on the viewer? • How does the use of autobiography provide insight into the lived experiences of girls such as Malala? • Did anything change because of Malala's shooting and recovery?

Lesson Materials	
Featured Secondary Source	Guggenheim, D. (2015). *He Named Me Malala*. Fox Searchlight Pictures.
Featured Primary Source	Lamb, C. and Yousafzai, M. (2013) *I am Malala: The girl who stood up to the Taliban and was shot*.
Technology/Media Sources	Guggenheim, D. (2015). *He Named Me Malala*. Fox Searchlight Pictures.
Other Materials and Supports	Copies of I am Malala *(2013), paper, pens, pencils, laptops, and graphic organizers.*

C3 Framework Inquiry Arc Dimension 2 – Standards Connections	
NCTE Standard for ELA	1. Students apply a wide range of strategies to comprehend, interpret, evaluate, and appreciate texts. They draw on their prior experience, their interactions with other readers and writers, their knowledge of word meaning and of other texts, their word identification strategies, and their understanding of textual features (e.g., sound-letter correspondence, sentence structure, context, graphics).
NCTE Standard for ELA	2. Students apply knowledge of language structure, language conventions (e.g., spelling and punctuation), media techniques, figurative language, and genre to create, critique, and discuss print and non-print texts.
NCTE Standard for ELA	3. Students conduct research on issues and interests by generating ideas and questions, and by posing problems. They gather, evaluate, and synthesize data from a variety of sources (e.g., print, and non-print texts, artifacts, people) to communicate their ideas.
C3 Framework Content Standard	D2.Civ.8.9-12. Evaluate social and political systems in different contexts, times, and places, that promote civic virtues and enact democratic principles.
C3 Framework Content Standard	D2.Civ.14.9-12. Analyze historical, contemporary, and emerging means of changing societies, promoting the common good, and protecting rights.

C3 Framework Inquiry Arc Dimension 3 – Analyzing Source Evidence	
Introduction/ Motivation	Using colored pencils, students will color countries on a world map where there are barriers to education for girls and women. A list of these countries will be provided by the teacher (Resource: UNICEF).

	C3 Framework Inquiry Arc Dimension 3 – Analyzing Source Evidence
Teacher Direct Instruction	1. After students have completed their maps, the teacher engages them in discussion prompting the students with questions such as "What surprised you? "What questions do you have after identifying the places in the world where education barriers exist for girls and women?" "What lengths would you go to for an education?" 2. The teacher will then give students approximately 20 minutes to read the Prologue to *I am Malala: The girl who stood up to the Taliban and was shot* (2013) or the class may read together. 3. Students are then asked to do a quick journal write of their first thoughts and impressions after reading the Prologue. Students will then share their thoughts in a large-group discussion. The teacher can offer prompts to generate student thought: *a. How does Malala's description of the sights, sounds, and smells of home on the day of the shooting affect you?" b. Malala compares her old life in Pakistan with her new life in England. Can you relate to this? Has there been a time when you had to change schools or move to another town, state, or country?" c. In the introduction, Malala focuses on her memories of everyday events the day of her shooting rather than focusing on her work as an activist. How do these details impact the reader's feelings?"* 4. The teacher then shows the class the first five minutes (5:26) of the film *He named me Malala*. The teacher will ask students to record in their similarities they see between the Prologue to *I am Malala* and the introduction to the film; *He named me Malala* in the notetaking chart and answer the reflection questions, "Why do you think so much emphasis is placed on name and identity in both the book and the film?" "what do you think were the outcomes or results of Malala's experiences? How does that make you feel?" **Note: The film, *He named me Malala*, runs one hour, twenty-two minutes, and thirty-seven seconds. The book, *I am Malala*, is 288 pages and divided into chapters within five parts. We encourage complete viewing of the film and a complete reading of the book; however, the book can be chunked by excerpts for close reads.**
Formative Performance Task/Student Structured Practice	Students will work in pairs or individually on completing the graphic organizer chart comparing the film and book, and reflecting on what they learned.

C3 Framework Inquiry Arc Dimension 3 – Analyzing Source Evidence	
Similarities- Book	Similarities- Film
	Reflection: Why do you think so much emphasis is placed on name and identity in both the book and the film?" "what do you think were the outcomes or results of Malala's experiences? How does that make you feel?"

C3 Framework Inquiry Arc Dimension 4 – Communicating Conclusions and Taking Informed Action	
Student Share	1. Students will then engage in a four-corners activity where the teacher asks them to go to a corner of the room that best connects to their response to the compelling question, "is education a right?" The four corners options are 1) strongly agree 2) moderately agree 3) moderately disagree, 4) disagree. 2. Students in each group must discuss why they chose their answer to the compelling question. After 5 minutes, the group will share their position to the compelling question to the class. 3. After each group shares their answers, the teacher will ask students again to choose a corner of the room that best describes their answer to the compelling question. If students change corners, they need to explain why. If students did not change corners, they need to explain why.
Closing	Students will complete an exit ticket outlining what they found surprising, interesting, and troubling (SIT method) about what they learned about education inequalities, Malala's experiences, and any connections to current issues or their own experiences they may have.
Summative Performance/ Extension	Students can research a topic about the history of education, as well as how education is supported today, in order to answer the compelling question about whether education is a right. Examples of topics to research include, but are not limited to, African Americans, women, indigenous peoples, religious minorities, or Latinx Americans.

The third documentary, *Writing with Fire* (2021), follows the all-female journalists of India's Khabar Lahariya ("News Wave") newspaper. The film follows the efforts of the Dalit (an oppressed caste in India) women who risk personal harm to deliver fact-based news. Through recorded meetings with the Khabar Lahariya staff, individual interviews, conversations at home with family, the film offers an intimate perspective of the political, social, and family barriers placed in front of these brave women who seek to defy those obstacles and do the work of journalists. Over the course of 14 years, chief reporter, Meera, leads her inexperienced colleagues from print to the world of smart phones and tablets to report the truth behind some of India's most polarizing events in politics and society.

Like the previous documentary, *He Named Me Malala*, *Writing with Fire* presents the struggle for women in a male dominated society in a still male dominated profession, journalism. Added to these struggles is India's caste system. All the women journalists working for Khabar Lahariya are part of the Dalit caste, previously known as the "untouchables." This film offers classroom discussion around women's rights in other parts of the world, the role of journalism in democracy, and the oppression and prejudice inherent in the caste system. Companion text suggestions can be found in Table 1.

Lesson Title: The Power of Journalism

Grade Level: 11-12

Length of Time: 5-6 days

C3 Framework Inquiry Arc Dimension 1 – Staging the Inquiry	
Big Idea	Freedom
Compelling Question	Is journalism important for society?
Essential Understandings/ Rationale	In a male-dominated media landscape in India, several women journalists, all belonging to the Dalit caste, risk their own safety to cover India's political and social news. A caste system is a social hierarchy that people are born into and separates a population by culture, religion, and practices. Once born into a caste, people are not allowed to leave it. India's caste system was officially dissolved in the 1950's, however, the 2000-year-old system is still recognized in many aspects of society. The Dalit caste, once referred to as "The Untouchables," is the lowest in the Indian caste system. In modern India, people in this caste are still denied certain jobs and access to many services. Students will be able to analyze the long-lasting impact of the caste system in India today through examining the role of journalism in society.
Learning Targets	• Students will be able to explain what a caste system is. • Students will analyze the limitations of resources and technology for women within the Dalit caste and the obstructions these limitations create. • Students will examine the challenges that exist for some to deliver and receive unbiased information. • Students will be able to debate what the role of journalism is in a society.

C3 Framework Inquiry Arc Dimension 1 – Staging the Inquiry	
Supporting Questions	• How does the use of video of the women journalists lives highlight the impact of caste in Indian society? • What are the challenges for journalists due to their caste and gender? • How do the journalists deal with these challenges? • What impact does the work of these journalists have regarding caste and gender?
Lesson Materials	
Featured Secondary Source	Article, "Jati: The Caste System in India," retrieved from https://asiasociety.org/education/jati-caste-system-india Thomas, R. and Ghosh, S. (2021). *Writing with Fire*. Black Ticket Films.
Featured Primary Source	Ramabai, Pandita (1887). *The High-Caste Hindu Woman*. Retrieved from https://chnm.gmu.edu/wwh/p/107.html
Technology/Media Sources	Thomas, R. and Ghosh, S. (2021). *Writing with Fire*. Black Ticket Films. Facing History and Ourselves, "Head, Heart, Conscience" activity https://www.facinghistory.org/resource-library/head-heart-conscience
C3 Framework Inquiry Arc Dimension 2 – Standards Connections	
NCTE Standard for ELA	5. Students employ a wide range of strategies as they write and use different writing process elements appropriately to communicate with different audiences for a variety of purposes.
NCTE Standard for ELA	7. Students conduct research on issues and interests by generating ideas and questions, and by posing problems. They gather, evaluate, and synthesize data from a variety of sources (e.g., print and non-print texts, artifacts, people) to communicate their discoveries in ways that suit their purpose and audience.
NCTE Standard for ELA	9. Students develop an understanding of and respect for diversity in language use, patterns, and dialects across cultures, ethnic groups, geographic regions, and social roles.
C3 Framework Content Standard	D2.Civ.8.9-12. Evaluate social and political systems in different contexts, times, and places, that promote civic virtues and enact democratic principles.
C3 Framework Content Standard	D2.Civ.14.9-12. Analyze historical, contemporary, and emerging means of changing societies, promoting the common good, and protecting rights.

CHAPTER 4

	C3 Framework Inquiry Arc Dimension 3 – Analyzing Source Evidence
Introduction/ Motivation	• Students in groups of four will receive handouts with the front page of three-four national and/or local newspapers. (The teacher should ensure the papers reflect diverse ideologies, example: *The New York Times* and *The Wall Street Journal*). • Students will be given five to ten minutes to examine the papers' front pages while making notes on what they notice. • In a whole class discussion, teacher will ask students about their observations about the newspapers and record their answers on the board. • Discussion questions include: Are there stories that dominate the majority of papers? How does the focus differ between national and local papers? What do you notice about how different papers discuss the same issues? Are these newspapers important to society? Why or why not?

Teacher Direct Instruction	1. The teacher will ask the class what they know about what the word "caste" means. Possible answers may include division, discrimination, and inequality.
	2. Teacher will show a diagram of the Hindu caste system on the board, and pass out copies of the article about the system for students to read from the Asia Society (https://asiasociety.org/education/jati-caste-system-india). Students will discuss the historical contexts in which the Hindu caste system, or jati, was created, the perspectives of gender, and why this system was significant to Indian society and culture in the past and present.
	3. Teacher can read aloud or pass out copies from Pandita Ramabai's writings against sati, or the custom of widow's jumping into their husband's funeral pyre: https://chnm.gmu.edu/wwh/p/107.html
	4. Students will reflect on the following questions:
	   • who would support this custom, and why?
	   • who would oppose this custom, and why?
	   • what role do you think journalism had in the debate for and against this custom in India?

C3 Framework Inquiry Arc Dimension 3 – Analyzing Source Evidence	
Formative Performance Task/Student Structured Practice	5. The teacher will then introduce the film, *Writing with Fire* (2021). The teacher will place students in small groups and instruct students to take notes as they watch the film. Students will focus on the following questions: • How does the context (where and when) when this film was created highlight the barriers these journalists face? • What are perspectives about the role of gender in posing these barriers in the film? • What are the perspectives and experiences of the families of the work and risks that these women journalists take? • What motivates these journalists to continue their work despite these barriers? 6. Students will discuss their thoughts on these questions and support their ideas with the notes they have taken with their small groups and engage in the "Head, Heart, Conscience" activity from Facing History and Ourselves (https://www.facinghistory.org/resource-library/head-heart-conscience) to examine the legacy and ramifications of caste on women in India. Students can record their answers on chart paper or as a computer-based presentation (i.e. using Google slides or Canva). A graphic organizer can be provided for students to complete or students can make their own: **Head**: • What information do you know about this event? • What information is confirmed? What remains uncertain? Are there any facts that are contested? • What additional information would you like to have to help you understand the event better? **Heart**: • What emotions does this event raise for you? • Are there particular moments, images, or stories that stand out to you? If so, why? **Conscience**: • What questions about fairness, equity, or justice does this event raise for you? • What choices did key figures make, and what values may have guided those choices? • How were people impacted by this event? Are there people who should be held accountable? If so, how? • What kind of informed action could you take?

C3 Framework Inquiry Arc Dimension 4 – Communicating Conclusions and Taking Informed Action	
Student Share	Each student group will share their "head, heart, conscience" responses to their notes and the film as a presentation to the class.
Closing	Students will reflect on the compelling question and explain their thoughts on whether journalism is important to society.
Summative Performance/ Extension	Students can research a contemporary issue by finding newspapers and other journalistic forms such as documentary films and implement the head, heart, conscience activity by explaining how the historical origins of this issue can impact taking informed action in the present.

Feature Films

For this chapter's purposes, we make the distinction between documentaries and films. In the section about documentaries, we include works that are non-fiction and that document the real lives and events that are historically significant. Under the category of feature films, we include works based on historically significant events that were dramatized and produced as full-length motion pictures. These films can be either those that are shown in movie theatres or streamed by services such as Netflix. There is so much rich scholarship on using films and television shows to teach topics in social studies and ELA. Katie recommends the book series "Hollywood or History?" that contains a vast collection of practitioner-based research on how to use popular movies and shows when teaching history and social studies. We put the link to these books in the Suggested Resources list at the end of this chapter that we hope you check out!

The use of film in the classroom is not new, however, in some educational circles they have received a poor reputation for their overuse or misguided use (avoiding instruction, killing time in the classroom). Like any instructional resource, films should be used purposefully and tied to learning targets and assessment. There is a time commitment with films that must be considered since most films run 120 minutes or longer. Student engagement also must be considered; activities created to support students in meeting the learning objectives tied to the film. Unlike documentaries, historically based full-length feature films are typically dramatized for entertainment purposes and directors and screenwriters may take artistic license such as creating conversations between historical figures that never actually took place. For these reasons, it is important for educators to view films in advance and prepare students fully so that they understand where historic accuracy ends, and artistic creativity begins. To help

Table 4.2 Some of Jennifer and Katie's Suggested Films

Title	Historical Context	Suggestions for classroom topics and activities
Cesar Chavez: Respect for All	Community Service Organization, Farm and migrant workers protests of the 1950's.	Primary source analysis of workers' rights, Brown Power movement, Chicano rights, migrant rights
The Grapes of Wrath	The Dust Bowl, migration to California during the 1930's and 1940's, the Great Depression	Read the novel Steinbeck, J. (1939). *The Grapes of Wrath*. Viking Press. Examination of photography of Dorthea Lang, WPA projects
Selma	The Civil Rights Movement, 1965 Voting Rights Act	Analysis of selected speeches by Dr. Martin Luther King Jr., John Lewis, photographs of the Edmund Pettus Bridge, read Voting Rights Act
Glory	54th Massachusetts Regiment, Civil War	Examine primary documents by or about William Gould Shaw, experience of former enslaved soldiers, Black experience during the Civil War
Lincoln	Abraham Lincoln and passage of the 13th Amendment	Analysis of Radical Republicans, Confederates, Democrats, Emancipation Proclamation, enslavement
All Quiet on the Western Front	Outbreak of World War I in Europe	Read the book Remarque, Erich Maria (2009). *All Quiet on the Western Front*. Vintage Books. Analysis of youth experiences as soldiers at the start and end of the war
Life is Beautiful	The Holocaust, anti-Semitism, World War II	Analysis of the geographical reach of the Holocaust and interment camps, Jewish diaspora, Allied liberation
Cinderella Man	The Great Depression	Urban plight during the Depression, Hoovervilles, scrutiny of Depression-era photographs and political cartoons, WPA projects

educators, we have selected a few films that we believe offer historically accurate narratives that support the teaching of historical empathy.

We also include a sample lesson for teachers on how to use the Steven Spielberg movie *Lincoln* to promote historical empathy. We chose this movie because the premise of the film, which is the focus on the 13th amendment, is part of the book *Team of Rivals: The Political Genius of Abraham Lincoln* by historian Doris Kearns Goodwin (2005). Students can read excerpts from the book as a secondary source while analyzing the primary sources Kearns Goodwin used to write her book to examine how the book and film compare and contrast regarding the portrayal of the historical context when the 13th amendment was ratified, and its lasting impact on the U.S. today.

Sample Lesson Plan

Lesson Title: *Lincoln* (2012) Film.

Grade Level: 10-12

Length of Time: 2-4 days (depending on length of instructional period)

C3 Framework Inquiry Arc Dimension 1 – Staging the Inquiry	
Big Idea	Compromise
Compelling Question	Is compromise worth it?
Essential Understandings/ Rationale	The Steven Spielberg film, *Lincoln* (2012) centers around President Lincoln's efforts to pass the 13th Amendment, which would surpass the Emancipation Act. Lincoln fears that the Emancipation Act might be dissolved after Southern states are allowed back into the Union after the war. Spielberg's film highlights the balancing act the President must complete to keep the support of the Radical Republicans such as Thaddeus Stevens, who do not want to negotiate with the Southern States, and moderate Republicans such as Francis Blair, whose support is necessary to pass the Amendment, and who refuses to support the Amendment without first negotiating for peace. This film highlights how very precarious an engagement this was for Lincoln who wanted to ensure that enslavement would be unconstitutional and that no African American could be re-enslaved and accomplish it before the end of the war.

C3 Framework Inquiry Arc Dimension 1 – Staging the Inquiry	
Learning Targets	• Students will explain the differences between the Emancipation Proclamation (1863) and the 13th Amendment. • Students will be able to analyze the role of compromise in ending the Civil War. • Students will examine the challenges behind passing the 13th Amendment.
Supporting Questions	• Why was the 13th amendment a key factor in ending the Civil War? • What challenges did Lincoln face when supporting the 13th amendment? • Who supported and who opposed his positions for ending the war? • What compromises were made to ratify the 13th amendment?

Lesson Materials	
Featured Secondary Source	*Lincoln* (2012) film.
Featured Primary Source	13th Amendment to the Constitution of the United States of America, NARA DocsTeach https://www.docsteach.org/documents/document/thirteenth-amendment Emancipation Proclamation, NARA DocsTeach https://www.docsteach.org/documents/document/emancipation-proclamation
Technology/Media Sources	Spielberg, S. (2012). *Lincoln*. 20th Century Films.
Other Materials and Supports	Highlighters, pens, pencils, notebook, Venn Diagram, guided notes graphic organizer

C3 Framework Inquiry Arc Dimension 2 – Standards Connections	
NCTE Standard for ELA	1. Students use a variety of technological and information resources (e.g., libraries, databases, computer networks, video) to gather and synthesize information and to create and communicate knowledge.
NCTE Standard for ELA	2. Students participate as knowledgeable, reflective, creative, and critical members of a variety of literacy communities

C3 Framework Inquiry Arc Dimension 2 – Standards Connections	
C3 Framework Content Standard	D2.Civ.14.9-12. Analyze historical, contemporary, and emerging means of changing societies, promoting the common good, and protecting rights.
C3 Framework Content Standard	D2.Civ.8.9-12. Evaluate social and political systems in different contexts, times, and places, that promote civic virtues and enact democratic principles.

C3 Framework Inquiry Arc Dimension 3 – Analyzing Source Evidence	
Supporting Questions for the Lesson	- Why was the 13th amendment a key factor in ending the Civil War? - What challenges did Lincoln face when supporting the 13th amendment? - Who supported and who opposed his positions for ending the war? - What compromises were made to ratify the 13th amendment?
Introduction/ Motivation	1. Students will be given a printed text of the Proclamation and asked highlight words and phrases that strike them as important. 2. The teacher will then invite students to turn and talk with their neighbor. The teacher will invite students to discuss with their partner what language they thought was most important and why. 3. Teacher will ask students to annotate the Emancipation Proclamation by examining the author, date it was written, and its main function. After, teacher will facilitate a discussion with students on what the achievements and limitations of the Emancipation Proclamation were, and why this document did not end the Civil War.

FILMS AND DOCUMENTARIES

C3 Framework Inquiry Arc Dimension 3 – Analyzing Source Evidence

Teacher Direct Instruction

1. The teacher will give students a printed copy of the 13th Amendment. The teacher will ask students work in pairs to analyze the language of the Amendment.
2. The teacher will then ask students to compare the language of the Proclamation and the Amendment. Students will complete a Venn diagram that identifies common language and ideas as well as language that is different.

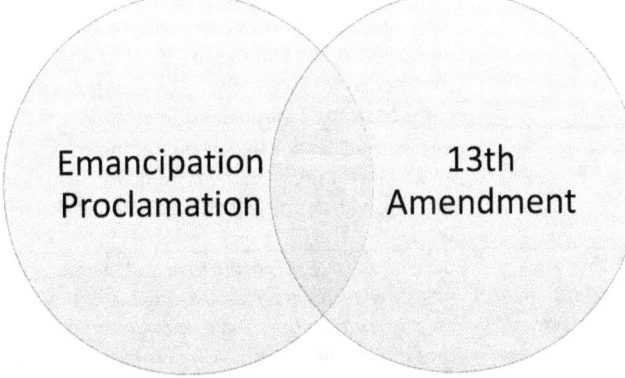

3. Students will reflect by either writing down the response, or share in a small group or whole group discussion:
   - What is the historical context of the documents? What was happening during the Civil War that impacted why they were written?
   - What perspectives are expressed in the documents?
   - How did the historical context impact why the documents were written?
   - What are some of your thoughts/feelings/connections you have from reading these documents?
4. Next, the teacher will hand out the film graphic organizer with guided questions (see Table 4.3.) As students watch the film, we suggest stopping at appropriate intervals for discussion and talk through questions. Each question is designed to encourage critical thinking about the choice of compromise. Students are asked to give their personal thoughts, evidence from the film, and to develop questions they have for discussion.

Formative Performance Task/ Student Structured Practice

- The film's running time is two hours and 30 minutes. Depending on instructional time (block or traditional) the film can be divided over the course of three to five days. After each viewing, students will discuss their responses in small groups in preparation for a snowball discussion (see dimension 4)

C3 Framework Inquiry Arc Dimension 4 – Communicating Conclusions and Taking Informed Action	
Student Share (snowball discussion)	Students will begin in pairs to discuss their response to the last question in the chart about whether compromises were necessary by sharing how evidence from the movie and documents support their answer. After 5 minutes, student pairs must join another pair of students which created a group of 4. The pairs continue to share their responses about compromises for another 5 minutes, then the groups of 4 will join another group of 4 to create groups of 8. The group of 8 will discuss their responses about compromises and join another group of 8 after 5 minutes of discussion. The teacher will continue to time 5-minute discussions as groups grow larger until the whole class come back into 1 group.
Closing	The whole class will decide on a group consensus- was compromise necessary for ratifying the 13th amendment, even when that meant working with people with different views on enslavement and the Civil War?
Summative Performance/ Extension	Students can read Lincoln's second inaugural address from LOC https://www.loc.gov/resource/mal.4361300/?st=text . Students reflect on a time where they had to make a compromise with someone that they did not agree with. Students can write a journal entry, draw a cartoon, create a poem or song, or act out a skit to demonstrate if that compromise was necessary and what they learned from the experience. Students will then connect what they learned from their experience to what they learned about the 13th amendment and explain the pro's and con's to compromise when it involves making tough decisions with people you disagree with.

Watching the movie *Lincoln* (2012) in clips can support ELA and social studies teachers who may not have the time to show the entire film. For example, teachers can show the scene where the House passes the 13th amendment and then read pages 686-690 from Team of Rivals to see how Doris Kearns Goodwin's use of primary sources to describe this event compares with how Spielberg depicted the scene in the movie. Additionally, teachers can distribute Lincoln's second inaugural address from March 1865 to examine how and why he made compromises, and whether those compromises were worth it, especially after his assassination in April 1865. There are many ways these primary and secondary sources can be used to promote historical empathy as students are compelled to consider times when they had to make compromises, whether making compromises with people they disagree with are necessary, and ultimately the short- and long-term ramifications of compromises, especially when those issues deal with major issues such as equality and freedom of people.

FILMS AND DOCUMENTARIES

Table 4.3 Guided Notes Graphic Organizer for *Lincoln* (2012) - by Jennifer Curl

Guiding Questions	Personal Opinion	Perspectives from the Film	Evidence from Primary Sources	Questions/ Thoughts/ Feelings/ Connections
What is significant to you in the first five minutes of the film? Identify descriptions of images and sounds, quotes.	Ex: The young Black solider tells the President that Black soldiers get paid $3 less than White soldiers. He embarrasses the older black soldier but then recites Lincoln's Gettysburg Address. Was he being disrespectful?	Ex: The opening scene shows the hand-to-hand combat of the war. Men are dying. Two Black soldiers and two White soldiers speaking to President Lincoln.	Ex. The Emancipation Proclamation stated that slavery was over in Southern states in rebellion, but it did not mean Black soldiers were treated equal in the North	Ex. How many Black regiments were in the Civil War? What were the conditions for combat at the end of the war?
Why do you think the filmmaker includes scenes between President and Mrs. Lincoln, between President Lincoln and his political opponents?				
What indications are given to suggest that the 13th Amendment might fail?				
What is the purpose of Lincoln's anecdotes (stories)?				
President Lincoln offers jobs to Democrats in his next administration if they vote for the 13th Amendment. Why would he do that?				

Table 4.3 (Continued)

Secretary of State William Seward meets with three men who have been hired to encourage undecided congressmen to vote for the 13th Amendment. Why would he do that? Explain your response.
Why was the second section of the of the 13th Amendment necessary?
Mrs. Keckley's son identified himself as a White man and enlisted in the Union Army before Black men could enlist. Offer your thoughts on her statement, "As for me: My son died, fighting for the Union, wearing the Union blue. For freedom he died. I'm his mother. That's what I am to the nation, Mr. Lincoln. What else must I be?"
What compromises are made? Were they necessary? Identify three and explain.
President Lincoln's 13th Amendment is ultimately ratified. Were those compromises worth it? Why or why not?

Katie and Jennifer recognize that some districts and administrators place parameters, perhaps even barriers to the use of film in classrooms. Like any instructional tool, if not used appropriately, film can become more of a distraction than a support. Criticism of film in the classroom such as the loss of instructional time is understandable when students are not asked to be accountable for what they view, if metacognitive and critical thinking skills are not activated, if the receptive literacies of viewing and listening are not identified in the lesson plan, and the value of media literacies highlighted. When used effectively as part of standard-based lesson plan, film can make lasting impressions on students and leverage their historical empathy. Katie and Jennifer hope the suggestions, resources, and lesson plan in this chapter will help teachers make that happen.

Television Shows

Television shows are not quite like feature films, but they still have as strong of cultural impact that can be impactful when teaching about historical time periods, social issues, and artistic genres. For instance, a teacher of civics or law may use old episodes of *Perry Mason*, or even clips from the film *Twelve Angry Men*, to engage students in critical thinking about not only the nuances and complexities of interpreting the law, but also how attitudes and beliefs during a particular time towards matters such as race and gender were portrayed in these shows that were watched by millions of people. The western drama *Gunsmoke* ran on TV for 20 years. Situational comedies, or sitcoms, from the 1950s and 1960s spanned from parody of contemporary Cold War politics with *Get Smart*, and commentary of gender and family roles with shows such as *I Love Lucy*, *Leave it to Beaver*, *The Adventures of Ozzy and Harriet*, and *The Dick Van Dyke Show*. Shows such as *Star Trek* were trailblazing not only for the visual effects and storytelling in the science fiction genre, but also highlighted social changes in the U.S., especially with one of the first interracial kisses on television between Captain Kirk and Lieutenant Ahura in the episode "Plato's Stepchildren." During the 1970s, shows by Norman Lear such as *All in the Family* and *The Jeffersons*, as well *The Mary Tyler Moore Show* and *M*A*S*H* addressing prevailing attitudes of gender, racial, political affiliation, war, religion, and socio-economics in both humorous and blunt ways.

Dramas and sitcoms from the 1980s and 1990s such as *Will and Grace* and *Ellen* amplified LGBTQ representation in mainstream television. Many period shows over the past 20 years such as *1883*, *Hell on Wheels*, and *Mad Men* portray life from decades ago in dramatized forms that in some cases upend nostalgia for years past. However, the nature of a TV episode being shorter in length than a full movie, using televisions shows can also be effective in supporting primary and secondary source analysis of historical time periods and people to evoke historical empathy.

Considerations for Using Documentaries, TV Shows, and Films

The use of films, TV shows, documentaries can mirror how literary analysis, digital media, and music can be implemented to engage students in historical empathy. Russell (2012) includes some very important guidelines for teachers, particularly highlighting that while laws are less restrictive regarding showing a movie in a non-profit or educational setting, educators are prohibited from using pirated films, profiting from showing the film, and using film for public performances (p. 28).

Additionally, teachers need to do their due diligence when choosing documentaries and feature-length films when teaching about historical time periods, people, and literary genres. Just be careful to watch all TV and movies before showing them with your students! Even the rating system can be pretty subjective regarding what is considered appropriate as "PG" or "PG-13." Get permission for every movie you show so that kids and parents can decide if watching the clip or feature is in their best interest. Teachers must make sure that episodes or clips that are shown are appropriate for children. Some shows on cable and streaming outlets may contain adult content that may be objectionable for use in school. We just want all teachers to use all powerful tools at their disposal to promote historical empathy without getting into professional trouble.

Another consideration teachers should keep in mind when using films and documentaries to promote historical empathy is examining whether students are more engaged in the emotive or academic aspects of historical empathy. For example, Bryant and Clark (2006) note in their examination of the television series "Canada: A People's History" that emotive empathy focuses more on affective responses, acceptance of facts at face value as presented in the film, identification with characters, and an understanding of the past through a contemporary or presentist lens; while historical empathy stresses cognitive responses, the interpretation facts as presented by evidence, making connections between content and context, and acknowledging that interpretations of the past change over time (p. 1044).

Furthermore, Buchannan (2014) notes in her analysis of four documentaries about the 1950s civil rights movement cautions that teachers need to help students "mov[e] past perspective taking to affective engagement" by analyzing multiple sources that can help students understand "external factors and their impact on a historical individual's or group's actions" (p. 91). Metzger's (2012) study of fostering historical empathy by showing the film *The Pianist* revealed that sometimes students can "over-empathize" with some of the characters in the film, which showed that too much affective responses could overshadow the intellectual or cognitive goals of historical empathy such as identifying historical contexts and using evidence to support claims and multiple perspectives. Additionally, Endacott et al. (2024) posit that movies are extremely effective in engaging students in experiencing what the past was like, which shows that using feature films are powerful tools that teachers can use to promote historical empathy by analyzing historical contexts, perspectives, and how students feel. As a result, we recommend that teachers include primary and secondary source sources when showing films and documentaries in order to put the film into context for students to critically analyze the portrayal and representation of the historical contexts and perspectives, and make reasoned affective connections and emotive responses to what they are learning from these films. (Endacott et al., 2024; Buchanan, 2014; Bryant & Clark, 2006).

As we mentioned in Chapter 2, films, documentaries, and primary and secondary sources found on the internet need to be vetted for accuracy, credibility of the film creators, bias, and alignment to standards. Some films and documentaries may have very explicit biases and opinions. For instance, there are **A LOT** of problematic stereotypes from classic shows and movies, particularly from the 1940s-1960s, that are absolutely up for debate, analysis, and discussion regarding how historical contexts impacted perspectives of people regarding race, gender, and ethnicity that not only may be viewed as harmful by today's standards, but also offensive to groups decades ago. When choosing either a Disney animation, a live action show, or clip from a movie, critically examining portrayals and depictions of marginalized people and groups such as Native Americans, Asian Americans, African Americans, and people of color is vitally important for students to examine the historical contexts of these sources, how the contexts shaped perspectives that were expressed, and how our today's world, values, and beliefs differ from what was acceptable in the past. In fact, movies can be used with students as a historiographic exercise in how socio-economic, cultural, and political climates impact the attitudes, beliefs, and values of people in the past and present.

Additionally, documentaries such Morgan Spurlock's *Super Size Me* and Michael Moore's *Roger and Me* have clear arguments about the issues they address. Additionally, movies such as *The Green Book* need to be used with caution when weighing the portrayal of Tony Vallelonga as a white savior who drove acclaimed Black pianist Dr. Donald Shirley on his tour throughout the South during the early 1960s. We mentioned Ken Burns earlier, as his documentaries have limitations on which perspectives are represented. There are many articles and resources for teachers on how to balance the portrayal of historical people, events, and places as historically factual versus taking creative license as a means to tell a story. The plot of the movie version of *The Sound of Music*, which we mentioned in Chapter 3, was not accurate regarding how the Von Trapp family left Europe for the United States (they didn't really climb the Alps). Disney films such as *Dumbo, The Jungle Book, Lady and the Tramp, Pocahontas, Aladdin,* and *Mulan* are often the subjects of such analyses. As a result, we recommend that when using films and documentaries, teachers engage students in examining the contexts when the film was produced, the perspectives and credentials of the directors, producers, and other stakeholders, and what type of primary and secondary sources were used (or needed) in order to evaluate how these factors impacted their telling of stories of people from the past.

> We compiled a list of articles that provide tips, strategies, and research about how to mindfully use films and documentaries when teaching ELA and social studies to promote historical empathy. This list is not the definitive collection of resources, so please add your own recommendations!
>
> Jim Crow Museum Anti-Black Imagery: https://jimcrowmuseum.ferris.edu/antiblack/index.htm
>
> Andrew Chow TIME Magazine article https://time.com/5527806/green-book-movie-controversy/
>
> Media Education Lab, Deconstructing Disney https://mediaeducationlab.com/index.php/deconstructing-disney-0
>
> Laura Hermoza Inside the Magic article https://insidethemagic.net/2023/08/how-disneys-representation-of-culture-and-diversity-has-changed-over-the-years-lh1/
>
> Larry Ferlazzo Education Week article https://www.edweek.org/teaching-learning/opinion-18-ways-to-make-social-studies-class-more-culturally-responsive/2022/09
>
> Matthew Farber Edutopia article using movies to teach social justice https://www.edutopia.org/article/using-films-teach-social-justice-issues/

Conclusion

In this chapter, we offer suggestions for ELA and social studies teachers to use documentaries and films to promote historical empathy. Documentaries and films are ideal tools for ELA and social studies teachers to use when promoting historical empathy. According to Russell, films are effective in "arous[ing] emotions, which helps students connect with and remember specific events and figures" (p. 22). There are excellent television shows and mini-series that are of a similar caliber of the cinematography quality of documentaries and films. There are some very powerful television shows, mini-series, and movies such as ABC's *Roots* (1977), HBO's *Band of Brothers* (2001) and *John Adams* (2008), and WGN/OWN's *Underground* (2006) that can really enliven learning about historical contexts and perspectives by visually representing the trials and tribulations of people in the past through film. Bryant and Clark (2006) state that the use of film can promote historical empathy by "humanizing history" (p. 1045). Buchanan (2014) notes "the emotional pull of documentary film has the capacity to encourage empathy among viewers…by engaging students' reasoning about and emotional involvement with historical individuals or groups and their experiences" (p. 91). Films and documentaries are impactful literacy modalities that can motivate students to engage in historical empathy in both ELA and social studies, especially when films and documentaries are based on books and other primary and secondary sources by or about historical figures and past events.

Film, whether biographical nonfiction or historically based fiction, offers students access to the lived experiences of historical figures and the lives of central figures in modern society. Visual images, particularly film, engage the emotional and psychological reactions of viewers thus offering educators opportunities to engage their students in deeper ways. Documentaries and films pair easily with texts that may already exist in school curriculum and can offer students further opportunities to employ skills of analysis, synthesis, critical thinking, and discourse. Finally, by watching historical events played out on screen, students gain a deeper understanding of how historical and current events are *human* events that have lasting impacts on the people who lived or are living those experiences.

Reflection

- How can documentary films and movies be used to support teaching about current events or historical events?
- How can documentary films and movies be used when promoting historical empathy with literature?
- What ideas do you have about using documentary films and movies when you teach social studies or ELA?

Suggested Film and Documentary Resources

13th Amendment. https://www.docsteach.org/documents/document/thirteenth-amendment

Edutopia, *Using Films to Teach Social Justice Issues*: https://www.edutopia.org/article/using-films-teach-social-justice-issues/

Emancipation Proclamation: https://www.docsteach.org/documents/document/emancipation-proclamation

Gonzalez, J. (2015). The big list of classroom discussions (snowball discussion). Retrieved from https://www.cultofpedagogy.com/search/snowball+discussion/#:~:text=Snowball%20Discussion%20%3E%20a.k.a.%20Pyramid%20Discussion,their%20ideas%20with%20the%20pair...

Information Age Publishing Cinematic Social Studies Book Series: https://www.infoagepub.com/products/Cinematic-Social-Studies

Information Age Publishing Hollywood or History Book Series: https://www.infoagepub.com/series/Hollywood-or-History

Ken Burns, PBS Classroom (Teacher Page): https://gpb.pbslearningmedia.org/collection/kenburnsclassroom/home/

Ken Burns in the 9-12 Classroom (Student Page): https://gpb.pbslearningmedia.org/collection/kenburnsclassroom/home/?student=true

Lincoln Second Inaugural Address: https://www.loc.gov/resource/mal.4361300/?st=text

Marcus, A.S., Metzger, S.A., Paxton, R.J., & Stoddard, J.D. (2018). *Teaching history with film: Strategies for secondary social studies.* Routledge.

Metzger, S. A. (2010). Maximizing the educational power of history movies in the classroom. The Social Studies, 101(3), 127–136.

Stoddard, J. D. (2012). Film as a "thoughtful" medium for teaching history. *Learning, Media and Technology*, 37(3), 271–288.

Teach with Movies: https://teachwithmovies.org/the-best-of-twm-u-s-history-for-high-school/

Zinn Education Project Teaching People's History with Film: https://www.zinnedproject.org/news/teaching-with-film/

Chapter References

Bryant, D., & Clark, P. (2006). Historical empathy and 'Canada: A People's History." *Canadian Journal of Education* 29(4), 1039-1063.

Buchanan, L.B. (2014). From freedom riders to the children's march: Civil rights documentaries as catalysts for historical empathy. *Social Education* 78(2), 91-95.

Burns, K., Burns, R. & Weta-Tv. (2002) *The Civil War: A film by Ken Burns.* Arlington, Va.: WETA.

Endacott, J.L., Warren, J., Hackett-Hill, K., & Lalonde, A. (2024). Arts integrated historical empathy: Preservice teachers' engagement with pluralistic lived experiences and efforts toward instructional application. *Theory & Research in Social Education* 52(3), 414-457.

Goodwin, D.K. (2005). *Team of rivals: The political genius of Abraham Lincoln*. Simon & Schuster.

Guggenheim, D. (2015). *He named me Malala*. Fox Searchlight Pictures.

Kroeger, B. (2023). *Undaunted: How women changed American journalism*. Penguin Random House.

Lee, S. (1989). *Do the Right Thing*. Universal Pictures.

Lewis, J., Aydin, A. and Powell, N. (2013). *March*. Top Shelf Publications.

Merritt, K.L. (2019). Why we need a new Civil War documentary. *Smithsonian Magazine*. Retrieved from https://www.smithsonianmag.com/history/why-we-need-new-civil-war-documentary-180971996/

Metzger, S.A. (2012). The borders of historical empathy: Students encounter the Holocaust through film. *Journal of Social Studies Research* 34(4), 387-410.

Porter, D. (2020). *John Lewis: Good trouble*. Magnolia Films.

Russell, W.B. III. (2012). The reel history of the world: Teaching world history with major motion pictures. *Social Education* 76(1), 22-28. https://www.socialstudies.org/system/files/publications/articles/se_760122.pdf

Spielberg, S. (2012). *Lincoln*. Twentieth Century Films.

Steinbeck, J. (1939). *The grapes of wrath*. Viking Press.

Thomas, R. and Ghosh, S. (2021). *Writing with fire*. Music Box Films.

Thoreau, H.D. (1849). *Civil disobedience*. Retrieved from https://blogs.law.columbia.edu/uprising1313/files/2017/10/Civil-Disobedience-by-Henry-David-Thoreau.pdf

Yousafzai, M. and Lamb, C. (2015). *I am Malala*. Back Bay Books.

CHAPTER 5

Photographs and Visual Arts

Brainstorming Activity

- How might photographs and other visual literacies deepen a student's contextual understanding of past events?
- Think of a photograph or other visual literacy that means a lot to you. How does thinking about that image make you feel?
- What might those feelings tell you?
- How might photographs and other visual arts promote or deepen historical empathy?

Introduction

Have you ever taken a picture while you were on vacation or just noticing something you hadn't before in your neighborhood? Have you ever showed these pictures with your students? When Katie taught undergraduate history at a college in Georgia, she took a selfie visiting Selma, Alabama, while driving to the National Council for the Social Studies conference in New Orleans in 2015. She included the pictures of the Edmund Pettus Bridge and of the Selma downtown in her slide deck when teaching about the Voting Rights Act of 1965 and the Civil Rights Movement during the 1960s. Katie knew that a simple Google search could find many photographs of the events of Bloody Sunday in Selma, but showing the students how she experienced this history by not only visiting the sites but even talking to community members who remembered those events as teenagers was impactful as students shared that they did not realize how this event from over 60 years ago had a visceral and lasting impact on that Selma and nation today.

Drawings, animation, and pictures are some of the first visual cues children receive and process. While we do not necessarily think of these images as text, they are examples of multimodal texts that rely on receptive literacy skills that

FIGURE 5.1 Historical markers, Selma, Alabama, November 2015, Photo Credit Katherine Perrotta

include viewing, reading, and listening. Visual literacies continue to provide cues for struggling and learning readers throughout development. The National Conference of Teachers of English (NCTE) has been calling on the inclusion of visual literacies in basic curriculum as early as the mid-twentieth century (NCTE, 2011). Social studies researchers Jim Garrett and Stacey L. Kerr (2016) note that the use of aesthetic texts such as poetry, fine arts, literature, photography, and music "can promote critical thinking, foster empathetic thinking, and aid historical analysis" (p. 505). Given that most of the teachers who read this book are probably using visual literacy regularly for their instruction, we aim to provide some examples and research-based methods that can support the implementation of visuals to effectively to promote historical empathy (Endacott et al., 2024; Clark & Sears, 2020; Brewer & Brown, 2009; Donahue & Stuart, 2008; Epstein, 1994; Gabella, 1995; Eisner, 1991).

Don't forget that the Library of Congress and the National Archives have plenty of digitized photographs and visuals with primary source analysis worksheets that teachers can use with their students! Feel free to flip back to Chapter 2 for more details about these digital resources! We include some more here to add to your list of strategies!

National Archives: Analyze a Photograph https://www.archives.gov/education/lessons/worksheets/analyze-a-photograph-novice

PHOTOGRAPHS AND VISUAL ARTS

National Parks Service: https://www.nps.gov/common/uploads/teachers/lessonplans/LEsson%201%20photo_analysis_worksheet.pdf

Pulitzer Center: https://pulitzercenter.org/sites/default/files/inline-images/zaFRrdTRZEDGXvERb737tW5bl0k8Afcij8KAmqGan48FUfLunC.pdf

Library of Congress Analyzing Photographs and Prints: https://www.loc.gov/static/programs/teachers/getting-started-with-primary-sources/documents/Analyzing_Photographs_and_Prints.pdf

Photographs and the visual arts are powerful primary and secondary sources that social studies and ELA teachers can use to engage students in historical empathy, as well as critical thinking about historical contexts, perspectives of the past, and the role of visual literacies in our 21st-century world. For example, one of Katie's favorite images to use when she is teaching about the American Revolution, and how to use images as primary sources with her social studies methods students, is Paul Revere's "Bloody Massacre." While this engraving is one of the most infamous documents of the colonial era, Katie never thought

FIGURE 5.2 Katie standing in front of the Edmund Pettus Bridge, November 2015, Photo Credit Katherine Perrotta

to think very deeply about the image until she was in one of her undergraduate U.S. history courses. She learned about how the events leading up to the Boston Massacre were much more complex than the colonists simply hating the British soldiers; often the British soldiers who were housed or quartered in colonial homes also had to seek out employment. Colonists, particularly in Boston, were very vocal about their disapproval of British taxes and quartering and they taunted the soldiers who were told to keep the peace. An object was thrown and hit a soldier, which led to an unknown shot being fired. The soldiers, believing they were ordered to shoot, killed five colonists including Crispus Attucks, a former enslaved patriot. John Adams defended the soldiers in court in order to demonstrate how there was a presumption of innocence in the American judicial system.

Obviously, Adams' defense of the soldiers was not taken well among patriots in Boston. His cousin Samuel Adams was involved in public protests and vigils where the soldiers were depicted as murderers. Bostonian Henry Pelham drew an engraving about the incident, calling it "The Fruits of Arbitrary Power, or The Bloody Massacre." However, Boston silversmith Paul Revere took a copy of Pelham's image and altered it, naming it "The Bloody Massacre Perpetrated in King Street Boston on March 5th, 1770." Both images are provocative, showing the British as gleeful offenders shooting into a crowd of innocent people. There is even a dog in the picture! These were contextual clues and details in an image that she saw many times before as a student, but never paid much attention to, especially since the engraving was meant to be anti-British propaganda. However, this image is a great resource to promote historical empathy—what were the motivations of the soldiers? Why were the colonists gathering around in Boston that evening? How was the socio-economic and political climate of March 1770 contributing to the violence that occurred? This chapter will focus on ways to incorporate photographs, images, and other visual art into lessons to foster visual literacies to engage students in literary analysis and historical empathy.

> Check out Henry Pelham and Paul Revere's engraving of "The Bloody Massacre" at these sites!
> - Boston Tea Party Ship and Museum: https://www.bostonteapartyship.com/john-adams-boston-massacre
> - Gilder-Lehrman Institute of American History: https://www.gilderlehrman.org/history-resources/spotlight-primary-source/paul-reveres-engraving-boston-massacre-1770

Visual Literacies

In a world that relies increasingly on media technologies and social media platforms, such as the examples we highlight in Chapter 2, we use visual literacies more than ever. Visual literacies, as defined by Wileman (1993) is "the ability to 'read,' interpret, and understand information presented in pictorial or graphic images" (p. 114). In terms of common classroom use, visual literacies include photographs, drawings or animation, protest posters like those discussed in Chapter 3, political cartoons, film and video from Chapter 4, paintings, and other forms of visual art. You may be thinking, "I've been using these for years!" Do your students understand that these are forms of literacy? Like many teachers, parents, and administrators, they may not. Informing students that their use of photography and visual arts are uses of text and employs literacy skills. Understanding that these skills are recognized in academic settings, as well as in the NCSS C3 Framework and NCTE Standards, instills in students a confidence in the skills they already possess. Students are able to tap into prior knowledge of content and life experiences that can contribute to development and demonstration of historical empathy in ELA and social studies.

Political Cartoons

Political cartoons are among the richest types of primary sources that depict the historical contexts and perspectives of individuals, groups, and nations. Political cartoons such as Benjamin Franklin's "Join or Die" from the French and Indian War (or Seven Year's War if you are teaching this from a world history perspective) served as critical propaganda to rally the British colonies to band together in defeating the French and their Native American allies in the war that in many ways led the way for the American Revolution. Political cartoons highlight not only commentary on political policies and platforms of political parties and politicians, but also the stance of interest groups, publications, courts, corporations, and other public or private sector entities.

Analyzing political cartoons as visual literacies in ELA and social studies involves several literary analysis and historical thinking skills. Cartoonists use symbols, exaggerations, and humor to depict people and express a point of view on an issue. For instance, the National Archives (NARA) has worksheets with strategies for students to specifically examine political cartoons for:

- Illustrator
- Captions or titles
- Words, symbols, and objects
- Feelings or messages portrayed

- Events happening when the cartoon was created
- Significance and meaning
- Other types of evidence to learn about the issue or topic expressed

There are numerous political cartoons that are housed on the NARA website. For example, the Clifford K. Berryman collection features his work about Washington D.C. politics from the late-19th century through the mid-20th century. NARA also has an interactive digital exhibit using Berryman's political cartoons to engage students in campaigns for running for office.

The Library of Congress also has resources for analyzing political cartoons that emphasize the process of observing the parts of the cartoon, reflecting on the meaning of the cartoon, and asking questions about the cartoon. Their collections include political cartoons as single images or in digitized newspapers spanning from the colonial era (including Join or Die!).

> Check out these resources for political cartoons and political cartoon analysis worksheets and strategies!
> - Library of Congress Cartoon Analysis Worksheet: https://www.loc.gov/static/programs/teachers/getting-started-with-primary-sources/documents/Analyzing_Political_Cartoons.pdf
> - Library of Congress Political Cartoons and Public Debates: https://www.loc.gov/classroom-materials/political-cartoons-and-public-debates/
> - National Archives Cartoon Analysis Worksheet: https://www.archives.gov/education/lessons/worksheets/analyze-a-cartoon-intermediate
> - National Archives Clifford K. Berryman Collection: https://www.archives.gov/legislative/research/special-collections/berryman#page-header

As mentioned in Chapter Two, both the Library of Congress and NARA have extensive digital archives that include political cartoons as primary sources that teachers can access to engage students in historical empathy. NewseumED is a digital resource created by the Freedom Forum that focuses on First Amendment education and media literacy skills that are essential for civic life. The Freedom Forum was founded July 4, 1991 by the Frank E. Gannett Newspaper Foundation, one of the nation's largest newspaper publishers, aimed at supporting the public's understanding of protecting First Amendment rights such as press and assembly. Teachers can sign up for a free account with NewseumED to gain access to online resources including videos, articles, lesson plans, and political cartoons. In a quick keyword search for "political cartoons" in their search function, teachers can select from a wide array of political cartoons from major time periods in U.S. history such as the American Revolution, Civil War and Reconstruction, suffragist movement, Cold War, and 21st-century. Furthermore, the NewseumED lesson plans are aligned to the NCSS C3 Framework, NCTE Standards, as well as other related curricular standards for literacy and technology.

> Check out the NewseumED site and the timeline of the Freedom Forum's founding!
> - Freedom Forum Timeline: https://www.freedomforum.org/about-freedom-forum/timeline/
> - NeweumED Political Cartoon Search Results: https://newseumed.org/search/?q=POLITICAL%20CARTOONS&

The works of Theodor Geisel, before he was known as Dr. Seuss, are also compelling examples of political cartoons that can be used to promote historical empathy. Geisel was a prolific cartoonist during World War II, often using racial and ethnic stereotypes depicting the Japanese, Germans, and other groups associated with the Axis Powers. Katie used to use Richard Minear's (2001) book *Dr. Seuss Goes to War* with her middle school students to not only show them about historical context and perspectives of the 1930s and 1940s, but also to encourage students to reflect on what they knew and wanted to know about Dr. Seuss in order to examine the extent to which his works during the war impacted his books for kids.

Although Seuss is an iconic author with classics such as *The Cat in the Hat* and *Green Eggs and Ham*, his images and messages have come under scrutiny. Sophie Gilbert (2017) writes in *The Atlantic* how Geisel's World War II and anti-fascist cartoons were being re-examined in light of Trump-era policies concerning foreign policy and the U.S.'s position in the world as a global economic, militaristic, and political superpower. Additionally, Geisel's cartoons and books have come under scrutiny due to his use of racial and ethnic tropes, particularly regarding Asian Americans. Mark Pratt (2021) reported for the Associated Press that six of Dr. Seuss' books were no longer going to be published by Dr. Seuss Enterprises due to his use of "insensitive imagery." Depending upon states' curricular standards and laws, teachers can use Seuss' cartoons and books to engage students in literary analyses and other forms of primary source research when considering how the historical contexts in which his images were drawn and books were written impacted his perspectives, and how we can grapple with the legacy of these works in the present-day.

> The University of California San Diego Library has a digital collection of Dr. Seuss' World War II political cartoons along with a statement on historical context and cultural sensitivity. You can check out that statement and these resources here:
>
> https://library.ucsd.edu/speccoll/dswenttowar/

Photographs

As we highlight in Chapter 2, many digital media resources include photographs that can be used as primary sources to engage students in historical empathy. The NARA, Library of Congress, as well as most museums, historical societies, cultural centers, and other humanities organizations have both digital and hardcopy photographs for researchers, teachers, and students to use. These institutions also have a plethora of teaching strategies, lesson plans, and worksheets to support students' analysis of photographs for historical contexts and perspectives that can be easily used for reflection of affective responses to the photograph and how the information they learn can be used to take informed action. Photographs, whether they be candid shots or posed for Jacob Riis or Dorothea Lange, are truly windows to the past as students can get a glimpse for historical context, perspective, and affect by observing the clothing, objects, settings, and facial expressions of people in these pictures.

> Check out some of these resources and strategies to analyze photographs as primary sources!
>
> - Society for American Archaeology: https://documents.saa.org/container/docs/default-source/doc-teachingarchaeology/lessonplan_photo.pdf
> - Minnesota Historical Society: https://libguides.mnhs.org/photos/primary#:~:text=Photos%20can%20be%20great%20primary,already%20know%20about%20the%20photo%3F

- Library of Congress Analyzing Photographs and Prints: https://www.loc.gov/static/programs/teachers/getting-started-with-primary-sources/documents/Analyzing_Photographs_and_Prints.pdf
- National Archives Analyzing a Photograph: https://www.archives.gov/education/lessons/worksheets/analyze-a-photograph-intermediate

Along with political cartoons, teachers need to be mindful of when they use photographs, political cartoons, or other types of images or visual art as instructional tools, particularly regarding copyright and usage permissions. Karen Lagola (2021) wrote a very informative article in *Edutopia* on fair use tips for teachers, highlighting that texts, audio, videos, and visuals that are in the public domain, such as the works of Shakespeare, or governmental materials sites such as the Library of Congress or Smithsonian are allowed for reproduction on worksheets, handouts, presentations, and other forms of dissemination. However, materials that are protected include published works under copyright or materials that are originally created by someone, including photographs you may take with your own personal camera. Therefore, teachers must be extremely careful when discerning which sources they use under the fair use doctrine or if they need to obtain permission to use certain creative works.

For example, Katie worked with a group of high school students who conducted primary source research about the historical significance of the COVID-19 pandemic. Students used the Library of Congress' archive and conducted their own local history research by collecting photographs, videos, texts, drawings, oral history interviews, and other artifacts from community members documenting their experiences during the pandemic. Their research resulted in an exhibit and companion book that was displayed in their community and was donated to the local school district for future programming. Students had to obtain written permission from every person they collected artifacts from, which included siblings, friends, teachers, community members, and family members. Katie and her colleagues got permission from original artists whose photographs and posters are digitized on the Library of Congress' site to use for conference presentations about this project and how students demonstrated historical empathy through doing this research. Although collecting all these types of permission was tedious, Katie knew that if the project was going to be done correctly, she and her colleagues had to model to the students that adhering to copyright and fair use, as well as citing sources for conventional expository writing or historical research, is a critical skill to cultivate both academically and ethically speaking.

In addition to teaching about copyright, the COVID project also served as a way for students to consider how everyday items such as emails, social media posts, and photographs are examples of primary sources that can be used to research about the historical contexts and perspectives of the past. The Library of Congress Teaching with Primary Sources "Leaving Evidence of our Lives" activity was an effective approach that Katie had the students complete when examining the artifacts that they collected for their research.

> You can check out the students' project "Same Storm, Different Boats: Documenting the Living History of the COVID-19 Pandemic" at the Student Leadership Johns Creek website! The Library of Congress' Leaving Evidence of our Lives strategy can be found on their teachers professional development site:
>
> https://www.loc.gov/static/programs/teachers/professional-development/documents/Leaving-Evidence-Our-Lives.pdf

Fine Arts

Like political cartoons and photographs, fine art in the modality of paintings, sketches, dances, performances, and drawings are compelling primary sources that can support fostering historical empathy in social studies and ELA. According to Burstein and Knotts (2011), fine art is an expression of a person or group's culture and identity, and "teachers can show how different societies live and evolve through their art…either in the past or the present" (p. 20). Arts integration in social studies and ELA is an interdisciplinary approach to not only engaging students in analyzing historical contexts and perspectives from an academic stance, but also considering how the purpose and meaning of art is a vital aspect of a people's history and contemporary values. For instance, a major part of teaching about the Holocaust is Hitler's purge of "degenerate" art that were in a modernist style or from a Jewish perspective. Such works included paintings and symphonic music that were destroyed or sold to foreign proprietors and museums. Moreover, the Nazi's used art such as radio shows, movies, and paintings as propaganda to promote their agenda of fascist politics and Aryan racial purity (Petropoulos, 2016). Historical empathy can be a powerful approach to examining how art was regarded as both dangerous and vital to the war effort in Germany, and why freedom of speech is an integral aspect of democratic life in the U.S. and around the world.

Dance as a visual art is a powerful modality that can incorporate empathetic, historical, and kinesthetic learning to social studies and ELA instruction. Examining dance as part of cultural traditions and customs such as for religious rituals or celebrating life milestones can be an engaging aspect of promoting historical empathy through observing dance choreography, costumes, singing, props, and music. If space, resources, and time allows, teachers can even have students demonstrate dances, or create their own, as part of studies of global or U.S. history and literature for in-class performances that can culminate as an interactive activity where students apply what they learned about a particular dance from primary and secondary source research to communicate conclusions and take informed action through movement. PBS Learning Media and KQED.org have several resources including videos and lesson plans that aim at promoting empathy through dance (see our suggested resources at the end of this chapter!).

> Studies show that dance in schools can improve students' empathy and overall social-emotional learning (see our chapter references!). Check out the resources by Dancing Classroom, a non-profit that services New York City schools through offering dance programs and professional development:
>
> https://dancingclassrooms.org

Museums can be important institutions where art can be contextualized for students and patrons to not only learn about the artistic, literary, and historic underpinnings of creative works, but also to promote empathy. The Norton Simon Museum in California has online videos and lesson plans that focus on how to use paintings to foster empathy through examination of the artists' life, historical context in which a painting was made, and reflecting on how the painting makes one feel. The Crystal Bridges Museum of American Art in Arkansas has its "Engaging Empathy" curriculum where the works of art at the museum are connected to promoting empathy and literacy for secondary students. Among the topics the Engaging Empathy curriculum addresses includes African American perspectives, gender issues, aging issues, Japanese internment, environmental issues, LGTBQ+ perspectives, and Indigenous perspectives.

CHAPTER 5

> Check out these resources to use art to promote empathy in literacy and social studies instruction!
> - Norton Simon Museum: https://www.nortonsimon.org/learn/schools-teachers/spotlight-on-art-videos-for-schools/cultivating-empathy-through-art/
> - Engaging Empathy curriculum: https://sites.google.com/teachingtransformed.com/engaging-empathy/home?authuser=0

According to historical empathy researcher Jason Endacott and his co-authors Jacob Warren, Kathryn Hackett-Hill, and Alexandre Lalonde (2023), arts integration played a major role in fostering pre-service secondary social studies teachers' engagement in historical empathy through encouraging reflection of affective responses to the historical contexts and multitude of perspectives expressed in aesthetic texts from the Vietnam War. Additionally, they found that focusing on the process in which art was (and is) created is an important aspect of examining historical contexts and perspectives of people in the past (Endacott et al., 2024). For example, showing a series of photographs of the assembly of the Statue of Liberty when it arrived by boat from France could be a way for students to think about why statue was given to the United States, what the statue represents, and how its construction changed not only the physical landscape of the New York City Harbor, but also perspectives, feelings, attitudes, and beliefs about issues such as immigration and freedom during the 19th century and today. As a result, using the fine arts as primary sources, albeit teachers need to be aware of when a painting or sculpture or other works of art were created, can be powerful resources to promote historical empathy in middle and high school settings, as well in teacher preparation courses.

> The First Thanksgiving by Jean Leon Gerome Ferris is a famous depiction of the Puritan settlers sharing their harvest with the native Wampanoag people in the Plymouth, Massachusetts colony. This painting is not a primary source when teaching about the first Thanksgiving because Ferris made it in 1912. A primary source about the first Thanksgiving would need to be produced by someone who was there at the event in 1621. However, if a teacher were to use Ferris' painting to examine how the contexts of 1912 impacted how he created this famous scene, then the painting would be considered

a primary source. You can find out more about depictions of Thanksgiving from Anne Savage's (2012) blog for the Library of Congress:

https://blogs.loc.gov/teachers/2012/11/library-of-congress-primary-sources-and-thanksgiving/

Visual Literacies for Differentiated Instruction

Visual literacies offer another aid for students who struggle with the written work, whether because they do not read, or do not read with fluency, the dominate language of the classroom, or because they struggle with written text for other reasons (Flattley, 1998 as cited in Stokes, 2008). Each time Jennifer introduced Romanticism to her ELA students, she would present Casper David Friedrich's (1817) *The Wanderer above a Sea of Fog* on the projector. With little or no contextualization, she asked students to describe what they saw. Generally, the responses were broad: "Lots of clouds," "Some mountains in the background," "A guy looking out over the clouds." Eventually, a student would dive a little deeper, such as "He's alone." The first comment like this would ignite something or nudge a reticent student to say more and before long, the class was engaged in thoughtful analysis. This small exercise had three outcomes: It introduced students to Romanticism, it engaged them in critical thinking, and it subsequently illustrated to them that yes, they could participate effectively in analysis. By allowing them to make observations about a work of art, not printed text, which of course in an ELA class comes with expectations, students felt little or no pressure to perform. Rather, it was simply conversation.

After the discussion, Jennifer would offer the big reveal and explain that by examining different elements of the painting such as color, detail, and depth, and by making inferences about the sole figure in the painting, they had in fact successfully analyzed the image. She further explained that analysis works the same way with printed text. Just as with the Romanticism activity, photographs, posters, paintings, and other forms of visual art can be used to scaffold skills such as analysis as well as make connections to the lived experiences of people in the past.

Connections to Standards

Photographs, visual art, and aesthetic texts are vital resources that enrich social studies and ELA instruction that can encourage historical empathy. Images are among the oldest forms of human communication, and the proliferation of digital media will create new venues for artistic and creative expression. Today, we may take for granted that we literally carry digital archies of photographs and other digital visual arts on our smartphones and other wearable devices. However, there is a rush of excitement, curiosity, and nostalgia when families dust off old photo albums that document family history, holidays, celebrations, and travels. Students can start with analyzing their own family artifacts to consider the historical contexts and perspectives of their ancestors, and whether those heirlooms align or challenge the depictions of people and groups in primary sources. Ultimately, students may be able to share deep affective responses to how their own heritages and identities contribute to their demonstration of historical empathy.

Photographs, cartoons, glyphs, fine arts, and other visuals are powerful tools to argue a point, send a message, express oneself, and celebrate something. For instance, it would be hard to truly grasp the gravity of the impact of the Vietnam War on the United States without seeing the images of protests, signs, clothing, and people who held very strong views about the war along with the other aspects of socio-economic and political tumult of the 1960s. As a result, the NCSS and NCTE standards widely support the use of images to promote historical empathy through the use of visual literacies that can be effective when differentiating instruction and promoting critical thinking through analysis of historical contexts and perspectives of art that can lead to informed action and deep student learning.

NCTE Standards and Visual Literacy

NCTE recognizes visual arts as part of a multimodal approach to literacy (2021). In Table 5.1, we have provided a list of NCTE ELA standards that align with using photography and visual arts to promote historical empathy.

NCSS C3 Framework and Visual Arts and Literacy

To reiterate, the NCSS C3 Framework was developed to help social studies teachers across the country teach content and skills that aligned with the Common Core ELA standards, which include history, for grades 6-12. As a result, the emphasis on literacy through teaching with multiple modalities of texts are evident in the C3 Framework Inquiry Arc. The term "literacy" appears in the document 120 times in reference to the Common Core Standards, as well as how literacy is a key component to teaching inquiry, historical thinking, shared language skills of reading comprehension, writing, speaking, and listening, particularly

Table 5.1 NCTE Standards Connections to Visual Literacies and Historical Empathy

Standard	Statement	Connection to Historical Empathy
1.	Students apply a wide range of strategies to comprehend, interpret, evaluate, and appreciate texts. They draw on their prior experience, their interactions with other readers and writers, their knowledge of word meaning and of other texts, their word identification strategies, and their understanding of textual features (e.g., sound-letter correspondence, sentence structure, context, graphics).	In NCTE's (2021) statement on multimodal literacies, they cite the use of non-printed texts such as music and visual arts. NCTE's standard 1 calls on students' prior experience which can be stimulated through images. It also recognizes strategies such as word identification through resources such as graphics.
5.	Students employ a wide range of strategies as they write and use different writing process elements appropriately to communicate with different audiences for a variety of purposes.	This standard acknowledges the use of strategies for writing. While this standard is broadly worded, images can serve as inspiration, cue prior knowledge, and help students draw personal connections to subjects, themes, and experiences.
6.	Students apply knowledge of language structure, language conventions (e.g., spelling and punctuation), media techniques, figurative language, and genre to create, critique, and discuss print and non-print texts.	Here, non-print texts are recognized as text for creating, critiquing, and discussion.
7.	Students conduct research on issues and interests by generating ideas and questions, and by posing problems. They gather, evaluate, and synthesize data from a variety of sources (e.g., print and non-print texts, artifacts, people) to communicate their discoveries in ways that suit their purpose and audience.	In this standard, NCTE recognizes non-printed texts as sources for research.
10.	Students whose first language is not English make use of their first language to develop competency in the English language arts and to develop understanding of content across the curriculum.	Images, whether photography or other visual arts, can offer cues for ELLs and other students who may struggle with printed text.

when considering perspectives, points of view, and arguments in various types of primary and secondary sources (NCSS, 2013, pp. 21; 87).

When examining the C3 Framework for specific types of visuals in its standards, photographs are explicitly included in the geography standards in Dimension 2 of the Inquiry Arc. The terms visuals and visualizations are more broadly used throughout the framework, most prevalent in Dimension 4 of the Inquiry Arc, which allows for more nuanced analysis of what kind of digital and print texts that historians and other social scientists use for research, communicating conclusions, and taking informed action (NCSS, 2013, p. 57; 64; 111). The C3 standards featured in this chapter have explicit and implicit connections to using visual texts, often referred to as "multiple sources," that can be used to promote historical empathy.

Sample Lesson Plan

To reflect the possible uses of photographs and visual arts, this lesson plan offers photography, political cartoons, and other images as examples of how visual literacies can be used to promote historical empathy.

Lesson Title: The Face of the Depression

Grade Level: 9-12

Length of Time: 1-2 days

C3 Framework Inquiry Arc Dimension 1- Staging the Inquiry	
Big Idea	Desperation
Compelling Question	Are all experiences of desperation the same?

Table 5.2 C3 Framework Connections to Visual Literacies and Historical Empathy

Inquiry Arc Dimension	Standard
1	D1.5.9-12. Determine the kind of sources that will be helpful in answering compelling and supporting questions, taking into consideration multiple points of view represented in the sources, the types of sources available, and the potential uses of the sources (p. 25).
2	D2.Civ.5.9-12. Evaluate citizens' and institutions' effectiveness in addressing social and political problems at the local, state, tribal, national, and/or international level (p. 32).
2	D2.Geo.2.9-12. Use maps, satellite images, photographs, and other representations to explain relationships between the locations of places and regions and their political, cultural, and economic dynamics (p. 41)
2	D2. His.9.9-12. Analyze the relationship between historical sources and the secondary interpretations made from them (p. 48).
2	D2.His.9-12. Critique the usefulness of historical sources for a specific historical inquiry based on their maker, date, place of origin, intended audience, and purpose (p.48)
2	D2.His.16.9-12. Integrate evidence from multiple relevant historical sources and interpretations into a reasoned argument about the past (p. 49).
3	D3.1.9-12. Gather relevant information from multiple sources representing a wide range of views while using the origin, authority, structure, context, and corroborative value of the sources to guide the selection (p. 54).
3	D3.3.9-12. Identify evidence that draws from directly and substantively from multiple sources to detect inconsistencies in evidence in order to revise or strengthen claims (p. 55).
4	D4.1.9-12. Construction arguments using precise and knowledgeable claims, with evidence from multiple sources, while acknowledging counterclaims and evidentiary weaknesses (p. 60)
4	D4.3.9-12. Present adaptions of arguments and explanations that feature evocative ideas and perspectives on issues and topics to reach a range of audiences and venues outside the classroom using print and oral technologies (e.g., posters, essays, letters, debates, speeches, reports, and maps) and digital technologies (e.g., Internet, social media, and digital documentary (p. 60)

CHAPTER 5

C3 Framework Inquiry Arc Dimension 1- Staging the Inquiry	
Essential Understandings/ Rationale	Students will analyze photographs and political cartoons to contextualize their close readings of passages from *The Grapes of Wrath* and *Their Eyes Were Watching God*. The big idea and compelling question will lead students into an examination of photography and political cartoons illustrated the desperation and extreme poverty experienced by many American during the Great Depression. These visual literacies will underpin the themes of desperation and poverty in the works of John Steinbeck's (1939) novel about Dust Bowl migrants and Zora Neale Hurston's (1937) novel about oppression, poverty, and race. While Hurston's *Their Eyes Were Watching God* is not specifically about the Depression in the way that *The Grapes of Wrath* is, students will gain insight into another part of the country within the Black community during the same time period.
Learning Targets	Students will be able to: 1. Compare and contrast visual and printed texts for depictions of Americans' experiences during the Great Depression. 2. Explain the historical contexts and perspectives of primary sources such as photographs during the Great Depression. 3. Identify the causes and effects of the Dust Bowl during the Great Depression. 4. Identify the role of geography where the Dust Bowl most impacted Americans. 5. Analyze the impact of the Great Depression on Americans.
Supporting Questions	1. How does Steinbeck (1939) depict the desperation of the Judd family and how they feel? How does this make you feel? 2. How does the photography from the Farm Security Administration files support the language used by Steinbeck about desperation? 3. How do the images of Oklahoma highlight how the context of the Dust Bowl shaped the experiences of Americans in The Grapes of Wrath? 4. How do the images of workers picking beans during the Great Depression compare to the descriptions provided by Hurston? 5. How do these sources help you to understand the human experience during the Great Depression?

PHOTOGRAPHS AND VISUAL ARTS

Lesson Materials	
Featured Secondary Sources	• *The Grapes of Wrath* by John Steinbeck (novel)/Teacher selected passages. • *Their Eyes were Watching God* by Zora Neale Hurston (novel)/Teacher selected passages.
Featured Primary Sources	Dorthea Lang Digital Archive (2024). The Depression. Dorthea Lang Digital Archive. https://dorothealange.museumca.org/section/depression/. • Library of Congress (2024). *Farm Security Administration/Office of War Information Black and White Negatives*. Library of Congress, Prints & Photographs Online Catalog (PPOC). https://www.loc.gov/pictures/collection/fsa/. https://www.loc.gov/pictures/collection/fsa/item/2017767006/
Technology/ Media Sources	The Library of Congress digital archives.
Other Materials and Supports	Highlighters, pencils, pens, sticky notes, KWLE chart, copies of the novels

C3 Framework Inquiry Arc Dimension 2- Standards Connections	
NCTE Standard 1 for ELA	Students apply a wide range of strategies to comprehend, interpret, evaluate, and appreciate texts. They draw on their prior experience, their interactions with other readers and writers, their knowledge of word meaning and of other texts, their word identification strategies, and their
NCTE Standard 5 for ELA	Students employ a wide range of strategies as they write and use different writing process elements appropriately to communicate with different audiences for a variety of purposes.
NCTE Standard 6 for ELA	Students apply knowledge of language structure, language conventions (e.g., spelling and punctuation), media techniques, figurative language, and genre to create, critique, and discuss print and non-print texts.
NCTE Standard 7 for ELA	Students conduct research on issues and interests by generating ideas and questions, and by posing problems. They gather, evaluate, and synthesize data from a variety of sources (e.g., print and non-print texts, artifacts, people) to communicate their discoveries in ways that suit their purpose and audience.
NCTE Standard 10 for ELA	Students whose first language is not English make use of their first language to develop competency in the English language arts and to develop understanding of content across the curriculum.
C3 Framework Content Standard, History	D2.His.4.9-12. Analyze complex and interacting factors that influenced the perspectives of people during different historical eras. (p. 47)

C3 Framework Inquiry Arc Dimension 2- **Standards Connections**	
C3 Framework Content Standard History	D2.His.9.9-12. Analyze the relationship between historical sources and the secondary interpretations made from them.
	D2.His.5.9-12. Analyze how historical contexts shaped and continue to shape people's perspectives.
C3 Framework Content Standard History	D2.His.9.9-12. Analyze the relationship between historical sources and the secondary interpretations made from them.

C3 Framework Inquiry Arc Dimension 3- **Analyzing Source Evidence**	
Introduction/ Motivation	1. The teacher will begin the lesson by checking for students' prior knowledge about the Great Depression in the United States by asking students to reflect and record what they "know" about The Great Depression. Students can record their responses this individually or in small groups in journals, notebooks, or other types of notetaking devices.
	2. Next, students will complete a gallery walk to examine photographs from the Library of Congress' Dorothea Lange collection. The teacher can print the images and hang them around the classroom.
	3. Students will walk through the gallery and take notes about what they noticed in the photos, the feelings that these images evoked for them, what they would still like to learn about the Great Depression. After writing down their thoughts in their notebooks or journals, students will share their responses to what they "know" and "want to know" as the teacher records a K-W-L Chart on the board or chart paper. The chart can be copied and distributed to students for notetaking as well.

Know	Want to Know

C3 Framework Inquiry Arc Dimension 3- Analyzing Source Evidence

Teacher Direct Instruction	4. If the students will only be reading passages from the novels, we recommend offering students summaries of the novels and perhaps biographical information about the writers. Notably, the novels were published within two years of each other (1937 and 1939). 5. Teacher can lead discussion by asking students about what the historical context of the late-1930s was like for white migrant workers and for African Americans, and how those contexts shaped the writings of Steinbeck and Hurston. 6. Background information to the books should highlight how families like the Judds in *The Grapes of Wrath* migrated to California because of the promise of work picking fruit and because their farms had either fallen to the effects of the Dust Bowl or foreclosure from local banks. Similarly, Janey and Tea Cake in *Their Eyes were Watching God,* go the Everglades in Florida for the promise of similar work, harvesting crops. 7. The teacher will ask students to complete a close reading and annotation of each passage, looking for language around desperation, and how the characters in both books had similar and different experiences with desperation during the Depression. Teachers are encouraged to choose passages based on their readers' abilities and interests, however, here are a few suggestions: Chapter 12, *The Grapes of Wrath* (pp. 118-119), Chapter 14, Their Eyes were Watching God (pp. 129-130).
Formative Performance Task/ Student Structured Practice	• After students have annotated the passages from each novel, the teacher will ask students to return to their journals or notebooks and re-examine the photos from the gallery walk. • Under each photograph (or the teacher can choose select images to give out to groups or pairs) the students are asked to compose a reflection where they explain their analyses of historical contexts, how those contexts impacted the perspectives of Americans during the Depression, and any connections, feelings, or experiences that relate to the image and the big idea and compelling question about desperation. • Students will choose one of photographs and reflections that they wrote that most resonated with them. Students will share why this photograph was impactful to them by creating a poem, song, short story, diary entry, illustration, cartoon, or another presentation modality of their choice. Students can work in groups or individually.

C3 Framework Inquiry Arc Dimension 4- Communicating Conclusions and Taking Informed Action	
Student Share	• Ask students to share their compositions. If working in groups or pairs, ask that a representative of the group or pair speak and discuss their composition choice and why they felt it offered an appropriate reflection of their photo.
Closing	• The teacher can lead the class in completing the chart from the beginning of the lesson, asking students to reflection on what they "learned" and what "enduring questions" they still have about the Great Depression. The chart can be collected as an exit ticket or as a segue into learning about the New Deal.

Know	Want to Know	learned	Enduring Questions

Summative Performance Task/Extension	• Students can work in cooperative groups to research primary and secondary sources that help them answer one of their enduring questions about the Great Depression. Students can connect their examination of the Depression to their reflections and share how the historical contexts and perspectives from that time bear relevance to their lives or to a current issue. Connections can be made to using Great Depression music from Chapter 4!

Conclusion

Not that long ago, cameras were considered luxury items that only the very wealthy could afford to own or to sit for a portrait. Obtaining fine art, whether they were original paintings or reproductions, was accessible only to the elites in society. Visiting an art gallery or museum or an opera house was an activity reserved for the upper classes. Purchasing instruments for visual, audio, and other aesthetic arts was a luxury few could afford. Technological advances and democratic movements throughout the centuries have led to the creation, dissemination, and consumption of art to be done by practically anyone. Art can be created by hand and the human imagination, and with the help of digital tools, to convey messages—to warn, to praise, to inform, to entertain, to critique— as well as to express personal feelings and emotions that connect people from all walks of life. Art can serve as powerful primary sources and visual literacies that engage students in critical thinking, self-discovery, and empathy of the experiences and perspectives of others. Although the arts can sometimes be dismissed as its own academic discipline, they are vital tools for understanding the past to make civic-minded and informed decisions in the present. Integrating visual arts into social studies and ELA instruction can truly enhance a literary or historical research experience by connecting human emotion, perspectives, and experiences from the past to a student's life and present-day world.

Reflection

- How might students find photography and other forms of visual arts more accessible than printed text?
- What are some of the benefits and challenges in using photography and visual arts in the classroom?
- How might you use photography or the visual arts in an interdisciplinary lesson plan to promote historical empathy?
- How can the use of visual texts support diverse learners, who may struggle with the written word, engage in historical empathy?

Suggested Photograph and Visual Arts Resources

Cruz, B.C., & Ellerbrock, C.R. (2015). Developing visual literacy: Historical and manipulated photography in the social studies classroom. *The Social Studies 106*(6), 274-280. http://dx.doi.org/10.1080/00377996.2015.1083932

Djangi, P. (2024). These manipulated photos are the original political deep fakes. National Geographic. Retrieved from https://www.nationalgeographic.com/history/article/political-photo-manipulation-in-history

Dukehart, C. (2013). 'National Geographic' celebrates 125 years of photography. *NPR*. Retrieved from https://www.npr.org/sections/pictureshow/2013/10/01/227871549/national-geographic-celebrates-125-years-of-photography

Endacott, J.L., Warren, J., Hackett-Hill, K., & Lalonde, A. (2024). Arts integrated historical empathy: Preservice teachers' engagement with pluralistic lived experiences and efforts toward instructional application. *Theory & Research in Social Education 52*(3), 414-457.

Getty images. Hudson River School Painting Stock Photos. Retrieved from https://www.gettyimages.com/photos/hudson-river-school-painting

Hensley, M., Waters, S., & Russell, W.B. III. (2023). *Visual literacy in the K-12 social studies classroom.* Information Age Publishing.

Kerr, S.L., & Adams, E.C. (2017). What do you see? Visual(izing) social studies for all students. *The Oregon Journal of Social Studies 5*(1), 30-41.

PBS. (2024). Social studies and world history through Music and dance. Retrieved from https://gpb.pbslearningmedia.org/collection/social-studies-and-world-history-through-music-and-dance/

Wadsworth Anetheum Museum of Art. Hudson River School. Retrieved from https://www.thewadsworth.org/explore/collection/hudson-river-school/

Zeeberg, A. (2016). How images trigger empathy. The Atlantic. Retrieved from https://www.theatlantic.com/science/archive/2016/01/cultivate-empathy-photograph/422793/

Chapter References

Burstein, J.H, & Knotts, G. (2010). Creating connections: Integrating the visual arts with social studies. *Social Studies and the Young Learner 23*(1), 20-23. https://www.socialstudies.org/system/files/publications/articles/yl_230120.pdf

Friedrich, C.D. (1817). *The wanderer above a sea of fog*. Retrieved from https://www.britannica.com/topic/Wanderer-Above-the-Sea-of-Fog

Dorthea Lang Digital Archive (2024). *The Depression*. Retrieved from https://dorothealange.museumca.org/section/depression/.

Endacott, J. L., Warren, J., Hackett-Hill, K., & Lalonde, A. (2023). Arts integrated historical empathy: Preservice teachers' engagement with pluralistic lived experiences and efforts toward instructional application. *Theory & Research in Social Education 52*(3), 414-457. https://doi.org/10.1080/00933104.2023.2279157

Garrett, H.J., & Kerr, S.L. (2016). Theorizing the use of aesthetic texts in social studies education. *Theory and Research in Social Education 44*(4), 505-531. https://doi.org/10.1080/00933104.2016.1211047

Gilbert, S. (2017). The complicated relevance of Dr. Seuss' political cartoons. *The Atlantic*. Retrieved from https://www.theatlantic.com/entertainment/archive/2017/01/dr-seuss-protest-icon/515031/

Hurston, Z. N. (1937). *Their Eyes were watching God*. J.B. Lippincott.

Lagola, K. (2021). A teacher's guide to copyright and fair use. *Edutopia*. Retrieved from https://www.edutopia.org/article/teachers-guide-copyright-and-fair-use/

Library of Congress (2024). *Ansel Adam's photographs of Japanese American internment at Manzanar*. Retrieved from https://www.loc.gov/pictures/collection/manz/.

Library of Congress (2024). *Curtis (Edward S.) Collection*. Retrieved from https://www.loc.gov/pictures/collection/ecur/.

Library of Congress (2024). *Farm Security Administration/Office of War Information Black and White Negatives*. Retrieved frohttps://www.loc.gov/pictures/collection/fsa/.

Library of Congress (2024). *Posters: Performing Arts Posters*. Library of Congress, Prints & Photographs Online Catalog (PPOC). Retrieved from https://www.loc.gov/pictures/collection/var/.

Minear, R. (2001). *Dr. Seuss goes to war: The World War II editorial cartoons of Theodor Seuss Geisel*. The New Press.

Dutro, E., & Collins, K. (2021). A journey through nine decades of NCTE-published research in elementary literacy. *Research in Teaching of English 46* (2), pp. 141-161. https://doi.org/10.58680/rte201118262

Petropoulous, J. (2016). Art and politics. *Facing History and Ourselves*. Retrieved from https://www.facinghistory.org/resource-library/art-politics

Prakash, N., Goodill, S., Sood, S., Vader, D. T., Moore, R. H., Beardall, N., & Shim, M. (2024). Examining the impact of dance/movement therapy on empathy, peer relationships, and cultural self-efficacy in middle school: A mixed methods study. *Social Sciences & Humanities Open, 10*, 100998. https://doi.org/10.1016/j.ssaho.2024.100998

Pratt, M. (2021). 6 Dr. Seuss books will stop being published due to racist imagery. *Associated Press*. Retrieved from https://www.pbs.org/newshour/arts/6-dr-seuss-books-will-stop-being-published-because-of-racist-imagery

Savage, A. (2012). Changing images of Thanksgiving: Library of Congress primary sources. Retrieved from https://blogs.loc.gov/teachers/2012/11/library-of-congress-primary-sources-and-thanksgiving/

Steinbeck, J. (1939). *The grapes of wrath*. Viking Press.

Stokes, S. (2008). Visual literacy in teaching and learning: A literature perspective. *Electronic Journal for the Integration of Technology in Education 1* (1), 10-19. https://wcpss.pbworks.com/f/Visual+Literacy.pdf

CHAPTER 6

Place-Based Education

Brainstorming Activity

- How do you define *place*?
- How would you describe *place-based learning*?
- What kinds of place-based sites and resources could you incorporate in your teaching?
- What are your favorite examples of place-based sites and resources that you can use when promoting historical empathy?

Introduction

Although it is a major cliché in education is that learning happens beyond the classroom, we believe this cliché to be true! Some of Katie's favorite lessons that she taught were the ones that she was able to connect to field trips and place-based learning opportunities with her students. In New York, the 7th and 8th grade social studies curriculum focused on U.S. history with emphasis on New York state history. Since she taught in Brooklyn, Katie planned several field trips every year where she took classes on the subway to visit places throughout the city that connected to the topics that they were learning in school. She took the 7th graders to Prospect Park to learn about the Indigenous Lenape people, Greenwood Cemetery to learn about the American Revolution and Civil War veterans buried there, Alexander Hamilton's grave at Trinity Church, Federal Hall, the Statue of Liberty, and the Museum of American History. During these trips, Katie reveled in seeing how the kids were able to make connections between what they were reading about in school to real, tangible places that were still vibrant aspects of their community.

However, one of the most impactful experiences that Katie was involved with was when she collaborated with the Brooklyn Library where the education specialist brought reproductions of primary sources to support 8th graders in conducting local history research for their end of year exit project. For three years, she worked with the Library to support students' research on topics such as the immigration, the Great Depression and Great Recession, and historical preservation of landmarks such Coney Island. At the end of the school year, students created presentation boards; some were displayed at the local branch library, and some were selected to be on display at the Grand Army Plaza main branch. Katie brought those experiences with her to Atlanta, where she took undergraduate students hiking at Kennesaw Battlefield and partnered with a student leadership organization to support high school students' local history research projects about a historically Black cemetery and exploring diverse experiences of community members living during the COVID-19 pandemic.

In this chapter, we will examine how historical can be implemented through place-based learning opportunities that engage students in making real-world connections to topics they study in school as a means of fostering inquiry and civic mindedness through taking informed action a la the C3 Framework. Although Katie's experiences took place in an urban setting, place-based learning can take place anywhere. For instance, the NCHE's Rural Experience in America program, which is grant-funded by the Library of Congress, offers teachers with professional development on promoting place-based education in rural areas across the country! Sometimes we are bogged down by the constraints of time, testing, and other building-level priorities that make it difficult to physically take students to visit historical sites on field trips. We understand that there are serious logistics to consider when planning a field trip that include cost of admission, transportation, parental or caregiver permission, chaperones, meals, and how to connect the place-based learning opportunity to the standards. However, we outline options for not only larger-scale place-based learning opportunities, but also local options and virtual field trip offerings that can support the goals of historical empathy in ELA and social studies instruction.

Place-Based Education

According to the Promise of Place website, place-based education (PBE) "immerses students in local heritage, cultures, landscapes, opportunities, and experiences, using these as a foundation for the study of language arts, mathematics, social science, science, and other subjects across the curriculum. PBE emphasizes learning through participation in service projects for the local school and/or community." In other words, PBE involves working within and with communities to connect content and skills that are taught in classrooms to real-world and relevant experiences in students' lives. David Sobel (2019), a prolific scholar of PBE, wrote in an article in *Yes! Magazine* that outdoor education has its roots in the progressive social reforms dating to the Second Industrial Revolution when the establishment of the National Parks and scouting organizations highlighted the need for conservation and preservation as part of providing health benefits of getting children outside.

Throughout the 20th and 21st centuries, the proliferation of television, video games, and internet-based devices exasperated concerns about children spending more and more time inside and isolated from nature and other people. Richard Louv (2005) raised the alarm about the onslaught of "nature deficit disorder" in 2005 with his book *Last Child in the Woods*. Since the COVID-19 pandemic, interest in PBE piqued due to concerns on how stay-at-home orders, school closures, and social distancing impacted student learning, socialization, and mental health. According to the Institute of Education Sciences, PBE can be adapted to mitigate the consequences of educational disruptions in all subject areas "by increasing social connections, through providing strategies and opportunities for building stronger relationships between educators, students, and the community by encouraging conversations, joint projects, and curriculum development with community members" (Conolly, 2020).

Connections to Community-Based Learning

PBE is an all-encompassing term that includes various types of outdoor learning that includes, but is not limited to, investigations of local ecology and environmental science studies, research of local architecture and historical sites, and identification of local issues or problems in a community. Community-based learning (CBL) and PBE share similarities, but there are distinctions. While both involve interdisciplinary approaches to promoting active learning and student engagement through visiting and interacting with environments outside of the school building, CBL has a specific civic focus, meaning a science or social studies lesson that takes place outdoors in a community has tenets of connecting the investigation or learning activity to addressing a local issue or problem, hence promoting civic engagement. For instance, Annie Whitlock's book on PBE when addressing the Flint water crisis is a strong example of CBL because of her emphasis on inquiry-based and interdisciplinary social studies instruction by connecting "community [as] an extension of the classroom" through asking compelling questions that are grounded in critical studies of local history and power such as "Why do people live where they do?," "Should elected officials always make every decision for their constituents?," and "Should we have to pay for water" (Whitlock, 2024, pp. 10-11)?

PBE does not necessarily have to have an explicit civic engagement component; however, we argue that CBL can be an explicit or implicit goal of PBE because tenets of citizenship such as caring for and about one's community is at the heart of connecting the local environment to kids' lives, especially when promoting historical empathy. For example, the Association of Fish and Wildlife Agencies' Project WILD 4th edition curriculum aims to "provide wildlife-based conservation and environmental education that fosters responsible actions toward wildlife and related natural resources" with standards-based resources developed by scientists and educators that include field investigation activities, exploration of STEM careers, and outdoor activities. The inventory methods that are outlined in Project WILD involve student engagement in the scientific method through observations of plants and wildlife in the school yard, and inquiry techniques that support students' stewardship by considering field ethics of conducting inventories and how these investigations can help local communities (Association of Fish and Wildlife Agencies, p. 540). Therefore, PBE that is grounded in fostering strong connections between students' identities and place in their communities is a strong characteristic of CBL and PBE.

> Project WILD offers several types of curricula including Aquatic WILD, Growing Up WILD, and Flying WILD with interdisciplinary connections to citizenship, physical education, and the arts! You can request materials and support from a Project WILD state coordinator!
>
> https://www.fishwildlife.org/projectwild/project-wild-resources

Place and Identity

So much of PBE, CBL, and historical empathy connects to students' identities and their conceptions of place. Research is growing about the role of students' identities on how they demonstrate historical empathy (Endacott & Brooks, 2018; Perrotta, 2018; Endacott, 2010; Epstein & Schiller, 2005). Identity, which can include students' racial, ethnic, religious, and gender affiliations impact how they see the world, experience the world, and ultimately interpret the significance and meaning of how historical contexts shape perspectives of people in the past and present. According to the National Council for Geography Education, the Six Essential Elements of Geography (formerly the five themes of geography), *place* refers to the physical and human characteristics of places, how people interpret the Earth, and how culture and experiences impact humans' perspectives on places and regions. In other words, place involves how people make meaning of the relative or absolute locations or spaces on the earth. For instance, the specific coordinates of latitude and longitude on a map indicates an absolute location of a space on earth. Relative location refers to when a location is determined in relation to another, such as how the borough of Staten Island is located near Manhattan. Space refers to the physical characteristics of a location. A space becomes place when people ascribe cultural, historical, economic, social, or political meaning to a location. Grasping the importance of place is key to promoting historical empathy through PBE. Students who engage in field trips, outdoor investigations, and other PBE opportunities need to have a sense of historical contexts of where they are studying in order to understand how multiple perspectives and experiences of people in a place changed or influenced a place, which leads to making reasoned affective connections to place while considering ways to take informed action in a community.

> The National Council of Geography Education's 17 standards are embedded in the six essential elements. Check out the standards here!
>
> https://ncge.org/teacher-resources/national-geography-standards/

According to Beverly Tatum (2017), who wrote the consequential book *Why do all the Black kids sit together in the cafeteria?*, identity is a complex term that refers to how people's concepts of who they are as individuals and members of a group are shaped by "individual characteristics, family dynamics, historical factors, and social and political contexts" (p. 9). Facing History and Ourselves (2021) has a great article geared towards history and ELA teachers that addresses the multiple types of identity. Social identity refers to how someone's sense of self is based on membership to a group based on aspects such as race, nationality, ethnicity, religion, and sexual orientation. Likewise, Facing History and Ourselves defines personal identity depends how someone defines themselves based on their beliefs. Identity rarely is static; it can evolve and change over the course of a lifetime based upon several factors such as a person's upbringing, movement from place to place, academic studies, hobbies, and relationships.

Researchers Aurore Marcouyeux and Ghozlane Fleury-Bahi (2011) state in their article in *Environment and Behavior* that "an individual's personal identity is built in relation to his or her physical environment, much like his or her social identity is built in relation to his or her belonging to social categories" (p. 345). Specific to PBE, *place identity* is "multidimensional" that is shaped by a person's attachment, dependence, and interactions in various environments (Marcouyeux & Fleury-Bahi, 2011, p. 347). Since identity is shaped by a person's experiences and perspectives on place, teachers need consider how students' identities, as well as their own, can impact their engagement in PBE to promote historical empathy. We cannot take for granted that all students will have an affective connection or intellectual curiosity to their school or the community where they live. Students may be new to a neighborhood, state, or even the country.

Additionally, some students may have negative experiences or beliefs attributed to a place based on trauma, hard histories, or economic downturn. As a result, teachers who plan and implement PBE as a way to foster historical empathy through CBL must immerse themselves into critical reflection of who they are and their biases and perspectives of the environments that they interact with, especially if they do not live where they teach by implementing an assets-based approach to local history, historical empathy, and culturally responsive, relevant, and sustaining pedagogies that affirm linguistic, racial, ethnic, gender, religious, and other forms of identity that is formed by one's relationship to a place. *Culturally-relevant pedagogy* is the appreciation of students' cultural backgrounds through sharing experiences and drawing upon students' prior knowledge. *Culturally-responsive* pedagogy refers to accepting and affirming students' identities through promoting critical consciousness with the content resources used for instruction. *Culturally-sustaining pedagogy* refers to how the multicultural and linguistic heritages and values of students of color are cultured, nurtured, and centered in curriculum. Check out Dr. Altheria Caldera's (2021) article from the Intercultural Development Research Association, which is listed in the chapter's references, is an important resource to support how teachers can promote historical empathy through engagement in these strategies that connect to students' assets, backgrounds, interests, and prior knowledge.

Connections to Historical Empathy

Making strong connections to students' identities, place identities, and communities are pivotal in effectively implement PBE when promoting historical empathy by 1) identifying historical contexts of the past, 2) examining how historical contexts shape multiple perspectives from the past, and 3) making reasoned affective connections to the past to take informed action in the present. While engaging students in outdoor environments is a hallmark of PBE, sometimes physical travel and taking time to go outside is not possible for all teachers. Katie remembers as a high school student after 9/11 that all field trips local and abroad stopped due to the impact of the terror attacks on concerns over public safety, as well as the impact on air travel. Likewise, the COVID-19 pandemic, which has increased attention to the importance of PBE in the wake of school lockdowns, has also impacted funding and ability for students and teachers to go visit sites. Gregory A. Smith and David Sobel (2010) highlight in their book *Place and community-based education in schools* five misconceptions about PBE that include adding more to a teacher's curriculum, disguising environmental education as PBE, and that PBE is more applicable for rural schools (p. ix). The persistent issue of time constraints regarding scheduling trips when balancing the demands of pacing guides, curricular standards, and standardized testing also makes PBE difficult for many teachers and students. These are real issues that present challenges to doing PBE. However, we hope that these challenges can be leveraged not as obstacles to promoting historical empathy with PBE, but as opportunities for teachers to be creative in connecting place to what they teach in ELA and social studies.

There are a variety of brick-and-mortar and digital opportunities that teachers can choose from that can engage students in PBE. For example, if travel is not possible, teachers can start with their school buildings where students are asked to consider the historical contexts of when and why their school was built, and even who the building is named after, the different perspectives that are reflected in the school's history, and how students' affective responses to researching the history of their school can lead them to taking informed action in their school community. When Katie taught U.S. history in Brooklyn, she did a small local history project where students researched who their school was named after. Using *The New York Times* search engine and the Library of Congress' Chronicling America database, students were able to find out that their school was named after a former principal of the school and president of the Principal's Association in New York City who was involved with the Teacher's Association to deal with issues of theft of faculty and staff personal belongings in schools (*New York Tribune*, 1908, p. 4; New York Tribune, 1907, p. 4). From that cursory investigation, Katie went on to partner with the Brooklyn Public Library, and even take students to visit the Library's archive, to research the history of immigration in their neighborhood and what this history means to them as citizens of their community, as the area in Brooklyn where Katie taught was historically a melting pot of European, Asian, and Latinx immigrants. Some students had their projects put on display at the main branch of the Brooklyn Public Library in Grand Army Plaza to showcase their research. This example is one way in which PBE can be done on a very local scale where connecting community history and assets to the standards in the 8th grade curriculum in order to engage students in making relevant and reasoned affective connections to what they were learning and the significance of local history on their daily lives.

In another PBE project, Katie worked with colleagues to plan a unit on how the history of baseball in Brooklyn connected to the 8th grade standards in math, ELA, science, and social studies. Students in Katie's class mapped out where baseball stadiums were located throughout the city, such as the Polo Grounds and Ebbet's Field, then read excerpts from the book Baseball in Blue and Gray about how Civil War soldiers used to play baseball games in between battles. Later on that school year, Katie took the kids to Greenwood Cemetery to learn about the Civil War veterans who were buried just 15 blocks from their school. These PBE projects are examples of how local history investigations can be integrated into teaching standards when misconceptions about PBE cause logistical challenges for teachers.

Museums

Museums are an excellent place to plan PBE experiences for students when promoting historical empathy, especially as museum attendance is declining. According to a 2023 incidence report from the American Alliance of Museums, white and Asian Americans visited museums at higher rates as compared to African American and Latinx patrons (Wilkerson, 2023). These gaps raise questions about the extent to which museums are accessible to people and whether museums are meeting the needs of communities. In recent years, museum education has been at the forefront of adopting historical empathy strategies in their programming because of the concerns and debates over how to contextualize hard histories such as Confederate monuments throughout the United States. Moreover, museums in western nations in Europe and the United States have undergone scrutiny over the repatriation of artifacts that were stolen or obtained during times of colonization from marginalized groups around the world. The shift to implementing historical empathy strategies in museum programming has been in response to these issues, as well as evaluating how their programming meets the needs of teachers, schools, and communities. As a result, the following suggestions of museums to utilize as PBE resources are not exhaustive, but representative on how large and small institutions can be critical supports of PBE when promoting historical empathy in ELA and social studies.

The Smithsonian and Smithsonian Affiliates

The Smithsonian Institution boasts on its website that it is the "world's largest museum, education, and research complex" that is made of 21 museums, the National Zoo, the Smithsonian gardens, and a multitude of affiliate institutions that includes the Air and Space Museum, the National Portrait Gallery, and the Museums of American History, African American History and Culture, Latino History, and Native American History. The American Women's History Museum is in the process of being built and contains many digital exhibits and educational resources. Although there is not a dedicated American museum for Asian American and Pacific Islander history, the Smithsonian Asian Pacific American Center (APAC) offers public programming in collaboration with other Smithsonian museums and affiliates.

The Smithsonian, which was founded in 1846 by British scientist James Smithson, provides "vast digital resources" and physical exhibits for research, teaching, and public interest pertaining to science, the arts, history, and culture. Among the artifacts that the Smithsonian houses span from the ruby slippers from *The Wizard of Oz*, Lincoln's stove pipe hat, and "Old Glory" flag from the War of 1812. Museum educators and staff provide blogs, podcasts, and mobile apps that are geared towards adult and youth audiences, as well as in-person programming for trips and PBE opportunities. If a trip to Washington D.C. is not possible, either for schools that are near the metropolitan area or schools that are far away, there are Smithsonian affiliates in all 50 states across the United States. Museums and historical sites can apply for Smithsonian affiliation in rural, urban, and suburban areas. These affiliates are invaluable resources to communities and schools to highlight local history and culture.

Arts and Science Museums

There are so many famous museums that offer free admission or group rates for school groups to visit. PBE with connections to earth science and history content are endless at this or any natural history museum that may be near where you live and teach! Many times, museums like the American Museum of Natural History in New York, the Franklin Institute in Philadelphia, and the Fernbank Museum in Atlanta highlight exhibits that focus on human-environment interactions that can align and support geography and science standards. Moreover, places like the Metropolitan Museum of Art in New York City, the Indianapolis Museum of Art Galleries, and the Philadelphia Art Museum are home to famous paintings such as Picassos, sculptures, and folk art of local communities. ELA teachers may find numerous connections to pieces of art to literature in the middle and secondary curriculum.

> You can visit the sites to these major natural history and art museums!
> Philadelphia Museum of Art, Philadelphia, PA: https://philamuseum.org
> Franklin Institute, Philadelphia, PA: https://fi.edu/en
>
> Metropolitan Museum of Art, New York, NY: https://www.metmuseum.org
>
> Indianapolis Museum of Art Galleries at Newfields, Indianapolis, IN: https://discovernewfields.org/do-and-see/places-to-go/indianapolis-museum-art
>
> American Museum of Natural History, New York NY: https://www.amnh.org
>
> Fernbank Museum of Natural History, Atlanta, GA: https://www.fernbankmuseum.org

There are also many military museums whose exhibits and programming are interdisciplinary by connecting to the arts, history, and science on a national and local level. For instance, the USS Intrepid in New York City focuses its educational programming on explorations of the aquatic habitats of the Hudson River. Over the past few decades, many military museums have broadened their focus beyond specific battles and branches of the military history to include diverse experiences and perspectives about the human, political, economic, and environmental toll of war. John F. Votaw (1994) states in an article in *Teaching History: A Journal of Methods* that the Catigny First Division Foundation created an immersive experience for visitors "'inside' the story and surrounds them with recreations of historical locations, artifacts, photographs, battle noise, soldiers' conversations, and lighting effects-all intended to reproduce the sensations of being a witness to historic events (p. 66).

The World War II American Experience Museum in Gettysburg, Pennsylvania has vehicles, artifacts, and stories of civilians from around the country about their experiences on the home front, Japanese Theatre, and European Theatre during the war. The expansive focus of military museums connects to PBE and historical empathy due to the inclusion of diverse perspectives about the experience of war, and how wars contributed to technological innovation, democratic movements, as well as consequential changes war causes environmentally, politically, psychologically, and emotionally, especially for the nation's veterans and soldiers who perished in battle.

There are many military museums whose exhibits and programming are interdisciplinary by connecting to the arts, history, and science on the national and state levels. Check out these museums' resources for in-person visits and digital resources!

- WWII Museum, New Orleans, LA: https://www.nationalww2museum.org
- WWII American Experience Museum, Gettysburg, PA: https://visitww2.org
- Air Force Museum, Dayton, Ohio: https://www.nationalmuseum.af.mil
- USS Albacore Museum, Portsmouth, NH: https://www.ussalbacore.org/education
- USS Midway Museum, San Diego, CA: https://www.midway.org
- USS Intrepid Museum, New York, NY: https://intrepidmuseum.org

Halls of Fame

Other museums that can support PBE and historical empathy instruction are sports, music, and cultural halls of fame. Halls of fame are critical places that teachers can engage students in not only experiencing exhibits, but also exploring critical questions such as who gets to be honored in these places. In May 2024, Major League Baseball (MLB) included the records of Negro League players in the official statistics of the MLB. The National Baseball Hall of Fame in Cooperstown, New York not only honors the history of the game and its pivotal players, broadcasters, and umpires, but also the historical contexts in which the game evolved into the "nation's pastime."

Additionally, the Rock and Roll Hall of Fame and Museum (RRHFM) is an important place in American music history as Cleveland, Ohio was where the term "rock and roll" was first coined by radio DJ's in the 1950s. Originally founded in 1988 and opening with its current location in 1996, the RRHFM's exhibits span from women in rock, to the Black gospel and rhythm and blues influences on British and American rock and pop music from the 1950s-1960s, to the 50th anniversary of hip hop (see Chapter 3 on Music!). To list every museum, cultural center, or hall of fame that can be a site for PBE would be exhaustive. We hope that our suggestions are a starting point to think about not only larger institutions that may be accessible to where you teach, but also to consider smaller regional or local museums that can support your instructional needs when engaging students in historical empathy.

Check out some of these music and cultural halls of fame throughout the US that have great primary and secondary sources that can support promoting historical empathy through place-based visits!
- Rock and Roll Hall of Fame and Museum, Cleveland, OH: https://rockhall.com
- Country Music Hall of Fame, Nashville, TN: https://www.countrymusichalloffame.org
- American Classical Music Hall of Fame and Museum, Cincinnati, OH: https://classicalwalkoffame.org
- National Radio Hall of Fame and Museum of Broadcast Communications, Chicago, IL: https://www.radiohalloffame.com
- Television Hall of Fame, Los Angeles, CA: https://www.emmys.com/awards/hall-of-fame
- Hip Hop Hall of Fame and Museum, New York, NY https://hiphophof.org

CHAPTER 6

Virtual Museums and Online Exhibits

Not every museum or hall of fame has a physical location. The concept of *virtual museums* arose during the 1980s and 1990s when personal computers and use of floppy disks, and later CD-ROMs, could run programs that reach diverse and expansive audiences. Katie remembers enjoying researching topics using Microsoft Encarta on her family's one desktop computer when she was middle school from 1995-1998. With the internet and improved digitalization technologies that aided in museum cataloging and creating archival finding aids that made physical objects accessible to visitors. Museum scholar Werner Schweibenz (2019) notes that the use of these technologies raised important questions regarding whether museums should only focus on physical objects, or if the museum itself is a larger microcosm of information dissemination that includes physical and digital objects. As a result, many brick-and-mortar museums established virtual exhibits that have grown into educational and public programming with virtual field trips, lectures and webinars, and professional development. Furthermore, other museums emerged as completely virtual spaces to promote widespread reach and to distinguish themselves from location-bound museums.

For instance, the National Women's History Museum (NWHM), which was founded in 1996, reaches "more than five million visitors each year" with its online exhibits, professional development workshops, public programming, and virtual field trips that aim at "uncovering, interpreting, and celebrating women's diverse contributions to society." Available online exhibits are organized by theme that include topics such as Women at NASA and a timeline of the Women's Suffrage Movement. Virtual field trips and guest speakers can be scheduled with an educator that can be tailored to the local needs of students and schools across the country. This virtual museum also has some place-based offerings in Washington D.C. such as a walking tour of Black feminist history and its Glass Ceiling Breaker exhibit at the Martin Luther King, Jr. Memorial Library.

If domestic or international travel is not possible, virtual visits to museums around the world are widely available. The Smithsonian, Library of Congress, National Archives, and Metropolitan Museum of Art all have extensive online exhibits and virtual offerings for PBE-oriented programming and research for school groups. The Louvre and The British Museum have vast online exhibits and programming that can connect to world literature, global history, geography, and global politics. The Frida Kahlo Museum in Mexico City takes visitors through her home, gardens, and self-portraits. The National Museum of Modern and Contemporary Art in South Korea takes visitors on immersive tours of the gardens and art from 1900 through the 21st century, including an interactive experience using Google Street View on how the building was transformed from a tobacco factory to Korea's first repository for art. The National Museum of the Democratic Republic of Congo has online exhibits in French or English that showcase indigenous games, musical instruments, masks, clothing, and tools. Visitors can virtually "walk" through the rooms to see the artifacts that are encased at the museum with captions.

> Check out the virtual exhibits, tours, and field trips offered by museums across the world!
> - Frida Kahlo Museum- https://www.museofridakahlo.org.mx/virtual/?lang=en
> - Korean Art Museum- https://artsandculture.google.com/partner/national-museum-of-modern-and-contemporary-art-korea?hl=en
> - The L'Ouvre- https://www.louvre.fr/en/online-tours
> - The British Museum- https://www.britishmuseum.org/british-museum-home
> - The National Museum of the Democratic Republic of Congo- https://matterport.com/discover/space/4BTkUBHpKiJ

Historical Societies, Libraries, and Cultural Centers

Historical Societies, Libraries, and Cultural Centers

Historical societies, libraries, and cultural centers, which sometimes have their own museums, tend to focus more on local communities and regions, which may be more accessible to support PBE in ELA and social studies when fostering historical empathy with students. All 50 states have state historical societies, but there are hundreds of regional and local societies that focus on micro histories of local communities that pertain to the general history of a place or specific topics that are significant to a place. Like the function of a museum, historical societies are typically non-profit organizations that specialize in collecting and archiving artifacts of a community's history that can be accessed by the public or professional researchers. The Massachusetts Historical Society (MHS) is the nation's oldest of these types of institutions that was founded in 1791. New York Historical Society (NYHS), located in Manhattan, is dedicated to being an archive, research repository, and exhibit space pertaining to New York history. The Georgia Historical Society, which is in Savannah, is a major repository of community events, teacher workshops, and school programming that focuses on Georgia throughout its five major geographic areas- the mountains, piedmont, coastal plains, and

Often, historical societies collaborate with other local institutions when locating, preserving, and making artifacts accessible to the public. For instance, library branches, such as the as well as university libraries, (especially if they offer access to the local community where a campus is located), also serve as vital places for not only accessing materials for reading pleasure, but also as meeting spaces for class trips, community workshops, meetings, and research. The Chicago Public Library system, like many other library systems, offer free passes for families to check out to visit museums or other cultural sites that require a fee for entry. Moreover, some of its community partnerships include YOUmedia, which provides library and studio space for teens at various libraries, high schools, and middle schools to "create [their] own music, video, 2D and 3D design, photos and podcasts with the help from skilled mentors."

Cultural centers are like historical societies and museums because they have exhibits, archival materials, and programming and community outreach opportunities. These places differ from museums and historical societies because these cultural centers are built specifically to host and facilitate performances, film screenings, art classes, and other opportunities for community gatherings to learn about a particular culture. The Polynesian Cultural Center in Oahu is an immersive place where visitors learn about native cultures, histories, and heritages of Hawai'i, including a traditional luau dinner with performances from native dancers and musicians. Additionally, some botanical gardens, which are planned intentionally for conservation, research, and educational purposes, are operated as part of larger cultural centers, historical societies, and museums. The Missouri Botanical Garden, which was established 150 years ago, offers several educational programming options that focus on plant adaptations, rainforest ecology, interdisciplinary math and science curricular kits and teaching resources, interpretive centers, and tours of the Tower Grove House that was built in 1889. Botanical gardens, called "museums without walls" by the Smithsonian, as well as cultural centers, are wonderful places to introduce students to local ecology, as well as PBE opportunities that can promote historical empathy by connecting global awareness to the diversity of cultures, plants, and wildlife around the country and world.

LINKS TO HISTORICAL SOCIETIES AND BOTANICAL GARDENS

- Missouri Botanical Gardens, St. Louis, MO: https://www.missouribotanicalgarden.org
- Smithsonian National Garden, Washington, D.C: https://www.si.edu/museums/smithsonian-gardens

- Snug Harbor Cultural Center and Botanical Garden, Staten Island, NY: https://snug-harbor.org
- New York Historical Society, New York NY: https://www.nyhistory.org
- Georgia Historical Society, Savannah, GA: https://www.georgiahistory.com/teachers-and-students/resources-for-teachers/
- Polynesian Cultural Center, Oahu, HI: https://www.polynesia.com
- Massachusetts Historical Society, Boston, MA: https://www.masshist.org/education

Conservation Centers, Parks, and Historical Sites

Although not all PBE is explicitly CBL, the place-based offerings of nature centers, science centers, and conservation centers can also serve as important places to engage students in historical empathy. Science has many strong interdisciplinary connections to ELA and social studies. For instance, the works of Thoreau can be read to glean insights about early 19th-century industrialization, citizenship, and nature both in literature and in historical contexts, and lay a foundation for students to do ecological studies on topics such as forest secession phases. Historical empathy can be woven through these PBE activities as students explore the historical contexts of natural environments and the perspectives of community members and stakeholders involved in preservation to make reasoned affective connections to how and why environmental studies are important aspects of PBE and how citizens make informed decisions when evaluating community issues such as land preservation versus development.

Nature Conservancies

Nature conservancies, which are typically non-profit organizations, are strategic partners with municipal and state governments to preserve parks, historical sites, and monuments that can be sites for PBE investigations and projects that can promote historical empathy. For instance, nature conservancies throughout the five boroughs of New York work in partnership with the New York City Parks and Recreation Department and the Gateway National Recreation areas to provide educational programming for schools and the public throughout the city's various forests, lakes, and beaches. Another example of a partnership between non-profit organizations and publicly funded parks, monuments, and historical sites is the Boston Freedom Trail (BFT). The BFT began as an effort between the city of Boston and residents in 1953 to protect buildings from development. Later, the National Parks, and the Freedom Trail Foundation joined this effort that resulted in a 2.5-mile walking path that highlights several historical sites to Massachusetts and U.S. history. Some of the significant places on the BFT include Paul Revere's House, the Old North Church, and the USS Constitution. The BFT's educational resources are expansive that include both in-person school trips, virtual programs, and distance learning resources to engage students in local history research and the American Revolution.

Zoos and Aquariums

Zoos and aquariums can be important places where students can engage in historical empathy through PBE investigations of local plant and animal wildlife that connect to topics such as globalization to interdisciplinary social studies, ELA, and science learning. San Diego Zoo Wildlife Alliance, which includes the iconic San Diego Zoo. has a multitude of science education curricular materials for in-person or virtual visits. Specifically, their "Take Action" site highlights ways in which people can make "small changes" to address issues such as ocean pollution and illegal trafficking of animals. Teachers can guide students through research on these issues to examine the origins of these problems, impact of these problems on plants, animals, humans, and environments, and how signing petitions, making informed decisions on where food and material objects are produced, reusing or recycling items, and reducing waste by shutting off lights when not in a room.

The Georgia Aquarium, which is the largest aquarium in the United States and fourth largest in the world, is a major conservation and research center that services marine locations in the Southeast. In addition to its virtual, community outreach, and in-person educational programming that incorporates conservation, marine science, and STEAM topics, the Georgia Aquarium also focuses on marine life rehabilitation and veterinary research. For instance, the Georgia Aquarium acquired Marineland, which was founded in 1938 near St. Augustine, Florida, as a location for dolphin care, rehabilitation, and education. Today, Marineland provides in-person programming, community outreach opportunities, and homeschooling resources to support PBE concerning the cultural history of Marineland as a film studio and conservation center that services the Atlantic coast in northern Florida.

National Parks and Monuments

The National Parks Service (NPS), founded in 1916, aims at caring for and safeguarding "these special places and share their stories with more than 318 million visitors every year." As part of the U.S. Department of the Interior, the NPS's mission explicitly connects both with PBE, CBL, and historical empathy due to its partnerships with "tribes, local governments, nonprofit organizations, businesses, and individual citizens [who] ask for our help in revitalizing their communities, preserving local history, celebrating local heritage, and creating close-to-home opportunities for kids and families to get outside, be active, and have fun." There are currently 64 national parks, which are part of the 400 sites that make up the NPS that include monuments, battlefields, forts, forests, beaches, heritage areas, and other significant natural and historical places throughout the country. The NPS has a mission to not only protect the nation's largest parks, but to work and collaborate with local communities to support preservation and PBE through service learning, civic engagement, and historical empathy.

Accessing the resources the NPS have on historical preservation and civic engagement can support authentic PBE and CBL instruction that supports historical empathy. For example, NPS has an entire section on their website titled "Teaching with Historical Places" (TwHP) that contains lesson plans and "curiosity kits" of articles and teaching strategies relating to important and topics in U.S. history such as Black Baseball History and Women Labor Activists. Additionally, the TwHP includes resources for teachers who are interested in participating in National History Day, research tips for student and teachers on how to use the National Register of Historic Places (Orr, 2018), and a Teacher Portal that contains a searchable list of lesson plans written by teachers that connect local communities across the country to the national parks, historical sites, and monuments.

Here are some of the NPS' website that contains educator resources including manuals and how-to guides on how to plan and teach CLB and PBE learning opportunities that promote historical empathy in local communities.
- Learning to Make Choices in the Future, by Delia Clark: https://www.nps.gov/civic/resources/2865_MBR_PBL_Book%20FINAL.pdf
- Benefits of Place-Based Education: A Report from the Place-Based Education Evaluation Collaborative, 2nd edition: https://www.nps.gov/civic/resources/PEEC2010_web.pdf
- Teaching with Historical Places (main page to additional sources): https://www.nps.gov/subjects/teachingwithhistoricplaces/index.htm
- Main NPS Page of Educator Resources (includes professional development, lesson plans, and field experiences information): https://www.nps.gov/teachers/index.htm

To even begin highlighting examples of national parks and associated sites here to facilitate PBE to promote historical empathy is a daunting task. For instance, examining the historical contexts of the formation of the Grand Canyon either with an in-person or virtual trip can lead to students' examination of life of the Navajo and native peoples in northern Arizona before and after the park was established in order to examine not only affective responses to the natural and cultural history of the Grand Canyon, but how students and the public can engage in informed action by raising awareness to the natural and historical splendor and significance of the native people, fauna, and flora of the Grand Canyon on the nation. However, if physically traveling to the Grand Canyon is not possible, you can browse the NPS site to find natural and historical sites that may be located near where you live and teach.

State Parks

State parks are also valuable resources to support PBE and historical empathy. Sometimes state parks get a bad rap as being inferior to the NPS. However, the thousands of state parks throughout the United States boast awe-inspiring canyons, coral reefs, waterfalls, mountains, and hiking trials. These places are home to not only stunning environmental and ecological science investigations, but also archaeological, sociological, and historical studies in local communities throughout the country. You can look up state parks using the List of Places site for all 50 states. This site also assists with searches of national parks in the United States and Canada.

State parks are critical to the economic, social, and cultural wellbeing of citizens and residents of states. According to the National Association of State Park Directors, there are over 9,000 state parks that welcome over 800 million visitors annually. Many state parks offer educational resources that support teachers and students' PBE with field trips and community outreach events that focus on civic engagement, historical preservation, and ecological and scientific discovery. For example, Picacho State Park in Arizona is the site of the Civil War battle that was fought farthest west. This state park offers geological tours and as well as self-guided youth activities that can lead to earning a Junior Ranger badge. The Great Salt Lake and Antelope State Park in Utah provide online resources for requested field trips, self-guided tours, and volunteer groups to engage in wetland exploration, and studying the prehistoric ecological history of the lake. Teachers can also check out a free toolbox to teach lessons about the beaches of the Great Salt Lake. Niagara Falls State Park is the oldest state park in the country that offers several PBE and field trip opportunities for on-site visits that include riding on the Maid of the Mist and visiting the aquarium to learn about the native fish and wildlife of western New York. The state parks play an important role in being stewards of natural and historic preservation in local communities.

> The U.S. Forest Service is part of the U.S. Department of Agriculture. See their sites for educational and conservation resources that can support teaching to promote historical empathy through place-based learning!
>
> https://www.fs.usda.gov/learn/educators
>
> https://www.fs.usda.gov/learn/conservation-education

Historical Sites and Markers

Historical sites and markers are other valuable places that PBE and CBL can take place that supports promoting historical empathy. Some of these sites are operated by federal, state, and local agencies with the purpose of landmarking places that bear historical significance to a local community. For instance, the National Register of Historic Places contains over 87,000 entries of places that meet the criteria for being designated a historical place that are to be preserved. Historical markers can be official signs or plaques on buildings or monuments. According to an NPR article, anyone can erect a historical marker, which has led to serious issues regarding historical inaccuracies of names and dates of events, the spread of discriminatory troupes, and outright lies about historical claims such as where anesthesia was discovered (Sullivan & McMillan, 2024). As a result, there are probably thousands of markers that claim a place to be of historical significance without much historical corroboration or evidence. J.J Pratts started the historical marker database in 2006 that is crowdsourced with photos and locations of historical markers across the country. As a result, museums, institutions, and historical societies have started their own marker programs to commemorate significant historical events and people in local communities.

The debates over the contextualization of the history of monuments and underrepresentation of marking the histories of marginalized people and groups throughout the U.S. highlights how place identity is very influential on how people can demonstrate historical empathy, especially regarding informed action and making reasoned affective connections in a civil manner. For instance, the Atlanta History Center's documentary *Monument* about the history of Stone Mountain, Georgia highlights the very real discussion of how, and whether, Confederate monuments should be preserved. Alabama and Michigan have state initiatives to erect new markers to honor underrepresented histories. The Washington State Historical Society is re-assessing and re-evaluating existing markers to broaden its inclusion of the diversity of the state (Chapman, 2023). Engaging students in PBE by critically examining historical markers and interpretations of historical sites can be a powerful exercise in historical empathy through conducting inquiry of primary and secondary sources about a place to actively participate in conversation and civic discourse on how groups determine what places and people are deemed significant, and what are appropriate and respectful ways to honor those places and people.

> Here are some resources on historical markers, contextualizing monuments, and locating historical places near you:
> - Smithsonian Magazine: https://www.smithsonianmag.com/history/why-historical-markers-matter-180982833/
> - National Parks Service: https://www.nps.gov/articles/prominent-places-for-historic-places-k-12-social-studies-curriculum.htm
> - Historical Markers Database: https://www.hmdb.org/about.asp
> - Texas Historical Commission: https://thc.texas.gov/preserve/preservation-programs/historical-markers
> - Florida Division of Historical Resources: https://dos.fl.gov/historical/preservation/historical-markers/
> - Monument: The Untold Story of Stone Mountain, Atlanta History Center- https://www.atlantahistorycenter.com/monument/
> - Georgia Historical Society Historical Markers Program: https://www.georgiahistory.com/teaching-with-the-georgia-historical-marker-program/
> - Monument Lab, Philadelphia: https://monumentlab.com/

Perspective recognition of different insights, thoughts, values, and beliefs **is not** condoning bad acts and excusing, or even sympathizing, with bad actions committed by past and present actors (Endacott & Brooks, 2018). Rather, engaging students in the process of historical empathy through the analysis of the historical contexts and perspectives expressed on historical markers, monuments, and other landmarks on historical sites can show how history is not static, but fluid, and that over time, individuals and groups learned that actions that were once considered acceptable are no longer in alignment with a community's values. Addressing these sensitive issues can put teachers in very precarious situations, especially if someone lives and teaches in a state where "anti-divisive concepts" laws curb, hinder, or prohibit teaching topics such as gender or race that can be considered polarizing and harmful to children.

Some museums, parks, monuments, and markers are strategically located on or near places with very difficult pasts that have led to generational trauma, economic and political instability, and serious social issues. As a result, teachers need to be extra diligent in planning PBE connections to standards if a visit to a place has connections to hard histories or controversial issues in history and contemporary times. For instance, the Birmingham Civil Rights Museum Institute, which is part of the Civil Rights National Memorial and Smithsonian Institute, is located down the street from the church where four Black girls were murdered when white men bombed the church in 1964. The Memorial for Peace and Justice, which is part of the Civil Rights Trail of the African American Freedom Movement throughout the Southeast, is a somber place commemorating Black men and women who were lynched. The memorial is part of the Montgomery Legacy Sites where visitors are asked to "with our history of racial injustice in places where that history lived. Almost 20 years ago, Katie took a group of 8th grade students to the Jewish Heritage Museum in lower Manhattan on a class trip to learn more about the global implications of the Holocaust. Even almost 20 years ago, she had to make sure that permission slips or consent forms sent to parents informed them that the kids might see disturbing images during their visit.

While we do not propose that these places should not be avoided, care needs to go into planning a trip to a museum whose exhibits may trigger trauma, cause discomfort, or inflame beliefs. For example, students may have family members who are war veterans or who died in combat. Without venturing into the argument of "trigger warnings," we support the notion that teachers should always be cognizant of the students and communities where they teach to plan PBE opportunities that foster learning and historical empathy that affirm and inform students, not harm them.

Connections to Standards

The rich connections between social studies, ELA, and other academic standards can make designing a PBE lesson or curricular unit that focuses on promoting historical empathy exciting! So many of the examples in this chapter deal with science education, particularly because of the ways the Six Essential Themes of Geography align with teaching environmental science, biology, ELA, history, and geography. As a result, we include connections to the Next Generation Science Standards (NGSS) in this sample lesson plan to support teachers whose goals of implementing PBE are to promote historical empathy through connections to science education.

NCTE Standards and PBE

The NCTE Standards for ELA address and support PBE to promote historical empathy in curriculum and instruction in several ways. The Language and Literacy Interactive Model connects with the goals of PBE and historical empathy with its three components—1) the purpose or why language is used, 2) the development of how language and literacy strategies are applied to daily life, and 3) the content that students should learn through multiple texts that are grounded in "personal knowledge, to schooling or technical knowledge, or to social or community knowledge" (NCTE, 2020, p. 10). In particular, NCTE (2020) states that "Literary works are valuable not just as informative or communicative vehicles, but as artistic creations and representations of human culture at particular times and in particular places... They show how individuals discover the significance of inner experience, social life, and history as they find their place in the world" (pp. 21-22). Major NCTE standards that support with PBE to promote historical empathy in ELA and social studies include, but are certainly not limited to:

These selected standards address the connections to PBE and CBL through examination of fiction and non-fiction resources pertaining to periods in literary history, explanatory texts, and works of literature that connect to citizenship, nature, and history. These texts that can foster historical empathy by connecting students' affective responses to content learned through examination of how historical contexts shape the perspectives of the authors who produce these texts.

NCSS C3 Framework and PBE

The C3 Framework have many strong connections to PBE relating to geography, civics and government, and history standards. Specifically, Dimension 2: Geography states that "each place on earth has a unique set of local conditions and connections to other places...Events in one place influence events in other places" (p. 40). Additionally, Dimension 2: Geography emphasizes the importance of geographical reasoning because these skills "brings societies and nature under the lens of spatial analysis, and aids in personal and societal decision making and problem solving" (p. 40). The prominence of place and its role in historical, political, economic, and geographic inquiry is evident throughout the C3 Framework Inquiry Arc as a way to engage students historical empathy through PBE strategies.

Next Generation Standards and PBE

The NGSS (2012) are designed to "give local educators the flexibility to design classroom learning experiences that stimulate students' interests in science and prepares them for college, careers, and citizenship." According to the Committee

Table 6.1 NCTE ELA Standards Connections to Place-Based Education and Historical Empathy

Standard	Description
1	Students read a wide range of print and nonprint texts to build an understanding of texts, of themselves, and of the cultures of the United States and the world; to acquire new information; to respond to the needs and demands of society and the workplace; and for personal fulfillment. Among these texts are fiction and nonfiction, classic and contemporary works (p. 19).
2	Students read a wide range of literature from many periods in many genres to build an understanding of the many dimensions (e.g., philosophical, ethical, aesthetic) of human experience (p. 21).
5	Students employ a wide range of strategies as they write and use different writing process elements appropriately to communicate with different audiences for a variety of purposes (p. 25).
7	Students conduct research on issues and interests by generating ideas and questions, and by posing problems. They gather, evaluate, and synthesize data from a variety of sources (e.g., print and nonprint texts, artifacts, people) to communicate their discoveries in ways that suit their purpose and audience (p. 27).
11	Students participate as knowledgeable, reflective, creative, and critical members of a variety of literacy communities (p. 31).

on a Conceptual for New K-12 Science Standards, "there is much work to be done to address the role of these sciences in the development of an informed 21st-century citizen" (p. 14). Through its three-pronged framework of core disciplinary ideas, crosscutting concepts, and practices, the NGSS are geared towards promoting interdisciplinary literacy among the sciences, as well as with math and engineering. Complementary to the goals of the NCTE Standards and C3 Framework, the NGSS high school standard *LS2D: Social Interactions and Group Behavior* support interdisciplinary instruction to promote historical empathy in ELA and social studies.

Sample Lesson Plan

Like our previous chapters, we use the IDBM template for our sample lesson plan so that teachers can adapt these skills, strategies, and activities for one or multiple days of instruction. This lesson plan focuses on the immediate classroom and school environment in order to meet the needs of teachers who may take instruction outside or to place-based settings or those who not able to engage in outdoor teaching and learning experiences. We hope that you find connections to previous chapters, especially with literary analysis from Chapter 1 and use of digital media in Chapter 2, to support analysis of Paul Revere as

Table 6.2 C3 Framework Connections to PBE and Historical Empathy

Inquiry Arc Dimension	Standard
1	D1.5.9-12. Determine the kinds of sources that will be helpful in answering compelling and supporting questions, taking into consideration multiple points of view represented in the sources, the types of sources available, and the potential uses of the sources. (p. 25)
2	D2.Civ.10.9-12. Analyze the impact and the appropriate roles of personal interests and perspectives on the application of civic virtues, democratic principles, constitutional rights, and human rights. (p. 33)
2	D2.Civ.14.9-12. Analyze historical, contemporary, and emerging means of changing societies, promoting the common good, and protecting rights. (p. 34)
2	D2.Eco.15.9-12. Explain how current globalization trends and policies affect economic growth, labor markets, rights of citizens, the environment, and resource and income distribution in different nations. (p. 39)
2	D2.Geo.2.9-12. Use maps, satellite images, photographs, and other representations to explain relationships between the locations of places and regions and their political, cultural, and economic dynamics. (p. 41)
2	D2.Geo.4.9-12. Analyze relationships and interactions within and between human and physical systems to explain reciprocal influences that occur among them. (p. 42)
2	D2.Geo.6.9-12. Evaluate the impact of human settlement activities on the environmental and cultural characteristics of specific places and regions. (p. 42)
2	D2.Geo.7.9-12. Analyze the reciprocal nature of how historical events and the spatial diffusion of ideas, technologies, and cultural practices have influenced migration patterns and the distribution of human population. (p. 43).
2	D2.Geo.10.9-12. Evaluate how changes in the environmental and cultural characteristics of a place or region influence spatial patterns of trade and land use. (p. 44)
2	D2.His.1.9-12. Evaluate how historical events and developments were shaped by unique circumstances of time and place as well as broader historical contexts. (p. 46)
2	D2.His.4.9-12. Analyze complex and interacting factors that influenced the perspectives of people during different historical eras. (p. 47)
2	D2.His.8.9-12. Analyze how current interpretations of the past are limited by the extent to which available historical sources represent perspectives of people at the time. (p. 47)
2	D2.His.11.9-12. Critique the usefulness of historical sources for a specific historical inquiry based on their maker, date, place of origin, intended audience, and purpose. (p. 48)

(Continued)

Table 6.2 (Continued)

Inquiry Arc Dimension	Standard
3	D3.1.9-12. Gather relevant information from multiple sources representing a wide range of views while using the origin, authority, structure, context, and corroborative value of the sources to guide the selection.(p. 54)
4	D4.7.9-12. Assess options for individual and collective action to address local, regional, and global problems by engaging in self-reflection, strategy identification, and complex causal reasoning. (p. 62)
4	D4.8.9-12. Apply a range of deliberative and democratic strategies and procedures to make decisions and take action in their classrooms, schools, and out-of-school civic contexts. (p. 62)

Table 6.3 Sample Next Generation Science Standards and ELA/SS PBE

Standard	Statement	Connection to Historical Empathy
HS-LS2-8.	Evaluate the evidence for the role of group behavior on individual and species' chances to survive and reproduce. [Clarification Statement: Emphasis is on: (1) distinguishing between group and individual behavior, (2) identifying evidence supporting the outcomes of group behavior, and (3) developing logical and reasonable arguments based on evidence. Examples of group behaviors could include flocking, schooling, herding, and cooperative behaviors such as hunting, migrating, and swarming.]	This standard focuses on how species evaluate their individual and group roles that can be consequential for survival. Although this lesson does not focus on the biological aspect of reproduction as a survival tactic, this standard supports the goals of this lesson because of the objectives of evaluating group and individual behaviors through examining evidence to communicate conclusions about historical significance and ecological impact

a historical and literary example for place-based inquiry to promote student demonstration of historical empathy.

Lesson Title: Paul Revere: Ordinary Person or Infamous Hero?

Grade Level: 9-12

Length of Time: 3-4 days

C3 Framework Inquiry Arc Dimension 1- Staging the Inquiry	
Big Idea	Bravery
Compelling Question	What makes someone brave?

C3 Framework Inquiry Arc Dimension 1- Staging the Inquiry	
Essential Understandings/ Rationale	The big idea and compelling question will support students' analysis of Paul Revere's role during the American Revolution though analysis of primary sources, secondary sources, and place-based research. Examination of bravery is the focus of this lesson in order for students to consider how someone can exhibit bravery, and how bravery can be a quality that leads communities to name places after a person.
Learning Targets	Students will be able to: 1) Identify Paul Revere's role in the American Revolution 2) Examine characteristics of bravery during the American Revolution with primary and secondary sources 3) Analyze how personality characteristics and historical contexts impact how and why a place is named after someone.
Supporting Questions	1) What was Paul Revere's role in the American Revolution? 2) How did the events of the American Revolution in Boston impact Paul Revere's actions? 3) Why was Paul Revere a significant person during the American Revolution? Was he brave or an ordinary citizen? 4) How do communities choose to name a place after a person?

Lesson Materials	
Featured Secondary Sources	• Longfellow, "Midnight Ride of Paul Revere" https://www.paulreverehouse.org/longfellows-poem/ • Map of colonial Massachusetts 1677, by National Geographic • Paul Revere biography, https://www.paulreverehouse.org/biography/
Featured Primary Sources	• The Bloody Massacre engraving, by Paul Revere • Paul Revere letter to Jeremy Belknap, https://www.masshist.org/database/viewer.php?item_id=99 • Map of Massachusetts Bay Colony, 1780* https://www.loc.gov/resource/g3760.ar088100/?r=0.327,0.211,0.354,0.153,0
Technology/ Media Sources	Paul Revere House website Boston Freedom Trail Virtual Experience MA Historical Society

Lesson Materials	
Other Materials and Supports	Notebooks, pens or pencils, guided imagery worksheet, KWL chart,

C3 Framework Inquiry Arc Dimension 2- Standards Connections	
C3 Framework Content Standard, Civics	D2.Civ.14.9-12. Analyze historical, contemporary, and emerging means of changing societies, promoting the common good, and protecting rights. (p. 34)
C3 Framework Content Standard, Geography	D2.Geo.7.9-12. Analyze the reciprocal nature of how historical events and the spatial diffusion of ideas, technologies, and cultural practices have influenced migration patterns and the distribution of human population. (p. 43).
C3 Framework Content Standard, History	D2.His.1.9-12. Evaluate how historical events and developments were shaped by unique circumstances of time and place as well as broader historical contexts. (p. 46)
C3 Framework Content Standard, History	D2.His.4.9-12. Analyze complex and interacting factors that influenced the perspectives of people during different historical eras. (p. 47)
NCTE Standard 1 for ELA	Students read a wide range of print and nonprint texts to build an understanding of texts, of themselves, and of the cultures of the United States and the world; to acquire new information; to respond to the needs and demands of society and the workplace; and for personal fulfillment. Among these texts are fiction and nonfiction, classic and contemporary works (p. 19).
NCTE Standard 2 for ELA	Students read a wide range of literature from many periods in many genres to build an understanding of the many dimensions (e.g., philosophical, ethical, aesthetic) of human experience (p. 21).
NCTE Standard 5 for ELA	Students employ a wide range of strategies as they write and use different writing process elements appropriately to communicate with different audiences for a variety of purposes (p. 25).
NGSS **HS-LS2-8**	Evaluate the evidence for the role of group behavior on individual and species' chances to survive and reproduce. [Clarification Statement: Emphasis is on: (1) distinguishing between group and individual behavior, (2) identifying evidence supporting the outcomes of group behavior, and (3) developing logical and reasonable arguments based on evidence. Examples of group behaviors could include flocking, schooling, herding, and cooperative behaviors such as hunting, migrating, and swarming.]

CHAPTER 6

	C3 Framework Inquiry Arc Dimension 3- Analyzing Source Evidence
Introduction/ Motivation	• Begin with a whole class discussion on what students think the term bravery means, and what characteristics or qualities a person who is a hero should have. Record responses on the board. • Segue into asking about who are some figures that come to mind when they think of heroes during the American Revolution. Answers can include, but are not limited to, George Washington, Marquis de LaFayette, Thomas Jefferson, Phyllis Wheatley, Betsy Ross, Benjamin Franklin, and Paul Revere. • Next, specifically focusing on Revere, ask students to complete a KWL chart to gauge what they know and want to know about Paul Revere. Instruct students to leave the L column blank. Have students turn and talk to share their responses, and then record student responses for the K and W columns on the board. { table: Know | Want to Know | Learned }
Teacher Direct Instruction	• Teacher will ask the class, "how do you think where the colonists lived impacted their role in the American Revolution?" Students may give answers that include a person's location to places with tensions like Boston and New York could impact their roles. • Teacher will give a brief mini-lesson introducing Revere's biography, giving the class context to his life before and during the American Revolution as a craftsman in Massachusetts. Use of the National Geographic Map of colonial Massachusetts will be shown to illustrate places that were integral to Revere's life in relation to the American Revolution. • Teacher will distribute copies of the 1773 Revere engraving "The Bloody Massacre." Students will examine the engraving for objects they see, people they observe, actions being depicted, words, and overall intent and message of the engraving by Revere. Teacher will have students discuss how Revere's location and relation to place (Boston) impacted his perspectives of the events of the Boston Massacre. • Next, teacher will read aloud Longworth's poem "The Midnight Ride of Paul Revere." Students will complete the guided imagery graphic organizer by recording their interpretations, feelings, and reactions to the people, places, and events in the poem.

What might you see?	What might you hear?	What might you smell?	What might you taste?	What might you touch?	What might you feel?	Where might you be?

Overall, how does your visualization of the Revere's midnight ride impact your assessment of what bravery is?

• Students will turn and talk or discuss their observations in small groups, then in a whole class debrief as teacher records responses on the board.

PLACE-BASED EDUCATION

C3 Framework Inquiry Arc Dimension 3- Analyzing Source Evidence	
Formative Performance Task/Student Structured Practice	• Students will work in groups and "take" the midnight ride using the interactive map on the Paul Revere House site: https://www.paulreverehouse.org/interactive-map-midnight-rides/ • For each "stop" on the ride, students will take notes on who they meet, what challenges they face, and where they are. • Next, students will read the letter from Paul Revere to Belknap and complete the graphic organizer comparing and contrasting, the events of the midnight from Longfellow's perspective from his poem and Revere's perspective from his letter 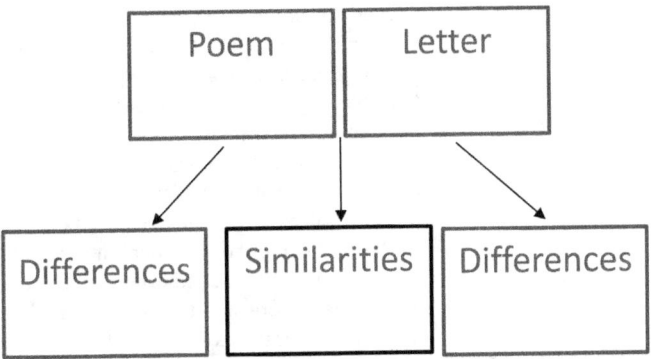 • Using the evidence from the poem, letter, and previous sources, students will cite supporting evidence to write a 1-page position paper answering the supporting questions "Was Paul Revere a significant person during the American Revolution? Why or why not? Was he brave or an ordinary citizen? Was he brave or an ordinary citizen? The paper should have at least one resolution where students consider the following, "how can the depictions of Paul Revere's life and role in the American Revolution from the Freedom Trail, Paul Revere House, and other primary and secondary sources connect to how we preserve historical places and people in our community? Brainstorm on one example from your community of a place that can, or should be preserved, and explain a plan of action on how that preservation could take place. • The position paper can include illustrations, maps, or any other student-created presentation materials such as Canva or Power Point presentations that highlight the connections between the preservation of the Paul Revere places to a historical site in their community. • If possible, teacher can take students on a walking tour or field trip to a historical site in their community to do reflections, take pictures, create maps, and consider connections to how Revere's ride and the preservation of his house on the Boston Freedom Trail can connect to preserving a historical site in a local community.

C3 Framework Inquiry Arc Dimension 4- Communicating Conclusions and Taking Informed Action	
Student Share	• Student groups will share their position papers and presentation materials.
Closing	• Teacher will ask students to complete the "L" column of the KWL chart and share reflections on the compelling question, "what makes someone brave?"
Summative Performance Task/ Extension	• If feasible, ask students to visit the place identified in the group research and take pictures and observational notes that include historical contexts, perspectives expressed at the place, and affective responses to why this place can or should be preserved. This could lead to a larger place-based observation on an individual project, group project, or whole-class project that involves trips to the site, research of historical, literary, and/or scientific characteristics of the place, and discussion with community stakeholders concerning ways of preservation and community awareness of the importance of the place. • If a physical trip or visit is not feasible, ask students to take a virtual field trip or tour of historical sites, museums, or park that is local (i.e., immediate neighborhood or city or county or state) in order to learn more about who and what places are named after, and how these sites are contextualized as places with historical, literary, or scientific significance.

Conclusion

Place-based education is a powerful approach to supporting student engagement in historical empathy through historical research, literary analysis, and scientific investigation. Although physically visiting a place may not possible for all students and teachers, the digital resources that local, state, federal, and international institutions provide can introduce students to concepts of place, place identity, and how and why the preservation of historical sites and natural environments is vital in connecting content learned in ELA, social studies, and even science and STEM subjects, to real-world situations. If going to a place, whether it be to a museum or historical site, or taking a walk through a school building and surrounding neighborhood, is feasible, we encourage teachers to think about how works of visual and literary art can support students' inquiry of the historical contexts and perspectives that are expressed with exhibits, artifacts, markers, and other types of primary sources. Getting students literally or figuratively outside of the classroom can make their school and learning experience more meaningful, constructive, and relevant to their lives.

Historical empathy involves analysis of how the past and present differ, and the way some places commemorated a person or event from the past may be reflective of the times when preservation efforts started and not of the values and beliefs of our world today. By implementing PBE and CBL approaches to promoting historical empathy, teachers and students can take an active part in examining how change over time occurs in places, and how the study and observation of these changes contribute to historical inquiry, artistic expression, scientific innovation, and civic engagement.

Reflection

- What are some benefits and challenges to planning place-based education as a way to engage students in historical empathy?
- What are some examples of places that you could take your students when implementing strategies that promote historical empathy with place-based education?
- Are there colleagues who teach in different subject areas that you can collaborate with when planning a place-based learning opportunity that can help students demonstrate historical empathy?

Suggested Place-Based Education Resources

Arizona State Parks https://azstateparks.com/geology-and-tours
Birmingham Civil Rights Museum Institute. https://www.bcri.org
Civil Rights Trail of the African American Freedom Movement. https://civilrightstrail.com/attraction/the-national-memorial-for-peace-and-justice/).
Facing History and Ourselves: Exploring the Concept of Identity. https://www.facinghistory.org/sites/default/files/2023-11/Exploring_the_Concept_of_Identity.pdf
Georgia Aquarium Research and Conservation: https://www.georgiaaquarium.org/research-and-conservation-overview/
Grand Canyon. Education. https://www.nps.gov/grca/learn/education/index.htm
List of Major State Parks: https://listofparks.com/pages/us-state-parks
Marineland Educational Outreach: https://marineland.net/education-outreach/
Montgomery Legacy Sites. https://legacysites.eji.org/about/
Museum of Jewish Heritage: A Living Memorial to the Holocaust. https://mjhnyc.org
National Association of State Park Directors. https://stateparks.org/about-us/

National Council for Geographic Education Standards: https://ncge.org/teacher-resources/national-geography-standards/

National Council for History Education, The Rural Experience in America: https://ncheteach.org/the-rural-experience/

Niagara Falls State Park https://www.niagarafallsstatepark.com

National Parks Service. Working with Communities: https://www.nps.gov/getinvolved/communities.htm

National Women's History Museum: About. https://www.womenshistory.org/about-national-womens-history-museum

Project WILD: https://www.fishwildlife.org/projectwild/project-wild

San Diego Zoo Wildlife Alliance: Take Action: https://sandiegozoowildlifealliance.org/take-action

Smithsonian Institution. https://www.si.edu/about

Utah Great Salt Lake State Park Field Trips https://stateparks.utah.gov/parks/antelope-island/pre-k-12-field-trip-requests/

Suggested Research Articles

Innes, M., & Sharp, H. (2021). Historical empathy and museum culture. *Journal of Museum Research, 46*(3), 307-320. https://doi.org/10.1080/10598650.2021.1954771

Karn, S. (2024). Designing historical empathy learning experiences: a pedagogical tool for

history teachers. *History Education Research Journal, 21*(1). https://doi.org/10.14324/HERJ.21.1.06.

Karn, S. (2024). Walking in their footsteps: Historical empathy and experiential learning on battlefield study tours. *Historical Encounters 11*(1), 30-42. https://doi.org/10.52289/hej11.103

Tatum, B. (2017). *Why are all the Black kids sitting together in the cafeteria and other conversations about race.* Basic Books.

Wakild, E., & Berry, M. K. (2018). *A primer for teaching environmental history: Ten design principles.* Duke University Press.

Chapter References

Atlanta History Center. (2022). *Monument: The story of Stone Mountain.* Retrieved from https://www.atlantahistorycenter.com/monument/

Caldera, A. (2021). What the term "culturally sustaining practices" means for education in today's classrooms. *Intercultural Development Research Association.* Retrieved from https://www.idra.org/resource-center/what-the-term-culturally-sustaining-practices-means-for-education-in-todays-classrooms/

Chapman, J. (2023). Dialogue in place: *Addressing historic monuments placed by the Washington State Historical Society*. Retrieved by https://www.washingtonhistory.org/wp-content/uploads/2023/04/WSHS-Monuments-1.pdf

Connolly, F. (2020). Integrating place-based education into classroom or distance learning during the COVID-19 pandemic. Retrieved from https://ies.ed.gov/ncee/edlabs/regions/pacific/blogs/blog33_integrating-place-based-education-into-classroom.asp

Endacott, J. L., & Brooks, S. (2018). Historical empathy: Perspectives and responding to the past, in Manfra, M.M. & Bolick, C.M., (Eds). *The Wiley international handbook of history teaching and learning*, 203-225.

Louv, R. (2005). *Last child in the woods: Saving our children from nature-deficit disorder*. Algonquin Books.

Marcouyeux, A., & Fleury-Bahi, G. (2011). Place-identity in a school setting: Effects of the place image. *Environment and Behavior, 43*(3), 344-362.

National Science Teaching Association. (2012). *Next generation science standards*. Retrieved from https://www.nextgenscience.org/

Perrotta, K.A. (2018). A study of students' social identities and a historical empathy gap in middle and secondary social studies classes with the instructional unit "The Elizabeth Jennings Project." *Curriculum and Teaching Dialogue 20*(1&2), 53-69. https://www.proquest.com/docview/2097606392?pq-origsite=gscholar&fromopenview=true

Schweibenz, W. (2019). The virtual museum: an overview of its origins, concepts, and terminology. *The Museum Review, 4*(1), 1-29.

Smith, G., & Sobel, D. (2010). *Place-and-community based education in schools*. Routledge.

Sobel, D. A return to nature-based education. *Yes! Magazine*. Retrieved from https://www.yesmagazine.org/environment/2019/12/13/nature-based-education

Sullivan, L., & McMillan, N. (2024). *Historical markers are everywhere in America. Some get it wrong*. NPR. Retrieved from https://www.npr.org/2024/04/21/1244899635/civil-war-confederate-statue-markers-sign-history

Tatum, B. D. (2000). The complexity of identity: "Who am I?." In Adams, M., Blumenfeld, W. J., Hackman, H. W., Zuniga, X., Peters, M. L. (Eds.), *Readings for diversity and social justice: An anthology on racism, sexism, anti-semitism, heterosexism, classism and ableism* (pp. 9-14). New York: Routledge.

The Promise of Place. (n.d.). *What is place-based education?* Retrieved from https://promiseofplace.org/

Whitlock, A. (2024). *Place-based social studies education: Learning from Flint, Michigan*. Teachers College Press.

Votaw, J. (1994). The military museum as classroom. *Teaching History: A Journal of Methods 19*(2), 65-70.

Conclusion

Why Historical Empathy?

We end this book with the question we asked in the Introduction, "why historical empathy?" because as the band Semisonic said in 1998, "every new beginning comes from some other beginning's end." Throughout this book, we highlighted various resources and strategies that social studies and English language arts teachers can implement when promoting historical in empathy high school students. We drew from our own experiences as classroom teachers and college instructors of teacher education to show how many of us teachers have been actively promoting historical empathy in our classrooms all along. There are a plethora of works of literature, digital media, music, photographs, films, and historical sites that can be incorporated into ELA and social studies standards that engage students in historical empathy that can lead to deep inquiry about why the past is significant to our lives today.

There are challenges to promoting historical empathy from an interdisciplinary approach in ELA and social studies. According to social studies scholar Tina Heafner (2018), the NCTE advocated for the curricular integration of ELA so that literacy skills could be learned and reinforced in multiple contexts. However, Heafner found in her case study of ELA and social studies instruction in an urban elementary school that unclear expectations for teachers on how to implement integration of ELA-specific reading skills with non-fiction social studies content. She also found that the lack of co-planning time, dedicated instructional time for social studies, and administrative expectations to prepare students for high-stakes assessment hindered effective integrated instruction. These are worrisome results for middle and high school ELA and social studies teachers. Without a strong foundation of ELA and social studies skills comprehension in identifying text features and engaging in reading to learn content, particularly in the upper elementary grades, students can struggle with engaging in historical empathy if they never were taught to apply those skills when analyzing primary sources and other literacy modalities for historical context and the relationship between those contexts to the perspectives of people in the past. Consequently, the lack of application of these skills in ELA and social studies can make engagement in the cognitive and affective dimensions of historical empathy difficult when students are unfamiliar with inquiry-approaches to teaching these distinct, yet related disciplines. While interdisciplinary planning is notoriously difficult to do for K-12 teachers, we do hope that this book can be a resource for teachers of all grade levels to see how ELA skills and social studies can be integrated with fidelity that can promote historical empathy that leads to the development of students into active and informed citizens.

Perhaps now more than ever, it is important to explore historical empathy as an instructional strategy in social studies and ELA. When historical empathy is implemented as a regular part of ELA and social studies instruction, students can immerse themselves in critical thinking about the meaning of texts, the complexities of the past, and how study of the past can be helpful in addressing current-day issues and problems. If history, according to historian David McCullough (1984), is to serve as a "guide to navigation in perilous times," then utilizing pedagogical strategies that promote historical empathy can prepare youth to consider how contexts shape perspectives and empathetic responses not only to people in the past, but how to address today's problems to create a brighter future.

Katie's Reflection

Throughout writing this book, I reflected a lot on my own career as a middle school social studies teacher and teacher education professor. At times, my reflections evoked nostalgia for the days when I taught in Brooklyn where I was not only able, but encouraged, by my school administration to take the kids outside the classroom to places where the history that they were learning could be brought to life. I thought about how much I missed being able to plan field trips and local history studies that I could incorporate into teaching the standards by taking her classes to throughout New York City to places that they perhaps might not visit. There are so many landmarks that we take for granted because we see them every day; my grandfather was born and raised in Brooklyn and never visited the Statue of Liberty! For years, I was doing place-based learning with historical empathy strategies without even realizing it. Learning about the theoretical and pedagogical aspects of historical empathy as a graduate student and teacher education professor helped me to see how my philosophical approaches of using field trips and local history research was grounded in historical empathy that can have positive effects on students' academic and individual growth.

While writing this book, I could not help but to also reflect on the major anniversaries that impact education, and events that will shape the country for decades to come. For example, the 70th anniversary of the *Brown v. Board of Education* decision was monumental given the Supreme Court's ruling that race-based segregation in schools violated Black Americans' 14th amendment rights. So many history books and school curricula depicted this time as when a challenge was overcome, and things got better. However, there are too many people who bore witness to the extreme backlash and intolerably slow desegregation efforts that persisted well beyond 1954. When I visited Selma, Alabama on my way to the NCSS conference in New Orleans, I got to meet two community elders who shared with me their experiences as teenagers joining the march across the Edmund Pettus Bridge. There was so much violence and resistance to desegregation that the 1964 Civil Rights Act was passed to prohibit discrimination in the workplace based on race, religion, and national origin (this definition has expanded over the years to include marginalized groups). However, this law was limited, particularly regarding voting and education. In 1965, the Voting Rights Act was passed to ban racial discrimination when voting. That same year, the Elementary and Secondary Education Act (ESEA) was passed as part of President Johnson's Great Society programs aimed at eradicating poverty and combatting racial discrimination in education. I find these anniversaries intriguing because they give teachers an opportunity to not only reflect on the historical significance of the past, but why the past continues to shape how we make decisions and live our lives today.

While not every anniversary is marked with cake and joyful celebrations, these anniversaries continue to touch every single person's lives in this nation. We still live with the ESEA with its reauthorization in 2001 as the No Child Left Behind Act and in 2015 as the Every Student Succeeds Act. During this time, I realized that I began teaching in the aftermath of the 9/11 terror attacks, economic ruin of the Great Recession, election of the first Black president, wars in Iraq and Afghanistan, Black Lives Matter, #metoo, COVID-19 pandemic, immigration and border issues, and consequential Supreme Court rulings about matters such as LGBTQ+ rights, reproductive health, voting accessibility, presidential immunity, healthcare, Title IX and the role of the U.S. Department of Education. What will future students, teachers, and researchers think about the history of the 2000s? None of us know. However, I hope that when these times in our modern history are taught as a long-ago past, teachers can implement historical empathy strategies with their students in order to help them grow into productive citizens who can be part of the American experiment of by studying historical contexts and multiple perspectives that can lead to reasoned affective responses that can push this nation forward towards becoming a more perfect union.

Jennifer's Reflection

Over the course of my career as a high school ELA teacher, I was fortunate to teach every grade level and every course. While I found something I loved about each, I will admit that I have a particular fondness for American Literature. I would tell my American Literature students that if I did my job well, hopefully they would find "their story," or at the very least, a story that offered a protagonist, a plot, a setting that reflected their own American experience. To meet this goal, I offered my students reading choices from a variety of authors and time periods and encouraged independent reading to explore different authors and different voices. I built and curated a class library, inviting my students to write book reviews on index cards to leave inside the books for the next curious reader. This process incorporated student input and reflection, encouraging them to think about the authors who were writing these narratives and the cultures and communities those stories reflected. Students engaged in book talks, offering their thoughts, whether good, bad, or indifferent, on the texts. I encouraged them to speak about their experiences in looking for books that reflected their own lived experiences. In this way, students were powered to discuss openly how they wished to be represented, not only in books they read for pleasure, but in texts required by teachers.

In my perfect world, teachers would have the time, flexibility, and autonomy to offer these informal explorations and experiences to their students, but Katie and I recognize that for most teachers, this is not the case. Many of us have experienced the frustrations of being tied to pacing guides, scripted lessons, and lack of choice when it comes to texts and curriculum. Many of my graduate students complain that they are tied to "teaching to the test" and district-created assessments that do not account for student diversity. How then, given time constraints and the pressure to deliver test results, can teachers engage their students in meaningful discussions, deep dives into texts, and offer thoughtful assessments that allow all students to reflect knowledge, skills, and learning? If the opportunities to diverge from pacing and curriculum do not exist or are unpractical, how can ELA teachers promote historical empathy and provide meaningful opportunities to think more critically about history and today's world?

Kaite and I hope that this book will offer teachers some practical strategies to promote historical empathy within the framework of existing curriculums. It is our hope that in these chapters, teachers will find ways to incorporate conversations, activities, and other forms of engagement that, as Katie reflected, help our students become more engaged in the world around them with a more nuanced approach to those who have different lifestyles, cultures, and lived experiences. Through technology, music, film, photography, and literary analysis, a frequently taught work such as *Animal Farm* by George Orwell (1945), can offer more than opportunity to discuss a literary work, but be an invitation to examine ideologies that continue to resurface and challenge our better angels. It becomes an opportunity for students to make connections through modes of literacy that are more accessible, such as music or digital media. As with all strategies, we encourage teachers to adapt those offered in this book in ways that best fit the needs of your students. As we know, each year and each class brings a different set of students with diverse needs, abilities, and prior knowledge. We hope you find this book helpful in promoting historical empathy in your students and engaging them in meaningful discussions.

What's Next for Historical Empathy?

There are always limitations to books, articles, and other manuscripts that are written, especially in education. New research and best practices constantly clarify or change our understandings of how students learn and how teachers teach. Our book focused on high school social studies and ELA because our professional backgrounds and academic training was grounded in secondary education. We couldn't include every idea we had in this book, otherwise we would be developing a manuscript longer than *War and Peace*. Despite these limitations, we hope that teachers and scholars consider some of these possible avenues for future historical empathy research and practice that can push ELA and social studies forward in deeper ways to engage student learning and empathetic living:

- Blake (1998) argued in a rebuttal to historical empathy scholars Stuart J. Foster and Elizabeth Yeager that a more accurate term for historical empathy is "empathy in history." While historical empathy as a pedagogical strategy is a legitimate instructional approach with growing theoretical and conceptual research supporting its implementation and impact on curriculum and instruction, we do not want a take-away from this book to be that these approaches are only applicable to humanities or liberal arts subject areas. In Chapter 6, we included some possible connections to the Next Generation standards to show how scientific observation and inquiry complements the goals of historical empathy when exploring historical contexts and perspectives and affective connections to outdoor settings. The field of the history of science is rich with many avenues that science teachers can try when examining the roles, challenges, and contributions of scientists throughout world history, namely women scientists and scientists of color. Recently Marie Curie's dissertation was auctioned off. Moreover, Stinson (2008) contends that critical analysis of marginalized mathematicians can be impactful. As federal and state initiatives promoting 21st century skills continue, we hope that STEM and STEAM teachers consider adapting historical empathy techniques can be an impactful and relevant approach in engaging students in examining the socio-economic-political and historical ramifications of scientific and mathematic discoveries and impact on environments, people, and societies.

- Our chapters and sample lesson plans mostly included examples from United States history, mainly because our teaching careers focused on teaching U.S. history and literature. However, comparative studies of world governments, literature, and emphasis on global history and literature can lead to rich opportunities to engage students in historical empathy by examining contexts and perspectives of diverse people and groups, particularly those who are colonized, marginalized, misrepresented, or excluded from mainstream narratives of the ELA and social studies curriculum. There are some great studies from countries such as Sweden, the United Kingdom, and Canada about effective historical empathy strategies that engage students learning about topics such as the Holocaust, World War I, ancient Greece, and Canadian battlefields (Karn, 2024). Historical empathy has been a more explicit curricular goal in Europe, especially the U.K., after World War II's decolonization movements, civil rights, and Cold War politics (Perrotta & Bohan, 2020). We encourage teachers and scholars to examine methods in which global history and literature in ELA and social studies can promote historical empathy in American classrooms not only through reading primary and secondary sources, but also visiting museums and historical sites in order to deepen students' understandings of the interconnectedness of the United States to the world, and vice versa.
- Since the COVID-19 pandemic, there has been a rise in pedagogical interest in social-emotional learning (SEL), affect, and the role of empathy in education. Teachers are doing a lot of work in the K-12 spaces in addressing SEL given the various mental health concerns that arose due to social distancing, remote learning, and increased usage of social media among children and teens. Eisman and Patterson (2022) make the argument that historical empathy can be effective in supporting SEL through engaging students in point of view exercises that can lead to the production of "justice-oriented citizens" (p. 128). Historical empathy strategies, especially those that focus on visual literacies that include dance, performance, and aesthetic texts, may be effective when engaging students in examining how people in the past experienced times of uncertainty, loneliness, and difficulty to draw connections to their own lived experiences as a means to improve their own wellbeing by serving the community.
- We live in the 24/7 news cycle that includes real-time comments, observations, and reactions to world events that are memorialized in social media posts. Social media has become its own form of digital archive of potential primary sources of contemporary history such as the COVID-19 pandemic. According to an article in the NCSS College and University Faculty Assembly research journal *Theory and Research in Social Education,* Miles and Gibson

(2022) perspectival presentism, which focuses on contemporary events instead of the distant past, can serve as "a historical approach to current problems and issues can make history more relevant, meaningful, and interesting for students" (p. 522). While there are scholarly debates on the extent to which presentism can, and should, be part of historical inquiry, teachers can incorporate contemporary examples of documents that consist of social media posts, news articles, photographs, and other forms of personal and collective memory that can help future historians and students learn about life in the 21st century through historical empathy methods. Additionally, historical empathy approaches can connect to Keegan's (2021) work on affective critical citizenship and Zemblyas' (2014) work on enriched critical citizenship education where students can engage in participatory action when preparing for voting and life in democratic society.

- Artificial intelligence (AI) is having its moment as being among the most revolutionary technologies in education. Although scientific and ethical research is currently being done about the use and potential of AI, teachers can use historical evolution of AI as a case study to examine its origins as a rudimentary post-Cold War technology accredited to the works of scientists such as Alan Turing to evaluate its current use in everything from art to music to influencing elections. For example, Hosseini et al. (2023) note that AI systems "do not 'know' the meaning or truth- value of the text they receive, process, and generate" (p.1). As a result, there are important ethical questions concerning how AI can and should be utilized. Examining the historical and current uses of AI through a historical empathy lens may help students to evaluate the technology's benefits and limitations in society, as well as the extent to which people make individual decisions to use AI in their professional and personal lives.

- Interdisciplinary efforts across content areas can be impactful in supporting pedagogical goals of historical empathy. While we highlighted the historical empathy or "empathy in STEM" can be extremely beneficial, we also encourage social studies and ELA teachers to tap into other content areas that can support these instructional aims. For instance, Jason Endacott (2023) and his research team found in a recent study on arts integration with preservice teachers that promoting historical empathy with an interdisciplinary focus can support prosocial behaviors among youth. Examining how teaching historical empathy methods to students of education may lead to greater understandings on how teachers' beliefs about historical empathy can impact how children learn and apply what they learn to real-world situations (Cunningham, 2009).

These examples are not an exhaustive list of future avenues for historical empathy research and practice. We hope that these ideas can serve as a jumping-off point for teachers, researchers, and anyone who is interested in learning more about the potential of historical empathy as being a pedagogical approach to ELA and social studies instruction to learn how these methods can support students' critical thinking, historical inquiry, and holistic development into caring, informed, and empathetic citizens in their communities.

A Caring Word

Professor Pei-Fen Sung (2022) at National Taipei University contends that the integration of a "post-modernist" view of historical empathy as grounded in emotion and imagination with the "hermeneutical" approach that encompasses the cognitive and reasoned affective aspects of historical empathy can help teachers to "make better judgement about their teaching orientations" (p. 3). Such an integration of emotion, academic study, historical inquiry, and human curiosity may be the ingredients needed to promote what Keith Barton and Linda Levstik (2004) advocate is historical empathy grounded in *care- caring about* relevant topics, people, and events; *caring that* something happened or something happened to someone, *caring for* people in the past and present, and *caring to* take action in the present, even though we can't go back in time to help those who were mistreated and suffered before us (pp. 229-238). We strive to teach so that students *care about* what they are learning. We hope to teach in a way that inspires students to *care that* something happened. We aim for students to *care for* people they know and do not know. We are supported to teach students to *care to* do something with the curricular supports in the NCSS C3 Framework and NCTE ELA standards.

As bell hooks (1994) said in her book *Teaching to Transgress*, "if we are all emotionally shut down, how can there be any excitement about ideas" (p. 154)? If historical empathy is a strategy that can benefit your students and enrich your teaching, then perhaps we can all play a part in restoring joy in teaching, learning, and being part of our human family.

References

Barton, K.C, & Levstik, L.S. (2004). *Teaching history for the common good*. Lawrence Earlbaum Associates.

Blake, C. (1998). Historical empathy: A response to Foster and Yeager. *International Journal of Social Education 13*(1), 25-31.

Cunningham, D.L. (2009). An empirical framework for understanding how teachers conceptualize and cultivate historical empathy in students. *Journal of Curriculum Studies. 41*(5), 679-709.

Eisman, J.I. & Patterson, T.J. (2022). A theoretical-practical framework for responding to presentist challenges in historical empathy. [Paper Presentation]. College & University Faculty Assembly of the National Council for the Social Studies 2022 Annual Conference. Philadelphia, PA, USA.

Endacott, J.L., Warren, J., Hackett-Hill, K., & Lalonde, A. (2023). Arts integrated historical empathy: Preservice teachers' engagement with pluralistic lived experiences and efforts toward instructional application. *Theory and Research in Social Education*. https://doi.org/10.1080/00933104.2023.2279157

Heafner T. (2018). Elementary ELA/social studies integration: Challenges and limitations. *The Social Studies 109(1)* 1-12. DOI: 10.1080/00377996.2017.1399248

hooks, b. (1994). *Teaching to transgress: Education as the practice of freedom.* Routledge.

Hosseini, M., Rasmussen, L.M., Resnik, D.B. (2023). Using AI to write scholarly publications. *Accountability in Research*. DOI: 10.1080/08989621.2023.2168535

Keegan, P. (2021). Critical affective civic literacy: A framework for attending to political emotion in the social studies classroom. *The Journal of Social Studies Research 45(2021)*, 15-24. https://doi.org/10.1016/j.jssr.2020.06.003

McCullough, D. (1984). Historian addresses Wesleyan. *The New York Times*. Retrieved from https://www.nytimes.com/1984/06/04/nyregion/historian-addresses-wesleyan.html

Miles, J., & Gibson, L (2022). Rethinking presentism in history education. *Theory and Research in Social Education 50(4)*, 509-529. https://doi.org/10.1080/00933104.2022.2115959

Perrotta, K.A., & Bohan, C.H. (2020). Can't stop this feeling: Tracing the origins of historical empathy during the New Social Studies era, 1950-1980. *Educational Studies 56(6)*, 599-618. https://doi.org/10.1080/00131946.2020.1837832

Semisonic. (1998). Closing time. *Feeling Strangely Fine*. Retrieved from https://americansongwriter.com/closing-time-semisonic-behind-song-lyrics/

Stinson, D. W., Bidwell, C. R., & Powell, G. C. (2012). Critical pedagogy and teaching mathematics for social justice. *The International Journal of Critical Pedagogy 4(1)*, 76-94.

Sung, P.F. (2021). What is historical empathy in history teaching? *Bulletin of Educational Research 67(2)*, 1-39.

Zembylas, M. (2014). Affective citizenship in multicultural societies: Implications for critical citizenship education. *Citizenship Teaching & Learning 9(1)*, 5–18. https://doi.org/10.1386/ctl.9.1.5_1

www.ingramcontent.com/pod-product-compliance
Lightning Source LLC
Chambersburg PA
CBHW061713300426
44115CB00014B/2664